THE VISION
A PAINTER'S LEGACY

PAUL POLSON

ISBN 978-1-957220-32-1 (paperback)
ISBN 978-1-957220-33-8 (hardcover)
ISBN 978-1-957220-34-5 (digital)

Copyright © 2021 by Paul Polson

All rights reserved. No part of this publication may be reproduced, distributed, or transmitted in any form or by any means, including photocopying, recording, or other electronic or mechanical methods without the prior written permission of the publisher. For permission requests, solicit the publisher via the address below.

Rushmore Press LLC
1 800 460 9188
www.rushmorepress.com

Printed in the United States of America

GALE W. McGEE
WYOMING

The Green River Star, Thursday, May 19, 1966

United States Senate
WASHINGTON, D.C.

OUTSTANDING AMONG ENTRIES in the State Industrial Arts Fair at Lander last weekend was the wood sculpture of Abraham Lincoln's head by Green River high school senior Paul Folson (right above), shown with his division and first place winner in Woods Classification, along with his instructor Rudy Gunter. Of the nine division awards at the state competition, Green River entrants won six and thereby claimed the traveling trophy for the highest points won. Many of the Green River winning entrants are displayed in a window of the Green River Mercantile building.

(STAR photo)

Congratulations and best wishes

Gale McGee

CHAPTER ONE

The Vision

My body was wracked with fever. I was only nine years old.

A world of darkness enveloped me. Huge dark spheres began to close in. I felt a fear that I had never felt before, and the reality I normally experienced was transformed. There was an overwhelming feeling of no upside down or right side up. The spheres had no size—nor did I. I could hold a sphere between my thumb and forefinger and roll it in circles as it diminished to nothing, yet the spheres were larger than the universe itself—all at the same instant.

Suddenly, the universe around me was filled with light. Orbs were floating in the void. One sphere had a shape emerging within it. The shape became a human figure, and my fear turned to calmness, peace, and enlightenment.

There it was! Right before me! It was the answer to our existence. It all made sense.

This vision repeated itself every year until I was nineteen, with no fever. I could come back to reality when I chose, but if I relaxed, I fell back in. I always wanted to write down the answer. I left a notebook and pencil next to my bed so I could do that. The problem was that I only knew what it meant while I was having the vision, and there was no reason to write it down. The moment I woke to reality, I could not describe it or remember it.

Even though I cannot put this "answer" to words, it feels like the yearly repetition of this vision was meant to impart some wisdom and awareness to my life. One effect it has had was to give me strength and confidence. Neither life nor death scares me because I have felt the true reality of our existence, even though I cannot describe it.

When I think back on fond memories, there are two that are particularly meaningful. They both describe a time when I felt the magic of the universe. These were moments when I felt completely at peace.

Our family of six lived in the tiny town of Grainger, Wyoming—population, 100. It nestled atop the Continental Divide that was also a high desert. This town existed due to a semi-grand railroad depot that was at the juncture of the major east-west routes. Trains didn't actually stop there. I think they did once. Grainger can boast of having the ruins of a Pony Express and stagecoach station. It was also the site of a UFO sighting that the whole town had the opportunity to view. The government said it was a missile test. Ha! We had all seen it; we knew.

During January of 1964, we arrived home late one evening, as we often did. The temperature was hovering at zero—quite warm for that time of year. Located thirty-five miles from the closest town, we did a lot of driving. My parents, two sisters, and brother shuffled through the snow to our toasty home. I crawled on the hood of our car, as I often did, and lay on my back to gaze at the stars. The warmth of the engine felt comforting as I stared at a panorama of our galaxy.

THE VISION

The door to our house opened, and Mom poked her head out.

"Paul, it's cold out there. Are you coming in?"

"I'm fine, Mom. I'll be in soon," I said with a glance in her direction.

Taking in the scene, she smiled and shut the door.

My eyes were finally adjusting to the night sky. The stars seemed to increase in number and detail. A satellite moved across the sky, and occasionally, a meteorite streaked toward the Earth. The Milky Way became a bright white band, and my mind wondered at the possibilities of travel to those distant islands. I thought of life and felt awed that we actually existed. What else is out there?

The second fond memory was actually three years earlier in another small, yet larger, town named Douglas, Wyoming—the home of the Jackalope.

"Paul, the missionaries will be here in an hour. Get ready for church," Mom yelled from the bottom steps of my attic room.

This was a great room. The stairs were thin, steep, and scary. No one wanted to climb them—total privacy!

"Oh, man!" I muttered to myself. Then yelled, "Do I have to go?"

"Yes, you do. They expect you to help today."

This was the Church of Jesus Christ of Latter-day Saints (LDS) or Mormon Church. Douglas didn't really have a church because the population was too small. The church was an annex of the school. Missionaries ran the different meetings and rituals. Everyone was required to play a part. I liked the missionaries. They were fun and came to visit often. We played games, offered them dinner, and joked around.

I looked out the window as I crawled out of bed and began to dress. It was snowing heavily, had been all night, and was at least a foot-and-a-half deep.

Even though this was a day I would always remember, it hurt my mother. I still remember her tears. I had always obeyed my parents. I'm not sure what came over me, except that I really didn't want to go to church that day.

Bundling up, I opened the window and stepped out on the roof. Planting my boots carefully in the snow, I walked to the edge and climbed down a fir tree. As I walked away, I noticed how surreal the world seemed. The flakes were huge, and I could only see twenty feet in front of me. A half-mile later, I was at the mouth of a small cave that I had noticed during my walks to school. The cave was five feet deep. I crawled in and sat in its mouth looking out at the white wall of slowly falling snow. There was no wind, and the quiet was deafening.

Being at peace with yourself is such an awesome feeling. Time did not exist and pleasant thoughts invaded my mind. Why do I exist in this world? I knew it was special. It seemed to me that this was the feeling you should have at church, but that didn't compare to the oneness I felt with God in this tiny secluded cave.

Remembering these two simple times of peace made me realize that they were quite opposite each other. The stars made me look out into the wonders of the physical universe, and the cave made me look at the universe inside myself. They both were endless and filled with infinite possibilities. These two experiences set the tone for the rest of my life. I have always tried to pursue those feelings of wonder and express them.

THE VISION

Who lives in Wyoming? If you have ever lived or stayed there for short periods, you would probably wonder why people choose to live in this godforsaken place. Some parts of the state are amazingly beautiful. Wyoming has a versatile landscape. There are rugged mountains, forests, plains, high deserts, and a vast sky that goes to a horizon you can see almost 100 miles away. The parks and diverse landscapes awe most people. Some people even move here. Unfortunately, after a winter with temperatures well below zero (minus twenty degrees is not uncommon) and continual winds of thirty to sixty miles an hour, new arrivals generally packed up and left.

Wyoming natives are a different breed of people who live a comfortable yet naïve lifestyle. Having never experienced anything else, they plod on, doing their mundane tasks, and criticizing the parts of the world they have never seen.

There are also people who come to the state to work in the oil industry or the mines. They work hard, make lots of money, and then hightail it back to civilization.

I just so happen to be the native type. I was born in Laramie, Wyoming, where my dad attended the University of Wyoming. Dad's side of the family is from the southwest corner of the state, a town called Mountain View. It is nestled at the base of the Uinta Mountain Range—the only east-west range in the United States. This was a town of 400 that supported the many ranchers in that broad valley, along with the towns of Fort Bridger and Lyman.

My grandfather owned a thriving lumber and hardware store. He passed away from a sudden heart attack in 1953 and left the business to his four children. My dad was the sibling who continued to run the store, and Mountain View became the town I grew up in until the eighth grade. Dad's brother and two sisters had moved to Utah and California. They were happy there and did not want to move back.

The world moved slowly and was comparable to the stories and art of Norman Rockwell. In the summers, I ran around town on my bare feet, visiting friends, climbing trees, and building forts to fight off imaginary Indians. We had our favorite swimming hole where the creek slowed and deepened on a curve. It was deep enough to dive in headfirst without the fear of hitting your head on a rock.

In the 4-H club, I raised sheep—a ewe and a lamb. People in town laughed and joked about the Polson boy who ran up and down the roads chasing his sheep. They always seemed to figure out how to escape from their little pasture.

I had three pigs, too. They often escaped their pen but behaved entirely differently.

In fifth grade, there was a knock on the door, and an office assistant poked her head in the room.

"Is Paul Polson here?"

I raised my hand.

"Your pigs are eating Betty Bullock's flower garden, and they won't let her get close. She tried to shoo them off."

I walked the two blocks to the Bullocks' house.

Sure enough, there they were, munching on Betty Bullock's flowers.

I would greet them with a whistle and a wave. They obediently fell in behind me, and I walked them back home.

THE VISION

I was very fortunate to spend these early years in southwestern Wyoming. The majority of my friends lived on ranches, and it was not uncommon to spend time and overnights at their homes. We went to bed early, got up at five o'clock in the morning, milked the cows, then put them out to pasture, fed the pigs and sheep, gathered the eggs, and—the most fun of all—rode horses. For fun at night, we wrestled in the hallways and bedrooms. Not surprisingly, most of us went on to wrestle in high school.

At a young age, I drove tractors. (My father sold them.) I also drove a push rake during haying season. A push rake, in our neck of the woods, was an old car with the body removed. The steering was detached and put on backward so the rear wheels did the turning. On the front (that was the back) was mounted a giant wooden rake with long sharp poles pointed forward and an equal number facing up. I dropped the rake as I drove down the rows of hay until it rose to a huge pile. Then I levered the hay off the ground and deposited it on a stacker.

A stacker was a truck whose front end was cabled to a system that would lift the hay as it backed up and drop it in one place. Another ranch hand would spread it out with a pitchfork to make the stack. I tried that job for fifteen minutes before collapsing in sheer exhaustion. I was unable to lift my arms for a day or so, but I could still drive a push rake.

None of this came close to my real driving experience in my dad's pickup.

Dad pulled up in front of our house with our flatbed truck. This was the truck he took to Salt Lake City every two weeks to restock our supplies and pick up special orders. I always went with him. He sang and told jokes the whole way. At the end of the day, we went to the ballpark and watched the Salt Lake Bees play baseball. We always spent the night at the Moxum Hotel. The following morning, we did the final loading of the truck and headed back across the Wasatch Mountains to Wyoming.

On this particular day—I must have been eleven years of age—my dad hopped out of the truck and entered the front door of our house looking for me.

"Hey, Paul, I have a job for you!"

Usually, that meant hard work, like unloading lumber. I liked helping my dad. Besides his cussing, he was pretty entertaining.

"The pickup won't start, and I need your help," Dad said as we walked outside. "Jump in the driver's seat, and I'll push you. You need to keep your foot on the clutch. When we turn onto the main road, we will speed up. Put it in second gear and, when I honk, release the clutch, and the truck will start. Drive to the store, and pull over to the curb."

"Sure! This will be fun!" Actually, I was a little scared. I climbed in the pickup, put it in second gear, and pressed on the clutch. Dad pulled up behind me in the flatbed.

The door to the house opened, and my brother Don ran out, followed by a little wiener dog that belonged to a neighbor who was gone for a few days. "I want to go! Can I go, Dad?"

Dad glanced at him. "Sure, you and the dog, get in the passenger seat with Paul."

THE VISION

Everything went as planned. The pickup started, and I drove the quarter-mile to our store. I pulled to the curb and stepped on the brake. Oops! The engine died.

"OK," Dad said. "I am going to push start you again. Drive back to the house, but, when you stop, push down on the clutch."

"Got it, Dad."

He pushed me again, and it started as before. This time, being proud of my driving ability, I sped up.

"You're going too fast, Paul," my brother blurted as his eyes widened in fear.

"Wow, this is fun!" I said.

As we approached the corner, I realized that, indeed, we were going pretty fast. Following my dad's instructions, I stepped on the clutch. Nothing happened. We were still barreling toward the intersection way too fast.

As we arrived at the corner, I jerked the steering wheel to the left. The pickup tilted up on two wheels, and the passenger side door sprung open. My brother and the dog rolled out of the cab. I barely glimpsed them as they both stood up and began running down the road.

I tried to correct the turn, but it was too late. Hitting a ditch, I shot up in the air and through a barbed-wire fence. The pickup was still going too fast as it headed straight for an open sewer.

"The hell with it," I thought, and I stepped on the brake.

The pickup came to an abrupt stop, and the engine died.

"Boy, my Dad is going to be mad!" I thought.

I crawled out of the truck just in time to see my dad pull up. He got out of the truck and literally rolled on the ground laughing.

"I'm sorry, Dad. I had to step on the brake!" I said, filled with embarrassment.

"That's OK, son, but next time, you need to step on the brake while you step on the clutch."

We looked toward the house. Mom was doing the dishes and saw the whole thing out the kitchen window. Her mouth was open in pure shock.

I swear, I felt so bad I couldn't sleep for two days.

There were many episodes, adventures, and learning experiences in this little town. I will leave that for another day.

This was all dampened by a little twist of fate. One of those experiences that makes you stop and take note with the realization that life often shakes things up so you can regain your footing and start anew.

The light in our bedroom suddenly went on at around one o'clock in the morning, and Mom stood there with a worried look on her face. Dad had left a day before to take the 300-mile trip across the state to watch the Wyoming Cowboys play football at the University of Wyoming in Laramie.

"Get up, kids! The store's on fire!"

THE VISION

We all ran out to the road and looked down the five blocks to the other end of town. The fire was huge! It lit the sky and the whole landscape. Housed in the same building, as our hardware store were two other businesses, a small café and a barbershop. We found out later that the fire started from a wood stove in the back room of the barbershop.

"Can we go watch, Mom?" I asked.

"No, honey." It was too dangerous to get close. You could hear all the ammunition that my father sold exploding like fireworks.

At least we had insurance. The problem was that my dad's brother and sisters preferred to split the insurance money since my grandfather originally left the business to all four children. The amount my father received was not enough to rebuild. It was time to strike out for a new career.

My father graduated with a Bachelor's degree in business but needed to pick up some education courses so that he could teach.

Regardless of not having enough credits for his BA in education, Dad was given a teaching job at Coal Mine, Wyoming. Coal Mine was not a town; it was an actual deserted coal mine. There was a small trailer at its edge for my dad to live in and a small outside shower about twenty yards away.

Coal Mine was a suburb of Bill, Wyoming—population one. Bill is actually on the map. It has a building that acts as a post office, general store, and gas station. There are many ranches in the area, and Bill acts as the supply center and the postal contact with the rest of the world. There is a small house next to the general store. I think Bill lives there.

My brother and I lived with our dad at Coal Mine. With the Wyoming winds, we were rocked to sleep every night. At six in the morning, we drove the three miles to the school where my dad taught. This was a beautiful little Norman Rockwell schoolhouse in a vast prairie of nothingness. We lit the potbelly stove to start the warming process and then drove to each ranch to pick up the students. Another parent picked up students as well. All of us, from first to eighth grade, were contained in the room. It was warm and cozy by the time we all arrived.

After school, we took the students back to their homes. It was common to be invited for supper.

After three months, I decided to live with my mom in Douglas, which was thirty miles south of Bill. Even though my parents got along great, my mom and sisters lived in Douglas out of simple practicality. Mom got a job, and my sisters went to school. Douglas had a population of close to 4,000—a thriving Wyoming city. It was exciting going to school there. I would have an actual social life. There were plenty of activities and there must have been thirty students per classroom—about 100 students per class—and girls! I wasn't even close to being confident in that area, so I just gaped in awe and walked into walls making a fool of myself.

A couple of jobs kept me busy before and after school. In the morning, I got up at four and delivered newspapers—delivering them before the sun rose in below-freezing weather. The snow was deep with drifts. After school, a friend and I shoveled snow for the downtown businesses.

I was actually quite the entrepreneur. Buying penny candy before school, I sold them for two cents each. There were a lot of students who were bussed in, and they were fine with the extra costs. My paper route provided me with boxes of rubber bands. I took them to school and sold ten of them for a penny. The teachers seemed to have a rubber band problem with the students. Looking back, I'm lucky I didn't go to school in a real city. I probably would have been a drug dealer.

My dad and brother came home every weekend. It was nice having the whole family together. For two summers, we stayed in Laramie so Dad could go to school. He finally got his education diploma and found a job in Grainger, Wyoming.

Grainger had a railroad station and a Pony Express station, and it definitely had its place in history. The Oregon and Mormon Trails passed through this town and, like the railroads, separated at that point. One trail went to the Pacific Northwest and the other to California. The population of Grainger hovered at around 100. I think the census was padded. Someone told me they included the dogs.

When the Indian railroad crews were in town on payday, we woke to their being passed out all over the streets from the night before. Occasionally, some of them froze to death or passed out on the tracks, but for the most part, there was no trouble.

Dad was the junior high school teacher, the basketball coach, and the principal. I was beginning my sophomore year and had to catch a bus to Green River—about thirty miles away. We crossed the county line and had to change buses. All the teenagers in that area were starved for something to do, and it was common to have students from the Grainger area heavily involved in school activities. Three out of five of the cheerleaders were from my area as well as three out of five starters on the basketball team. We placed first in the state in basketball my senior year. Not me; I was captain of the wrestling team. The band

and theater classes were filled with kids from Grainger and Little America. The Grainger school district sent an activity bus to pick everyone up after our activities were over. We usually made it home around eleven at night.

Oh, yeah. My Dad drove the activity bus.

My mother didn't have an easy time in Grainger. She was raised in Las Vegas, Nevada, and met my father when he was at Edwards Air Force Base during World War II. Her whole family was there. It was common after I graduated from high school for our family to go to Las Vegas in the summers so that Mom could be with her family.

There wasn't much to do in Grainger. Her favorite time was the spring thaw. The melting snow washed off a layer of topsoil, revealing arrowheads and spearheads. She had quite the collection. Sea fossils were also somewhat common, and the area was a hotbed for dinosaur bones.

At the time, I didn't realize how hard living in Grainger was for Mom. She eventually became one of those Valium-addicted moms of that era. She was prescribed the medication after a suicide attempt. My brother found her in the bathtub when he got home from school. I had never seen my dad cry before, and when he picked me up at school, I heard the story and broke down in tears as well.

On winter evenings, the whole family sat around our only stove, told stories, and joked. Those were happy and close times. It became a usual practice for me to rub my mom's neck and shoulders every evening. I also rubbed her feet after a little persuasion on her part and could see her relief.

The rest of the house was pretty cold, and at the end of each evening, we braved the frigid air as we made our way to our beds, put on our pajamas, and crawled under the covers. Within ten minutes, our beds were warm and cozy from our body heat.

Dad bought me an old 1951 Plymouth. He allowed me to take it to school on occasion. This car was like a jeep. Neighbors would make comments to my dad.

"Wow, Ed, that is some car you bought your son. I keep seeing it driving across the desert at a pretty fast clip, climbing hills, and driving straight across shallow riverbeds."

This was true, and it was loads of fun. My favorite thing to do was drive down the creek when it was frozen over. There were no worries about breaking through. The creek froze all the way to the bottom. This activity taught me amazing control over icy roads. I would purposefully yank the steering wheel to one side and do 360s for pretty long distances before coming to a quick stop against the bank. Boy, they don't make cars like that anymore!

Summers were a delight after the harsh winters in Wyoming. Three of those summers, during high school, were spent in the Uinta Mountains. Dad had a summer job with the National Park Service. On the first day of June, we would snowplow our way to a small cabin on a beautiful lake—Bridger Lake, it was called. The cabin was on the cusp of a wilderness area that led to the high Uintas. This was a magical place above the timberline. I would wake early every morning, go fishing, and have trout and eggs for breakfast.

We had a generator that provided light during the late evenings. Other than that, we relied on a large fireplace for heat throughout the night.

Those three summers were an exception. From that point on, our family spent the summers in Las Vegas. We did this for Mom.

Wyoming in the winter and Las Vegas in the summer—you couldn't find more extreme weather—most people would prefer the reverse.

I was in the habit of drawing and painting on any surface I could find—usually oilcloth with a vinyl coating over a canvas material. My parents bought me my first oil painting kit, and I painted on the unprimed canvas side of the oilcloth. I took an art class every year during high school and could do a whole painting in an hour, always finishing by the time the bell rang. Usually, it was a landscape—not from life, but from my memories of the beautiful forests, mountains, and cloudy skies of Wyoming. My teachers were delighted, and many of them bought my work. I had never taken Home Economics, but the Home Economics teacher bought one of my paintings in exchange for seven lemon meringue pies. There was one waiting for me every Friday in the fridge. Being involved in sports, I showered after practice and led my Grainger teammates into her classroom. We all dove into the pie.

There wasn't much art to appreciate in Wyoming. Looking at books of famous artists fascinated me. Saving the grand sum of eighty dollars, I bought a huge gold-covered book of Salvador Dali's paintings. It was in a bookstore in Salt Lake City. I spent many hours looking at his work.

That area of the country wasn't completely devoid of artistic expression. I have memories of a friend of my father who painted western-themed oils. His name was Harold Hopkinson. I have often wondered if this painter was not as good as I thought, my being so young. It turns out he was not only a good artist; he was an excellent western painter. He even has work in museums. I confirmed this by looking it up on today's internet. He lived in Wyoming from 1918 until his death in 2000. His work amazed me.

THE VISION

We had friends in Salt Lake City whom we visited on occasion. They had a daughter my age. We had a mutual interest in each other but didn't know what to do with it. Her father did oil paintings of the human figure. A couple of these paintings hung in their house. I was not allowed to go to his studio to see any more of his work. Again, what I did see was extremely good, according to my memory. Of course, I was a naïve and inexperienced artist at the time.

And! There were murals, paintings, and sculptures on the LDS temple grounds. This work was stunning. The best work was hidden inside the temple that, to this day, I have been unable to see—having not advanced far enough in the church to be allowed in.

Walking alone across the high desert that surrounded Grainger was a favorite pastime. I found old roads that were falling apart. They hadn't been used in decades. Along these roads were old liquor bottles, car parts, and other ancient trash.

If you could float a mile above this area and look down, you would see what appears to be a coastline going from one horizon to the other. The area is flat, even though it is on the Continental Divide. There is a twenty-foot difference from the top level to the lower one. I don't know if it was caused by seismic activity or if it was an ancient coastline. There were countless ocean fossils in the area.

One day while hiking from Little America to Grainger, I slid down a steep slope to the lower level of this geologic structure and ended up sitting on my butt in a small enclosure—about the size of a living room—with a passage to my left that would take me out to the lower level of this vast plain.

Before I was able to stand up, I noticed a bobcat ten feet in front of me. The cat would need to get even closer to me to exit the passage. I did not want to stand and walk (or run) out since it could be interpreted as threatening. This resulted in a twenty-minute standoff. Both of us stared at each other. Finally, the cat—very slowly—walked toward the exit. When it was close enough, it darted out.

We both survived the incident. It was a strange feeling while we stared at each other. I felt no fear and even talked calmly to it.

"Hey, cat. What's up? Sorry to barge in on you like this. Would you mind leaving first? I'll just sit here until you decide."

Being a wrestler, I visualized moves I could make if attacked. I have no idea if they would have worked.

Scenario 1:

The cat attacks! Of course, it will go for my neck. I roll backward, bringing my foot into his midsection kicking as hard as I can. I jump up and dart out of the opening. The cat will not follow. It realizes I am no longer there and no longer a threat.

Scenario 2:

I jump up screaming, flailing my arms, and snarling. If he takes the escape route, fine enough. If he attacks, I punch him in the nose and hope for the best.

Scenario 3:

I go for communication. I explain to him that I am a wrestler and would be happy to show him some moves. Kneeling beside him, I put my right arm around his waist, grip his left front leg with my left hand, and whisper in his ear, "When I say go, try and get away."

Nah. Looking back on this, I tried being nice like that to both of my ex-wives. It wouldn't work. Of course, it wasn't quite the same situation. What I did with the cat worked.

"Is Paul here?" the voice said from the face that poked into the room during study hall.

I was in my third period of the day at Lincoln High School in Green River.

I raised my hand.

"You're wanted in the principal's office."

"What did I do?" I thought to myself as I stood and walked toward the door.

"Paul's in trouble!" a few voices taunted as I left.

I walked down the hall, down the stairs, and knocked on the principal's door.

The principal was sitting behind his desk talking to Mr. Gunter, the wood and metal shop teacher. Rudy Gunter was also an amazing sculptor, although he didn't teach that at school.

"You have study hall this period, right?" the principal asked.

"Yes?" I stated cautiously.

"We are pulling you out of study hall. You will take wood shop instead." He nodded toward Mr. Gunter.

Mr. Gunter smiled. "I have requested that you take my shop class this year. You are not learning much in art other than doing your paintings. I want you to carve a bust out of wood—your choice of who you want it to be. You are too talented to not be given this opportunity."

My choice was Abraham Lincoln. After all, our school was named Lincoln High School. As it turned out, I won first prize in the state's annual competition, then donated the bust to the school at graduation. I also received an invitation to an art school in Chicago to work on paintings and sculpture for a week, which would determine the number of grants and scholarships awarded to potential art students. I didn't apply for this, which led me to believe that Mr. Gunter was the one who actually sent in the application. Unfortunately, my parents wouldn't let me go. They wanted me to go to UW. They wanted me to have a "well-rounded" education. Thus began my official art education.

CHAPTER TWO

My dad drove me the 300 miles to school. The University of Wyoming is a well-funded school—a beautiful campus built from the natural stone of the area. The campus is as big as the rest of Laramie, the place of my birth.

We found our way to the second floor of Crane Hall. I said goodbye to my dad and began unpacking.

My roommate was an avid golfer and had immediately joined a fraternity—Sigma Nu. The university put us on the same floor as the freshman football team. They kept things alive with their antics.

We went through three proctors that first year. One of the football players would rouse everyone from bed at one in the morning to plan our next attack on the poor soul who was only trying to do his job so he could get his room for free.

We would do silly things during our lights-out curfew. Once we stood by our open doors, slammed them shut at the same time, turned off our lights, and hopped in bed as if we had all been sleeping. The proctor made the rounds and found everyone snoozing away.

This was followed by placing an M-80 firecracker in a shoebox full of shaving cream in front of his door. We knocked and did the door slam routine again. The worst damage we did was to prevent the guy from going to his final exams by wedging pencils in the crack of his door. This effectively locked him in his room. We didn't have telephones in these rooms, and he couldn't call for help. The one phone on each floor was in the dayroom.

I was dubbed "The Artist" and was responsible for decorating the football players' casts from football injuries. My favorite one was when I painted a stretched-out shoe that matched a player's real shoe. A nude female was also a common pick for decoration, along with the players' favorite sayings.

I did portraits of the players and their girlfriends for five dollars each. Many of them would give me a photo of a favorite girl or least-favorite girl and have me draw a nude body on it in various poses.

One evening, there was a loud pounding on the door. When I opened it, all I saw was a huge body that disappeared above the doorframe at the neck area. He leaned forward so he could fit his head inside my room.

"You the artist?" he said in a low gruff voice.

He turned sideways and wiggled his huge frame into my room.

"Uh, yeah?"

"See this photo?"

"Uh, yeah?"

"This is my sister," he said as he glared down at me.

"Oh, my God," I thought. "What did I do?" I didn't recognize the photo, but I had drawn so many, I could easily have not recalled her.

"I want you to do her portrait."

I felt relieved. I was ready for the worst. He followed me to my desk and hung his head over my left shoulder. I could hear—and feel—his wheezing as he fixed his gaze on the empty piece of paper I placed in front of me. This was not the most comfortable situation for doing a portrait. I started the sketch, trying to ignore him. Usually, a football player would drop a photo off, and I would deliver the portrait to their room when it was finished.

When I was done, he took the drawing and, with a huge smile on his face, said, "Wow, man. You're a good artist!"

He plopped down a twenty-dollar bill and squeezed back into the hall in obvious delight—almost skipping down the hall.

It took me about fifteen minutes to calm down. This could have been disastrous. I better watch out for who I am depicting.

In the cafeteria, I usually sat with twin brothers from Cheyenne—Ron and Marty Miyamoto. They were Japanese but well Americanized; in fact, they hated sushi. Visiting their house once, I noticed that they had an authentic samurai sword over their fireplace that had been passed down through the family. Other than that, I didn't see much of their heritage in their home. They said something about their father being in a Japanese unit of the United States Army.

"Have you thought of joining a fraternity?" Marty asked one day.

"Not really," I said. "I'm not sure how the free spirit of an art major would work in a structured organization."

"We're not the usual fraternity. First of all, our house is off-campus. We are subject to the university requirements, but not the housing or resident halls' rules and restrictions. We also have the highest-grade point average compared to the other frats on the row."

"What's it called?" I asked.

"Delta Sigma Phi," he said, as he leaned back and pointed to his tee-shirt. "You should at least come over and meet the guys."

Accepting an invitation to dinner, I found myself in a group of friendly and conversation-motivated guys. The Miyamoto twins' older brother, Glen, was president. The sales pitch was persuasive: normally, you have to stay in the dorms your freshman year, but I could move in the second semester. The costs were less than on-campus housing. They had quiet hours and free tutoring from members if you had difficulties with any class. There were year-round intramural sports, and it was easy to get teams together.

They also had a cook. The new pledges served and did dishes. On Mondays, they had meetings and a formal meal with a housemother while attired in a sport coat and tie. They also took advantage of the early fall and spring weather by driving to the mountains for keg parties at Vedauwoo or Happy Jack Recreation Area at least every other week.

It was a great sales pitch. I decided to join.

Four of us were not drinkers—yet—and we were not encouraged to do so. It was the end of my sophomore year before I chugged my first beer.

We easily gathered the players for basketball, softball, touch football, and wrestling. Oh, yeah, we had a kick-butt bowling team—the Miyamotos' favorite sport.

I loved sports and thrived. Being in sports in high school had prepared me well. I was an outstanding player, only because the rest of the fraternity had not played sports much.

My favorite activity was playing drums. The house had its own band, and the drummer showed me beginner beats. I was a natural and picked it up fast. I would stand next to or behind drummers from other bands in the Laramie area to see how they played. I also learned a lot watching rock bands in two of our Colorado party towns: Fort Collins and Greeley. After observing real drummers, it helped me understand the beats on the new albums hitting the top of the charts.

After one of our "quiet hour" breaks, a fellow frat member cranked up the new Jimi Hendrix album. Wow! What the hell was that? In a couple of weeks, I couldn't get enough. In the late sixties, new music was abundant. It was magic! The Beatles didn't excite me until "Sgt. Pepper's Lonely Hearts Club Band." There were The Doors, The Rolling Stones, The Who, Cream, etc.

Eventually, I became the drummer in the fraternity band. The first drummer was a senior and had just gotten married. He was happy to drop out of the band to concentrate on his studies. Graduating became his number-one priority. I easily fit in, and he let me use his kit.

One spring day, we were sitting on the porch and heard a guitar and a wonderful female voice from the neighbor's house. I walked across the street: Lo and behold! My first wife! I don't mean to jump that far ahead yet, but that is how it turned out. Barbara and I got along great. She became one of the lead vocalists in the band. We had a regular gig at the Bum Steer in downtown Laramie. They always wanted us to play unless we were busy playing somewhere else. We packed the place with college students. It became a regular source of income.

My brother loaned me his 1949 hearse. It was maroon in color with velvet curtains, and it had a siren. It was used as an ambulance in those days. It turned out to be our traveling vehicle. We would load our amps, guitars, drums, keyboards, and the rest of the equipment in the side and back doors, then travel to junior colleges and high schools to play. Small crowds watched us unload; most had seldom seen a real rock band.

We added little theatrics when one of the band members was chosen to be unloaded. He played like he was a corpse as we unloaded him, put him on a wheeled gurney, covered him with a sheet, and pushed him into the gym (or whatever venue we were using).

Now, "Why did I go to the University of Wyoming?" Oh, yeah—to study art. My social life was obviously packed.

I truly enjoyed the art department and the other students. Many classes lasted three hours. These were figure-drawing and sculpture workshops, along with other classes that needed creative time. My first nude-model experience was novel in a couple of ways. It was a three-hour class on Tuesday and Thursday evenings from six to nine o'clock. A woman fully undressed wasn't as exciting as I predicted. It might have been her age—about fifty-five. She had been a regular at UW for a long time and was on a first-name basis with the students and instructors.

The weather that evening was heavy with snow. The studio was warm and cozy, and we each picked our drawing horse to sit and prop our large tablets on. One tablet was newsprint, and the other was a finer acid-free paper for longer drawings. We started with one-minute sketches, and, by the end of three hours, we were doing twenty- to thirty-minute drawings.

During the second hour, two students burst through the door and pelted the model with snowballs.

"You jerks!" she yelled.

She jumped up in a rage and chased them down the stairs, out the door, and almost to the end of Prexy's pasture. We watched through the second-story window as she gave up and stomped back—elbows out and fully nude in the thick falling snow. Surprisingly, she walked in with a smile on her face and a rosy tint to her loose skin. She seemed to have enjoyed the attention.

We had all types of models—male, female, young, and old. Variety added to the understanding of the figure.

The system used by the art instructors was interesting. The university provided them with a large studio, and they did their own work when they weren't teaching. UW made a point of generously funding all of the colleges on campus. The state of Wyoming had many resources, and the university was one of their proudest achievements. You could expect a good education with great facilities and instructors.

And then there were girls! I had always been a little shy. I knew girls were interested in me; I just didn't know what to do with them. Since junior high, I had always had opportunities to go further in the touching and kissing department, and the girls were frustrated that I was afraid to make that first step. In high school, they couldn't have been more obvious as to their intentions, but again, they waited for me to pick up their cues. Plenty of opportunities presented themselves, but in the long run, I was glad I waited. My life could have easily taken a different turn. Living in Grainger and being so close to my family helped shelter me. All it would have taken to get me more involved would have been an aggressive female that was willing to plant a huge kiss on my lips while clutching my crotch with her hand. I would have been lost to the passion.

Being at the university tipped the scales for me, but it still took a while. I met Sandy the first week in school. She was pretty aggressive and worked hard to arrange situations where we could be alone and cuddle. She was born in Turkey, and her parents were Americans working for the United States government. Sandy was a sorority girl who was definitely smitten with me. We did do a lot together, but it always fell short due to my still lingering shyness. She never gave up—for three years—and I still didn't allow it to get too far. Thinking back, that was the one that got away. I didn't know what I had.

The same year, two of my fraternity brothers and I triple dated. That was when I first was able to get physically closer. My date was much more playful and aggressive than anyone I had experienced. We drove into the country—two couples in the back—my date and I in the front. It began with cuddling and kissing. Before I could get control of the situation, she had unzipped my pants and had a firm grip on my erect penis.

"Oh my God," she said, loud enough for everyone in the car to take notice. "What is this?" She smiled and gave a little spurt of laughter.

"OK. What's going on up there you two?" a voice sniggered from the back seat.

THE VISION

When my date turned her head, she released me and said, "A lot more than what's going on back there."

By the time she turned back around, I had just enough time to force my goods back into my pants and fasten them.

"Would you stop that?" she said, as she quickly undid my belt and zipper to resume her grip.

Luckily, gripping was all she did. One short stroke and I would have released my manhood all over the car and myself.

"Don't start anything you can't finish," I said. (That was a hollow threat.)

She just gave me a smile and a nudge. We then continued our banter with the two couples in the back seat. They had no idea what was going on.

Thirty minutes later: "Well," I said. "Let's go back to town." My date released her grip, I buttoned up, and we headed back to Laramie. How anti-climactic!

We dropped the girls off, and us guys headed back to the fraternity.

If you have ever experienced a case of blue balls, you would understand what I went through for the next couple of hours. So much for my first experience with my sexuality. Ouch!

That was about the time I started a more serious relationship with Barbara. Sexual trysts happened often, and they highlighted our relationship for the next two years. We began our mornings with my going to her house after her parents left for work. She answered the door in her robe, and we climbed the stairs to her bedroom. Thus, we ventured into a world yet unknown.

There were other promising aspects to our relationship other than sexual. Well—now that I look back on it—maybe not.

Pursuing an art career was at the forefront of my interests. I often talked about my plans with Barbara. She was excited about doing the same; she had a beautiful voice. She was going to school in music with a vocal major and was also interested in the performing arts. We talked about how ideal that would be with our artistic directions being different enough not to conflict. The arts all took the same level of discipline, and if we married, we could move to a larger city with outlets and opportunities. We could support each other and live an artist's lifestyle.

We also agreed that if we had children, they would have the opportunity to have parents that would follow their dreams. We would be role models, rather than be parents who sacrificed everything for their kids so their kids could sacrifice everything for their kids. People had become too materialistic and just focused on making money. Our kids would be well taken care of even if we had to take side jobs, which we would surely need to do, especially at the beginning.

Things did not always go well. There were the proverbial red flags that no one ever looks at until it is too late.

One was when the two of us drove to Grainger during spring break. Barbara had never met my parents, and we were excited about the trip across southern Wyoming. We had midterms during the day and planned a late start rather than waiting until morning. My Dad bought a brand new 1969 GTO and let me have it for the spring semester. We headed out about nine o'clock that night. It takes about three and one-half hours to make the drive.

THE VISION

A few miles out of Laramie, I checked my speedometer. We were going a little over eighty miles per hour, which seemed slow in this car. I looked over at Barbara, and she was sprawled out in the passenger seat with her legs crossed and resting on the dash.

"Put your seat belt on, please."

"No," she said.

"I'm not kidding, Barbara. Put your seat belt on."

"Nope."

There was silence in the car for about forty-five minutes. I was getting angrier as the miles rolled under us.

"Barbara, I'm driving and responsible for my passengers. Put your seat belt on."

Again, came the usual reply: "Nope."

Silence.

I could see the lights of Rawlins getting closer. When we arrived at the next exit, I took it, crossed the freeway, and headed back to Laramie.

Silence.

For me—at that time—our relationship was over. I planned to drop her off at her house and tell her to get out. We were done.

Finally, we were only a few miles from the first Laramie exit. She put her seat belt on and said, "OK. My seat belt's on."

I don't know why, but I took the next exit, swung back towards Grainger, and sped west—again.

That pretty much ruined our trip. Not a word was said the whole time. We arrived at my parents' house. I showed her to her room and went to mine. The few days we were there, we didn't talk. I'm sure my parents picked up the tension. They didn't say anything.

As we returned to Laramie, our anger subsided, and we began communicating again. She did wear her seat belt on the way back, and things were back to normal by the time we returned to school.

Spring semester, 1969, I asked Barbara to marry me. The date was set for the end of the upcoming summer, just before school started.

When summer arrived, Barbara went to Las Vegas with me. My parents had bought a house in North Las Vegas a couple of years earlier, and we both found summer jobs. Barbara worked at a department store, and—for the second summer—I did watercolor portraits at Circus Circus on the strip. I remember swiveling around in my chair while waiting for another customer and looking at the TV located in a small bar across the aisle. That is how I watched the first Apollo landing on the moon.

I came by this portrait job a year earlier when Mom found a job clipping in the newspaper early in the summer of 1968. A few portrait artists from Disney were starting the business of supplying the different casinos with artists. They charged fifty dollars for a two-week class. Dad was skeptical. "They just want to take your money." Mom was the opposite. She raked up the money and gave it to me.

Over twenty-five people took the class. We had to bring our own model, so I took my little sister Sally. I was used to the art school style of drawing—a quick gesture and then going back and defining shadows and highlights. The watercolor added a nice flowing effect, but, as is usual for the medium, you need to paint a lot to understand drying times and effects. Vegas had a very dry climate, causing the water to dry faster than normal.

The Disney artists loved my work but taught me the style they needed. It was fast—five minutes. It was designed to get people's attention. You started drawing with an umber wax-based pencil to resist water. Starting with the eyes, you made a dark deliberate line and moved quickly to the nose and mouth—then on to the contour, hair, and the clothing. Leaving the white of the paper for highlights, I painted a flesh wash over the face. Then I moved on to the hair and collar before going back to the face, where I applied the shadows in quick dabs and strokes. If you added the shadow color too early, it would bleed across the face. If the wash was added too late, it left an ugly line where it met the dry color. The timing was important.

After the first week of lessons, they put me on the stand at Circus Circus. At the end of the two weeks of lessons, no one else was chosen. Even though my work was acceptable, within two weeks, I was smoking hot with the technique mastered and the time under five minutes. The next summer, when Barbara accompanied me to Vegas, it was like starting all over again. It took two weeks to get in the flow.

Not getting as many artists as they hoped, my boss asked me if I knew anyone else who could do portraits.

"Sure!" I said. "My Aunt Mary."

Aunt Mary started the following week and put me to shame. She took a bit longer than five minutes, but she did an amazing job.

To viewers, it looked like we always created an amazing likeness. The model and their family liked the work, but the personality wasn't what they hoped. The face and head details were accurate but something was missing.

They were right, of course. An artist needs to get to know the model, so they can pick up that unique detail of one slightly raised eyebrow or a twisted smirk at the corner of the mouth. Essentially, they were like driver's license photos with a three-quarter view.

Our wedding was in a beautiful church in Laramie. From a distance, it looked like a white sail with one upraised corner supporting a tall, slim cross. My older sister Kay (a bridesmaid) caught her hair on fire with a candle as she leaned over to pick up something she had dropped. Other than that, nothing else happened that could provoke later laughter or stories. My sister! Always looking for attention.

The reception was held at the fraternity house. There were many people and piles of gifts.

Tom, my designated "little brother" in frat lingo, walked up to me with a sly smile on his face.

"So, big brother, what car are you using for your honeymoon?"

"And why would you ask that?" I said cautiously, wondering what was up.

His smile widened as he told me the plan.

"Everyone in the house is assuming you are taking the GTO. At the moment, it is filled with empty beer cans—stuffed floor to ceiling." He reached into his pocket and handed me his car keys. "Take mine,

I parked it right next to yours. My chance to pull a fast one on the fraternity."

When we left, the whole party followed us to the back parking lot. Everyone was laughing and whooping it up as they watched us make a B-line to the GTO. Then came the shocked sounds of "Whu? Huh? Hey, what the fuck!"

We jumped in Tom's car, backed up, and tore out of the parking lot with one frat member frantically grabbing a door handle, then quickly letting go as our forward momentum outpaced him.

We had a great honeymoon at Estes Park, Colorado. That was beautiful country—what we saw of it outside our honeymoon suite. After diving in bed to consummate our already consummated wedding and frolicking around like a herd of rabbits, we fell back in exhaustion. Barb ran to the bathroom, and when she returned, she sat on the edge of the bed.

"Paul, I have a little problem. I thought I was starting my period, so I put a tampon in this morning. I can't get it out. Will you help me?"

I tenderly scoped her out, found a string, and slid it out. "Hmm, no blood. Didn't we time this so this wouldn't happen?"

"I just saw a little blood this morning. I think I'm pregnant."

Wow, that was fast!

Then it was back to school, an apartment in the basement of Barb's grandmother's house, and our rock and roll band.

December 1969 sparked off a controversial and much-disliked event that changed the lives of many young men: the first military draft lottery. The battle was intensifying in Vietnam, and the need for new recruits was growing well beyond their ability to enlist fresh young bodies. It was organized by birth dates, and the TV presented it like a game show: "And now for our next lucky winner!" I was upstairs studying.

"Hey, Paul, the draft is starting! Get your butt down here."

I ran downstairs and plopped on the floor in front of the TV, getting there as they announced number nine. I can't remember that first birth date, but I intently followed the dates as they read them off. After 365, I thought, "I must have missed it."

Sure enough, in the paper the next morning, there was my birthday: September 7, number eight. Rumor had it that the first 100 would more than likely be drafted.

It didn't take them long to notify the lucky winners. They loaded us in a bus and drove to Denver so we could get our physicals. I passed with flying colors and was later notified by mail that I would need to report for duty as soon as I graduated—the following May 1970.

For some reason, I wasn't bothered by the news. The Army sounded like a great adventure. I could be in a real war! However, the country wasn't exactly letting anyone know the reality of the situation. It sounded to me like we were kicking ass, and the lottery was to get the men to finish it off. Being in Wyoming, I did not know a soul who was over there at the time. There was no firsthand news.

I knew I had options. I could join the Navy or Air Force. My dad had been in the Air Force during World War II.

THE VISION

When I picked up the ringing phone, it was my father-in-law. It just so happened that Dean was a chief warrant officer with the local National Guard unit. It was said that there was a two-year waiting list if you wanted to go that route.

"Hello?"

"Hello, Paul. I just thought I would let you know there are two immediate openings in the Guard. One is for heavy equipment maintenance, and the other is for a grader operator."

"So, do you think I should take one?" I asked.

After a short laugh, he said, "I most certainly do, but it's your choice."

"Do you recommend one over the other?"

"Heavy equipment maintenance would be my choice. You can always get work as a mechanic when you get out."

I'm sure that his daughter being pregnant had a lot to do with his decision.

So, the deal was done. I went down to the local Guard unit and signed up. That meant going to weekend meetings until I was called to active duty. I received my orders to Fort Campbell, Kentucky (home of the 101st Airborne), for basic training in early September, then on to Fort Belvoir, Virginia, for my school.

Since signing the papers to join the Guard in 1969, I still had nine months before I needed to report for active duty. Things had changed a lot since my first year at the university. A Nehru jacket and a medallion replaced the sport coat and tie that we wore at our frat meetings and Monday meals.

It was an easy last semester before graduation. The majority of it was consumed by my student-teaching assignment In Casper, Wyoming. A couple of weeks after starting, my supervising teacher was in a car accident and was laid up in the hospital for the rest of the semester. His wife would march into the classroom, literally throw her huge purse on the desk, and sit in the chair with her arms folded watching my every move. I felt like I was being punished for something.

Student teaching was enjoyable. I did make some errors, but that was why I was there—to learn and get actual experience. My son Kevin was born on April 26, and I took a day off, combining it with a weekend to travel to Laramie and be with Barb and my newborn son.

On the last day of classes, I had the students help clean and organize the room. They gathered their year of art assignments to take home. I did the needed paperwork for their grades and anything else I needed to do to end the school year. My supervising teacher sent a list for me to follow.

The next day—after the students were gone—I made sure I had accomplished the chores on the list. The teacher showed up and at first started chiding me for not completing the list of my duties. Then he looked around and, realizing that I did do what was required of me, said, "I still want you to come in tomorrow. Here is the sealed letter that the university is expecting. I okayed the completion of student teaching, and you are clear to graduate. I have a much better report for you to take if you show up tomorrow."

The next day was fitting day for my cap and gown, and the school needed to see my teacher's evaluation before I could get on the graduation list. My ride was leaving at the end of that day.

I didn't much care about why my supervising teacher wanted me to wait another day. He said he wanted me to make up the day I missed when I went to see my newborn son. All I could think of was graduating, being with my new family, and going to Vegas to do portraits before flying to Fort Campbell for my basic training. Ignoring my supervising teacher, I left that day and delivered my evaluation without looking at it.

CHAPTER THREE

My third year of doing portraits was overshadowed by my impending date with the military. A couple of portrait artists from Disney approached me and wanted me to take off with them and travel the country. They wanted to travel to major events such as Mardi Gras in New Orleans and any other national expos or events that would allow us to earn money from our skills.

"No," I said. "I need to report to active duty this September."

"That's not a problem," said one. "We know a lawyer you can talk to. He supports young men wanting to avoid the war, and he only charges a hundred bucks."

"So, how is he going to do that?"

"He just takes a compromising photo—in action with a gay guy. It always works!"

"Actually, I think I will take a pass. I'm married and have a new son."

"That's all the more reason to figure a way to get out. They might lose you altogether."

"No thanks."

Fort Campbell, Kentucky was still pretty hot and humid in September. I was both mentally and physically fit for this adventure. Humility was always an asset of mine, even more so after basic training.

I had the distinction of being the only recruit to hit the drill sergeant's hat, fifty yards away, with a hand grenade. He bet the platoon that no one in this sorry-ass mess of humanity could hit it. He was both pissed and somewhat excited that he accomplished something: finding someone with an accurate arm.

I was also unique on the bars. We had to swing from bar to bar, screaming our heads off. The only thing I could yell, at a high enough volume, sounded like I was herding cattle. It got a laugh out of everyone.

There is not much to be said other than what everyone would suspect. All experiences were confined to the base since we were not allowed to take leave. At the firing range, I started as a marksman and finished as an expert. My final test was in a huge field. There were pop-up targets that ranged from ten yards to almost 100 yards. I hit 100 percent.

We crawled in the mud through barbed wire with live rounds one foot above our heads. We learned to use a variety of weapons—M-16s, claymore mines, M-60 machine guns, rocket-propelled grenades, and bazookas.

We were yelled awake at five in the morning and had five minutes to get dressed before lining up in formation. Our first duty of the day was to run a mile as we carried our weapons and backpacks. In short, we were all pretty fit by the time it was over.

The school at Fort Belvoir, Virginia, was also very competent in its objective. We learned to tear apart and maintain all sorts of engines, both diesel and gas. We could troubleshoot various forms of heavy construction vehicles as well as tanks, jeeps, and deuce and one-half trucks.

Sometimes, the training was almost as dangerous as the battlefield. When we loaded our squad in the back of a deuce and a half to relocate one morning, the driver, trying to show his competency as a stock car racer, rolled it while rounding a corner. There were twenty of us in the back. It seemed like slow motion. As it rolled, another GI on my opposite side landed on my butt as I was rolling backward, resulting in a bruised hip.

Everyone survived. We were all lined up and checked over by medics. The medic who looked at my hip said, "Just a bruise. Sign this form and get back to your unit."

Three months after returning home from active duty, I was playing tennis and suddenly collapsed on the court. My friends helped me off the court and took me to the doctor. After X-rays, they found that my hip had been dislocated. I experienced a decade of lower-back problems due to the accident. The cartilage had built up around the bone. Every time it was popped into place, it popped right back out. When I attempted to see if I could get help from the Army, I realized that the red tape, delays, and just plain incompetence discouraged me from pursuing this logical route.

Another fun event occurred while at Fort Belvoir. The whole company of 250 men came down with food poisoning at one o'clock in the morning. What a mess.

THE VISION

One asset of our location was its proximity to Washington, D.C. On weekends, I took leave and traveled fourteen miles to the National Gallery of Art and the National Portrait Gallery. It was amazing to see the beautiful buildings, monuments, and sculptures. They stood in stark contrast to the slums that surrounded the Capitol—the dirty derelict buildings, crumbling almost before my eyes. The poverty was astonishing.

During a barracks and locker inspection, the Commanding Officer noticed that my locker was filled with nude drawings of women I had done during downtimes. He paced back and forth in front of the two bunk beds associated with the four lockers.

"Who the hell did those drawings?" he yelled. Everyone stood at attention in stunned silence until I admitted to the crime.

"Meet me in my office immediately after this inspection, soldier," he yelled, two inches from my face.

When I walked downstairs afterward, his demeanor had changed to a smile.

"Give me a list of supplies. I want you to decorate the day room with a mural."

I also learned to play the system. It reminded me of the "MASH" episodes I later loved to watch on TV.

The schooling reached its end, and we were given leave before reporting to our permanent duty assignment. They kept delaying our departure. As a result, we had more guard duty assignments. With just a day to go, I noticed that I was the fourth on the list. There were two soldiers to be picked for this duty but the three before me had conveniently disappeared on leave. I knew that when one o'clock arrived, the sergeant would approach their bunks to shake them awake. When he realized they were gone, I would be the next on the list.

It just so happened that across the hall was the empty bed of a much-feared Hawaiian. He had taken leave as well but was not in danger of being called. I merely relocated to his bed and had a great night's sleep. I was only interrupted by a yell: "Where the hell is Polson?" The sergeant checked the list and grabbed the next unlucky soul for the job. I really didn't mind guard duty, but I began to enjoy a little game playing, just for entertainment.

Then there came the tensest moment that every soldier of that era feared: the list of permanent duty assignments. It was placed on the bulletin board next to the CO's office. All 250 names were listed in alphabetical order.

The first eight names were going to Vietnam. The next one was Germany. The next twelve were going to Vietnam. Then two were assigned to Germany and one to South Korea. The next nine to Vietnam, and so on until it reached my name: Paul Polson, permanent duty station: Laramie, Wyoming.

I didn't truly appreciate what my father-in-law did for me until that moment. Five years later, I appreciated it even more when I realized that many of my classmates did not come home. The rest were permanently affected—falling to alcoholism, suicide, or if they were lucky, just plain lethargy.

It was great being back home. I had missed Barbara and my son Kevin. From Fort Belvoir to the airport, I kept looking behind me. I was sure the military police would see me and drag me back to the barracks. "Two more weeks, son. You can't go home just yet."

THE VISION

After spending time with family, I accepted a job at the Wyoming State Hospital in Evanston, Wyoming. I worked under a registered occupational therapist, Judy Eron, teaching arts and crafts to the patients. The shop I worked in had a kiln for clay work, woodworking tools, and lapidary equipment. I taught these to the small groups of patients from each ward. These were the lucky ones who could leave their units. I also taught art, leatherwork, weaving, and knitting.

Judy was my age and had a profession that allowed her to work wherever she chose. Occupational therapists were in demand. She moved to Evanston to live the western lifestyle, beginning by buying a horse. She practiced barrel racing and in a short amount of time was racing at rodeos. She also had a guitar and loved to sing.

I immediately felt at home working with her. We took a tour of the hospital and all the units: Alcoholics, Social Rehab, Adolescent, and Drug Rehab. There was also a geriatric unit and a locked ward for the criminally insane. Each group had their time at the shop except the locked ward. I took a variety of "safe" craft supplies for them to work on in their unit.

All the groups were small. When new patients were admitted to the hospital, Judy and I went to their admittance meetings to learn their history and devise a plan of treatment. To start, all the patients were given a collage project. We had many old magazines, and each person could choose the clippings of their choice. This showed the imagery they were interested in. You could also see how detailed they were and how much patience they had. Some tore out the images, and some neatly cut the images out in minute detail. That first project, along with their history and treatment plan, determined the projects with which they could be successful.

Our new family found a small, cozy home on a corner, just two blocks from downtown Evanston. This was our first real home together. We went to church on Sundays. I was asked to be the scoutmaster.

We also found that Barbara was pregnant with our second child. I would come home after work, anxious to share my hospital experiences. The first order of business was to pick Kevin up from his crib and let him run around; he was delighted to see me. Barb was still in bed.

"Hey, Barb, are you okay?" I said as I greeted her with a hug and a kiss.

"Yes, I feel great. I just enjoy being in bed."

Understanding the part she played in nurturing her pregnancy, I let her relax as I fixed lunch and dinner for the three of us. To be fair, once or twice a week, she did motivate herself enough to make a meal. I began thinking that it was unhealthy for her to be so lethargic. She acted depressed although she denied it. She just liked idling around and sleeping.

This was my first time having a real domestic life other than my family upbringing. Was this how it was supposed to be?

The more this continued, the more disenchanted I became with home life. I loved coming home to Kevin, and his excitement in seeing me made it all worthwhile. I missed lively discussions. Conversations with Barb were shallow and felt manipulative. We were like aliens from different planets, unable to communicate or even understand where the other person was coming from. She was expecting me to do all the house chores. Going back to work became a much more attractive and interesting destination and environment.

THE VISION

Things changed and life became much more exciting when Kimberly was born. We found another house, larger, with three bedrooms, and the move, along with the change of environment, livened things up again. This was like a rebirth. Now I had two healthy beautiful children, and Barb was much more involved.

Unfortunately, that didn't last. Barbara gradually returned to her lethargic attitude. Returning from work, I walked into the house and heard Kevin yelling, "Daddy!" I walked into their room. Kim bounced up and down and had a large grin on her face. She stood along with Kevin inside their crib.

"Come on, you two," I said as I lifted Kevin out, gave him a big hug, and put him on the floor. He ran to his potty in the bathroom and then excitedly ran into the living room. Kim wasn't walking yet, but she was an avid crawler. I carried her into the living room, put her on the floor, and changed her diaper. She joined Kevin playing with toys that were scattered across the floor.

Barb was fast asleep. I sat on the bed next to her.

"I'm home, hon. Get up!"

Her eyes opened, and she changed her position—facing me.

"I'll be up in a minute; let me rest a while longer. It sounds like the kids are fine. They've been crying and yelling all day."

"Have you been up at all today?"

"Yeah, a couple of times."

I didn't come home for lunch that day. I met a group of co-workers in the hospital cafeteria. It was enjoyable being around fun people whose occupations were all about communication. This eventually became a regular routine, justifying it by convincing myself that I was becoming an enabler when I went home. It was forcing Barbara to get up and be involved with the kids.

"Hey, Barb, this can't be good for you. You need to get in a routine."

"Why? I like sleeping."

"It would be nice to come home with you active and involved with the kids. I would also enjoy being greeted with a hug and a welcome home."

She shut her eyes a moment and then looked up at me. "Why don't you make dinner? Let me know when it's ready, and I'll get up."

"This is bothering me," I said with a tinge of frustration in my voice. "Maybe you should get a job. We can get a babysitter."

"But I'm their mother. The kids need to be with their mother."

I drew my head back, looked at her, and sadly shook my head.

"But you're not with them if you sleep all day. They need to interact with you."

"I know," she said. "I'll start doing that."

Wyoming winters were not the best environment to encourage activity. After spending most of the time avoiding the weather, it became necessary to bundle up and go somewhere—anywhere. You can go crazy locking yourself inside. The winds were strong, and below-freezing temperatures were common.

I felt like something needed to be done.

"Remember when we were in school, and we talked about our dreams? I think it's time we pack up and relocate to a city where we can pursue our art careers."

Looking a bit annoyed, she said. "We have children now. You need to get a better job that pays more. Your art can be your hobby."

"We talked about that. You know how I feel. We both agreed to follow our art. It would be good for the kids to have artistic parents who pursue their goals."

"Do you remember my telling *you* what my high school music teacher said? I would never make it as a vocalist. My lung power and small frame are not strong enough. I could never make it as a vocalist."

"That's bullshit! You don't have to do opera. Have you heard of microphones?" I asked sarcastically. "You were our lead singer in our rock band. You were great!"

As spring arrived, I had too much energy to stay at home. The home environment was depressing me. I had to get out.

The first thing I did was purchase a dirt bike—a Kawasaki 175. After greeting my family when I went home after work, I jumped on my bike and headed out of town.

There were a lot of cross-country enthusiasts in that area. I loved hill climbing and would just pick a point on the horizon and drive as fast as I could, handling the obstacles as I came upon them. Racing was big in Wyoming. I tried a horseshoe track where competitions were held each week. I thought I was doing well until a ten-year-old passed me twice every time I did a lap.

I met a friend, Steve, who worked as a social worker in the adolescent unit. He had recently returned from Nam. He was a Navy corpsman who was placed in a Marine unit. He had experienced the worst the war had to offer. He didn't talk about it. Later, he wrote me a letter describing his ordeal.

He eventually quit the hospital to rejoin the Navy and was stationed at Miramar Naval Air Station in San Diego. The psychological aspect of pilot training was of major importance.

On occasion, Steve and I would get together at Sam's Tavern, just outside the city limits. Sam's was a unique bar where the human remnants of the Sixties hung out along with hospital staff. They were mostly pretty open-minded and enjoyed the conversation. This bar was the opposite of the cowboy bars in downtown Evanston where there were fights and yahooing—guys trying to prove they were real men in childish ways.

Steve was also the person I could unload on. I inundated him with the problems and concerns I had with my home life and my cravings to focus on my painting and sculpture. He was more than willing to listen—with patience. He had the ability to make me laugh and not take life so seriously—this coming from a man who had more experiences and stories to tell than I ever would. I realized, later on, how self-centered I was as if I was the only one who had problems.

Judy, my supervisor at the hospital, also provided that link of needed conversation. She helped me grow up. She would point out sexist remarks I made without my feeling I was being attacked. There were many aspects of my personality that she shed light on. This was the beginning of my self-awareness. After she visited her fiancé back east, she brought me a book, *Jackson Pollock: Psychoanalytic Drawings* by C. L. Wysuph. It made my mind explode and introduced me to Carl Jung, who I did not know existed. This led to several years of reading all the books in his volume set along with other Jungian authors and novelists. His work was slow to read but packed with insight.

The time came when Judy was ready to move on. She put in her two-week notice, and her fiancé drove out to pick her up. The hospital was okay with my running the shop.

The morning they were supposed to leave, there was a knock on our door. When I opened it, Judy was standing there with tears in her eyes. She had walked from her house, a half-mile away.

"I need to talk to you," she said.

"Sure. I'll give you a ride back to your house."

"I really don't want to leave," she said, as she wiped the tears from her face. "I'm not sure I want to get married. I've grown so close to you that I'm confused. I know you're married. I don't know what I'm thinking."

Judy and Geoff had plans to move to Nashville and get involved in the music scene. She had already landed an occupational therapy job at Vanderbilt University Hospital.

"I thought you were excited to leave. I had no idea you felt this way."

I drove her to her house. "There really isn't anything we can do about it right now."

She knew it too. I gave her a big hug, and we said goodbye.

Something had to be done. I didn't feel good about avoiding my own home. One asset of my job was being acquainted with qualified therapists. Before meeting Judy, I wouldn't have considered it, but I knew that Barb and I needed counseling. I talked to Barbara about this, and she reluctantly agreed. If nothing else, it would get her out of the house and involved in something.

It felt good to talk. I could say anything and everything that was on my mind. Barb wasn't as forthcoming as I had hoped, but frankly, I don't think she really knew what she wanted. The more we talked, the more it became apparent how different we were. I was enthused about the world and what it had to offer. Barb was complacent, and hanging out at home was fine with her.

One thing that added more distance between us (I was forewarned before I became involved) was learning transcendental meditation. This gave me more confidence and awareness. When I discussed this with Barb, she was okay with me doing it, but she wasn't interested. Looking back, that could have been just what she needed, what "we" needed.

Our counselor understood this, too. It became time to try a more radical approach. I moved to a basement apartment two blocks away. Barbara was hired at the hospital as an aide, and they arranged her schedule so that I had the kids when she worked and she had them when I worked. I loved this freedom, and it relieved my guilt of not wanting to go home. Barbara became a real person again. It was nice seeing her on a schedule, meeting friends, and being involved in something other than sleeping.

This was also the straw that broke the camel's back. Barb became convinced that I wanted to move out so I could get involved with other women. That's when the game playing started.

The phone rang in my apartment.

"Hello?"

"Hi, Paul. Could you come over and give me a hand? There's water leaking under the sink, and I don't know where it's coming from."

"Sure, I can do that. Is now a good time?"

"Could you come over at three? I need to run a couple of errands."

"Sure, three it is."

When I arrived at three o'clock, I walked in. She and some guy were making out on the couch.

"Oh," she said as she jumped to her feet with a surprised look on her face. "I wasn't expecting you."

I turned around and left.

It got worse than that. A couple of weeks later, I contacted her. I needed some of my belongings, so I called Barb and asked when I could come over. We set a time in the evening. When I walked in, there were two nineteen-year-old outpatients from the drug rehab unit. They had Barbara sandwiched between them. They both quickly removed their hands from under her blouse. Barb's response was to point her finger at me and laugh. They all three looked pretty stoned.

Kevin and Kim were crying and yelling from their crib. I walked into their room, changed Kim's diaper, and gave them a hug. When they calmed down, I gave them a kiss and left. The trio was still on the couch. The kids started crying again after I shut the door.

I felt so stupid afterward. The best thing I could have done would have been to remove Kevin and Kim and take them to my house. It was unacceptable for my children to be in that environment.

The next day, I saw a lawyer to file for divorce. I also made an appointment with our counselor and told him what was going on. He said that now was a good time to move to a larger city and pursue my art. When I brought up the kids, he said that Barbara had a job, a car, and a job. She would be OK.

Barbara didn't show up at the divorce hearing. My lawyer said it didn't matter. She would get custody anyway. Mothers always got custody in this state.

That evening, I hopped on my bike and joined a friend at the edge of town, and we pointed our bikes in the direction of a small butte. Opening up the throttle, we drove straight for it. It didn't seem like we were going that fast—enough to just handle the obstacles. The sun had set, leaving a glow in the sky. After several minutes, we came across an old dirt road that allowed us to open up a little more.

The first thing I remembered about this incident was the barbed-wire fence, six feet in front of me and barely visible. "Shit, I'm dead!"

I had an unusual response to this moment in time. The thought flashed in my mind that I would not survive this. I felt anger, intense anger I had never felt before. I gave it even more gas, tensed my upper torso, and hit the fence as hard as I could.

I was lying face down. No pain—yet. Can I breathe? Yes, I can breathe. Feeling my throat, I removed my hand; it was coated in blood, dripping in the desert sand. By that time, my friend was helping me to my feet. The bike had traveled ten yards past the fence. I had traveled about twenty-five.

Did I luck out or what? The post next to the area I hit was the starting point of the next roll of wire. My collision yanked all the U-nails out. The wire whipped across my neck and upper body, completely tearing off my outer sweatshirt.

THE VISION

I climbed on the back of my friend's bike, and we headed for Evanston. Again, the kind heart of fate spared me. My major arteries were intact.

I sat in the emergency room. No one rushed over to help. A head with a nurse's hat popped from around a corner every now and then. I'm sure I was in shock, but the nurses seemed more so than I. The doctor finally showed up. He had already gone home for the day. Wow, it was Doctor Daines! The same doctor I had as a child when my family lived in Mountain View. It had taken him ten minutes to get there. He must have lived on the other side of town.

After a few jokes about the headless horseman and almost losing my head over the deal, he patted me on the shoulder. "You'll be fine. I put fifty-two stitches on the outside and only six inside. After a couple of weeks, you can take the stitches out yourself. They will slide out easily when they are ready to be removed."

I put in my notice to end my employment at the hospital.

A few days later, I heard through some friend that Barbara and the kids had moved out of the house and that she was on her way to Laramie to live with her parents. I didn't have an opportunity to say goodbye to Kevin and Kim. What a heartless woman!

Evanston, being as small as it is, spewed gossip as well as any other Wyoming town. The word quickly got to my friend Judy. I received a letter from her. She had secured a job for me at Vanderbilt University Hospital in Nashville. It was really tempting. I actually thought about it for a few days, but I decided to go west and follow my original plan. I had no idea where I was going. I just had my confidence and curiosity.

CHAPTER FOUR

The Vision

I keep thinking of the vision I had every year during those ten years of my youth.

I shared this with friends later in life. The men would usually give me a questioning look—not say much and frankly didn't know how to respond.

On two occasions, women I talked to looked at me and said, "Oh, that was your birthing experience."

They had a point! I visualized what it would be like growing in a womb. How aware were we? And then suddenly be thrown into the light of our world. It made a lot of sense; but, to this day, I know there is much more to it than that. There has to be.

The feeling of no upside down or right side up seems like the environment that a fetus would be nurtured in. Would a pre-born feel fearful darkness? The spheres must mean something. It plainly made the point that size did not exist; after all, it was just a few months earlier that the fetus was a microscopic cell.

Maybe it's one of those things that do not follow the laws of physics in our three-dimensional world. If totally understood, this could be a clue to wormholes. If size did not exist, distance would not exist—just a thought.

When I left Wyoming for the great unknown, I didn't really know where I was going. It was the first of February, and the weather was cold with icy roads. My van was loaded with a bed and all my necessities packed around it (drum set, motorcycle). Inserting my eight-track tape into the stereo system, I headed straight for San Francisco. The tape was the best of rock and roll and also included my favorite folk singers Bob Dylan, Cat Stevens, and Neil Young.

The sun was just rising as America's "A Horse with No Name" blared in the speakers followed by Paul Simon's "Mother and Child Reunion." Tears rolled down my cheeks. I felt an overwhelming sadness.

On a positive note, a great weight was lifted off my shoulders. I looked forward to the coming adventure. The trip began with the beautiful and familiar Wasatch Mountains. I passed through Salt Lake City, followed by the salt flats, heading toward Reno. Even though I had driven a lot around southern Wyoming, Utah, and down to Las Vegas, I had never taken this road. The landscape was new to me.

Between Reno and Sacramento, the weather drastically changed. It went from below-freezing to tee-shirt weather and clear blue skies. The most obvious sensation was the salt smell in the air. I had only seen the ocean once in the last twenty years on a quick trip to San Diego.

As I neared San Francisco, I was thrust into the mayhem of rush-hour traffic. This was not the bumper-to-bumper crawl I later became used to. It was the fast, over-the-speed limit—still bumper-to-bumper—craziness that I had never experienced in Wyoming. Cars and trucks crowded the lanes on both sides of me. I gripped the steering wheel and stayed in the lane I was in.

The freeway led me south of San Francisco. At this point, I headed straight to the ocean. Pulling off the road at the first opportunity, I walked to the ocean's edge and sat down, gazing at the sight for two hours. The sunset was beyond description. My mind felt the same peace as the stars or falling snow. It definitely recharged my batteries. Finding a rest area, I pulled over and settled into my bed for the night.

Waking to the fresh salty ocean air with the sound of waves breaking and crashing against the rocks was music to my ears. I climbed out of my van and sat on the rocky ledge above the shore. What a beautiful sight! What a wonderful feeling! Having been born and raised in Wyoming, I had never realized the warmth and sensations that converged on me. I could sit here all day smelling the air and watching the hypnotic motions and details of the waves.

It was decision time. Do I drive north to experience San Francisco and then on to Seattle? Seattle seemed a magical place to me. I don't know why it appealed to me except for the fact that it was pulling me like a magnet.

South was my choice. My plans were to eventually go to Seattle, so I thought I might as well explore the coast and then end in the Northwest. The coastline mesmerized me when I saw the film *Play Misty for Me* prior to leaving Wyoming. Big Sur, Carmel, and Monterey looked like paradise. It was like being on an alien planet. Everything was lush and green. The cliffs turned me into a speck on the hillside, and surfers skimmed along the waves, then paddled vigorously through the white water to the swells forming outside. I wanted to find a job in that area and settle into the lifestyle, but I was much too antsy. My wanderlust had not been satisfied. I could always come back.

As I drove farther south, the population increased, and I found myself back in the world of jammed freeways. Los Angeles was huge, an ant colony of scattered direction and purpose. Each person was on his or her own agenda with their own unique life. I wasn't drawn to this area at all. A person could get swallowed up and lost.

Then came San Diego. It was in the early seventies, and the atmosphere was much more relaxed. Each area was like a small town.

My friend Steve Lytle from Evanston had moved here. The time I had spent with him at Sam's Tavern included his selling points on this area of the planet. He knew my marriage was falling apart when he rejoined the Navy. He also knew my passion for the arts. This was no New York or San Francisco, but it offered the outlets I was looking for.

Looking up his address in the phonebook, I found his home in a section of town called Hillcrest. I knocked on his door. When the door opened, there was Steve with a huge smile on his face. "I knew you would come to your senses and end up here," he said, as he put an arm around my shoulders and led me inside.

That evening, we cruised by a liquor store and bought a bottle of red wine. We continued north to La Jolla and found a small secluded cove, opened the bottle, and sat back to watch the sunset.

"I had a feeling you would show up sooner or later," Steve said, as he leaned back on a rock wall while sitting on the still-warm sand. "I'll show you around tomorrow."

"Sounds good. I still have my eyes set on Seattle, you know. My money won't last forever. I need to get a job."

"Save your money. You can stay rent-free with me for a few months until you have the time to see what's happening. My guess is that you will be here a while. I'll cover your food too. Buy some art supplies, and start painting."

My style at the time was oil painting on wood panels. I would buy a sheet of Masonite, sand it down, and apply two coats of gesso. Using a cross stroke with my brush, the primer formed a loose textured background. I placed the panel on the floor, leaned it against the wall, and dove in. Whenever I visited my parents, I would do the same thing—buy the materials, push the furniture aside, and paint. My Mom and Dad loved it!

Being away from the Wyoming environment, I found myself with patience and focus on detail I had never experienced before. The paintings I did turned out better than I could have imagined. The enjoyment I felt in the act of painting was through the roof!

Steve took me to the San Diego Art Institute in Balboa Park. They have regular monthly, juried shows, and weekly figure-drawing workshops. They had a great gallery, and I was excited about the workshops. The first month I entered a painting. It was accepted, and it immediately sold. The next month, they had a Southern California juried show. I was accepted, received a purchase award, and was asked to bring in another painting, which sold immediately.

Wow, what a great start—and all in the first two months in San Diego!

All of this excitement was tempered by the phone ringing. It was Barbara. I had been calling Kevin and Kim weekly. They were excited to talk to me. I missed them.

When I answered the phone, the first thing out of her mouth was: "Now that you realize you are a failure, why don't you come back?"

"Actually, things are going great! Why would you assume it wouldn't be? Why don't you pack the kids in the car and move out here? We could start fresh and leave all the Wyoming baggage behind."

"Nope" was her curt reply.

A strange thought surfaced in my mind: the memory of my asking her to put her seat belt on in my Dad's GTO before we were married—something about red flags.

"Nope."

This became a regular reply of hers. Unfortunately, it became the word she used from that point on whenever I called and asked to speak to the kids. "Nope."

I loved a small art supply store in Pacific Beach. It was my favorite place to buy needed materials. It had a unique character to it. It was old and rustic. It had an aura about it that felt like all the ghosts of art history were hanging out there. The shop was owned by Xavier Romano. Since I had lived at Steve's for three months, I asked Xavier if they were hiring. He had me fill out an application. I did it while at the store. I bought my needed supplies and headed home, after a stop at the beach to watch the surfers and the gorgeous babes in bikinis.

Besides the therapeutic value, my association with Steve turned out to be a drinking one. I actually felt that it was a "much-needed" medication at the time. Just before leaving Evanston, I had become acquainted with pot. Steve didn't use it—alcohol all the way for him.

Every now and then, we would visit our favorite spot in La Jolla, but mostly it was bars and taverns. I really enjoyed the difference in the people compared to Wyoming. Their attitudes and their humor were alien to me but exciting. Everyone was tan, and the women were beautiful and flirty.

Actually, that could have been because Steve carried this aura, or magic, that drew women to him. This was all done by his intelligence and wit. He was actually a little homely. He wore large glasses and had a larger than normal nose, and while the back of his hair was trimmed in military fashion, the front was combed to the point of covering one eye. All it took was a little wink and a verbal taunt to lure a woman into a conversation, and we had a female drinking partner for the evening.

Steve seemed to have a pretty unique and interesting job in the Navy. After a couple of months, he invited me to his workstation at Miramar and ran me through the same tests he gave new pilots. They made me feel a little foolish but showed actual problems a pilot would encounter.

Recently, there had been problems with the F-14 jet airplane as it was introduced to the Navy. During practice, they would do touch and gos. This was when a jet would fly in for a landing, touch its wheels on the tarmac, and take off again, banking to the left (or right) and then gain altitude. The problem was, after touching down, they would bank, and the roll didn't stop. The roll continued until the plane was upside down and still rolling. Pilots instinctively hit eject, and they were slammed into the tarmac from thirty feet above the ground.

Steve showed me the ejection seats. The seat itself took the impact with little effect. It was a different story with the pilots. The seats were covered in dried blood.

I received a call from The Fine Art Store as I was sitting with my legs crossed in front of a painting. It was Xavier. "We would like to hire you, but it will be at the main and much larger store in Kearny Mesa."

I was delighted.

It just so happened that Xavier graduated from the Art Institute of Chicago. He opened his store and expanded with two other art supply and framing stores from different areas of San Diego. There were three stores total. The Fine Art Store was the name that resulted from the merger.

Xavier did the hiring. He only wanted employees who had degrees in art or were accomplished artists. As a result, I met a great group of people who would always be devoted friends. We were about the same age and had an art career as our ultimate goal.

I started out in retail, which I had never done before. I learned a lot since it was the largest art supply store in Southern California. I don't know why, but I felt uncomfortable. The owner of that particular store noticed my struggle.

There were several areas of the store. In the front retail area, there was a design room where customers would bring their artwork to be framed. In the back, there was a large fitting area where they cut mats and assembled pieces into the frames. The largest area was stocked with every type of frame molding you could imagine, and a couple of employees cut and joined the frames. The rest of the building was a warehouse, where the art supplies were stored. An order desk was in a central location to assemble orders to be trucked to various locations.

The Fine Art Store was the major supplier to all the galleries, schools, and navy bases, as well as any other art-related businesses, such as illustrators and designers.

The owner of the Kearny Mesa store (another Steve) asked if I would drive the delivery truck. It was a Ford Econoline, the same year and model as mine. I jumped at the chance. It gave me the opportunity to intimately know the San Diego area.

I eventually came to know the owners and employees of all the art supply and framing customers. I loved that job and was very good at it since I am an orderly and efficient person. It also gave me access to all of the work areas of the store, which provided a great social life. I was free to roam around to each area when I wasn't driving. The other employees and I were always joking as we greeted each other with smiles. Flirting with the women who worked there was a blast. They flirted with me, too.

One task that had to be done at The Fine Art Store was to cover the back of the framed piece, add the wire, and wrap it in Kraft paper. A young man named Luis did this job.

Luis became an immediate friend. He was Hawaiian and Mexican in heritage, and his mom was a successful model, providing him with an upbringing in a beautiful house in a nice area. His dark hair flowed down to the middle of his back. Luis was an avid surfer and did well in competitions.

"Hey, Paul, want to go surfing with me this weekend? I have several extra boards."

"I've never surfed before."

"I know, Mr. Wyoming," he said with a smile. "I'll teach you."

It wasn't long before I became addicted to surfing. I would show up at Luis's house at six every Saturday morning, and we would hop in his surfer truck, decked out with boards and wet suits. I loved the smell of the coconut wax we used to cover our boards. He also had

THE VISION

a stereo system that he would crank up with Iron Butterfly filling the cab. We checked out all the local beaches while puffing on joints and deciding which waves were the best. By noon, we opened our first bottle of wine, kicked back on the beach, and watched the other surfers as they paddled out and rode waves. Luis was quick to point out the good ones and their unique styles.

I was in great shape and loved sports of all kinds. On my first day out, my arms were so tired I couldn't hold onto the board as I walked out of the water—this coming from a person who did fifty push-ups every morning and had for years—different muscles, I guess.

Watching the sunrise and set every day while sitting on my board became my new daily habit, regardless of the waves, flat or stormy.

I eventually had enough money to move out of Steve's apartment and find a place of my own.

A couple of employees at work found a nice house with a view overlooking Ocean Beach. They asked if I would move in with them. It was five blocks from the shore, and you could see the pier with all the coastal activities from our picture window. A large glass-enclosed patio was on the north side of the house. This became my first studio.

I soon became involved with Sue, a fantastic artist who is a couple of years older than me. She worked at The Fine Art Store in the fitting room, and I thought of it as a comfortable match. I really enjoyed being with her, and we had mutual respect for each other's artwork. Sue had a one-person show scheduled at a great gallery in La Jolla. Her paintings were large. They were unique because of the glazes she used. Her style had an amazing effect with a floral theme.

We were together for only a year when she mentioned that she would like to move to East Hampton, New York. It was on the eastern tip of Long Island. She had a couple of friends there. She didn't intend to stay permanently, just for a year or two.

It was a long trip, and she asked me if I would help her drive. I asked for a two-week vacation, which I had coming anyway. We packed her car and headed east.

My only request was to go through Wyoming so I could visit Kevin and Kim. It was a fun drive. We had taken a trip to San Francisco a couple of months earlier. Sue had relatives there, and it had given us an opportunity to explore the Bay Area. We traveled well together. I had never been to New York.

It was exciting to visit my kids in Laramie. They were really glad to see me. My ex-wife was still in punishing mode (which she never got over) and only let me visit for twenty minutes while she stood there glaring at me.

"OK," I said. "Can I come to visit them tomorrow?"

"Nope. I have to go to work, and I need to take the kids to the babysitter."

"That's perfect. I can watch them tomorrow, and I will have them waiting here when you get home!"

"Nope."

Sue and I spent the night at the fraternity, rose early, and continued on our way. I had never experienced the country east of Wyoming before. It was an easy, fun trip.

THE VISION

It was hard to not think about my son and daughter. I was pretty sad and quiet. Sue understood, and we traveled in silence for a while.

New York was an awesome experience. Long Island was beautiful and quite the contrast from the city. I spent three days with her before she drove me to the airport.

"I do plan on going back to San Diego," she said. "I love you, but I have always wanted to do this; I need to do this."

"I'll miss you, Sue." I wasn't sure she would follow through with her promise to return, but what could I say?

CHAPTER FIVE

My journey back to San Diego began with a flight to Nashville. I wanted to visit Geof and Judy. Judy picked me up and we drove to her place outside of town. It was a comfortable house in the middle of the woods. I took a walk by myself and found a really cool turtle shell. When I showed it to Judy, she laughed and said they were really common in that area. When she lived in Wyoming, the same thing had happened. She came to work one day with a cow skull. I laughed and said, "You can find those everywhere."

That night, they had a gig in a small town about thirty miles away. I helped them set up. They were *really* good. I had heard her play the guitar and sing in Wyoming. She was talented and had come a long way. The two of them worked well together. They also played in Nashville, and Judy ended up recording her original songs on two LPs.

A couple of days later, they drove me to a freeway on-ramp so I could hitchhike home.

I was a little nervous when I stuck my thumb out for a ride, but my first experience put me at ease. My Army duffle was crammed full and heavy. It would be a long trip, so I decided to relax and take the rides and the days as they came without being too anxious to reach my goal. I was also carrying a book: Carl Jung's *The Spirit in Man,*

Art and Literature. Reading his whole volume set was a goal of mine. It was slow reading but packed with profound enlightenment.

My first ride was in a noisy open-air jeep. It was a friendly atmosphere. The driver was only going to Jackson, 130 miles away.

The next ride was from a young man in a Chevrolet Monza. This was also an easy, friendly trip. It was a smooth, quiet car with great music. He dropped me off in Memphis. He was headed north and dropped me off on the freeway without taking an exit.

I was only there ten minutes before a state patrolman pulled up in front of me and stopped. He kicked his door open and jumped out of his cruiser in an angry and aggressive stance. He had a Smokey the Bear hat on like the drill sergeants I had experienced a few years ago in the Army.

"What the hell are you doing on the freeway, you ass!"

He stomped toward me with his elbows out and glazed eyes like he was going to kick some butt.

Before I could respond, he yelled, "Pick up your bag and get in the back seat."

He grabbed my upper arm and roughly escorted me to his car. He opened the door and threw me—bag and all—in the back seat. He slammed the door and climbed into the driver's seat. He turned to face me and started yelling with his finger pointing and wagging.

"Don't you know better than to hitchhike on the freeway?"

"I was just dro—"

"Shut the fuck up. I don't want to hear a word from your mouth."

"Yes, Si—"

"What did I just say, numbnuts? Keep your mouth shut! I want you to get the fuck out of my car now! I'll be back in ten minutes. If you're still here when I return, I'm taking you straight to jail."

He let me out, hopped back in his cruiser, and peeled out.

"Damn," I thought. "I can't make it to an exit ramp in ten minutes." I was on a freeway bridge. My previous ride had left me on the side of the westbound freeway, at least fifty feet above the ground.

I walked swiftly, toting my heavy bag and thumbing the traffic.

I believe I have a guardian angel. Too many convenient things happen in my life, as happened that evening. Within a couple of minutes, an old beat-up pickup pulled over. There was an elderly fellow driving.

"Throw your bag in the back and hop in," he yelled through the open window.

"Thanks!" I yelled back above the noise of traffic.

We immediately crossed the Mississippi River into Arkansas and headed west.

"Thank God you're here. I need help driving."

"How far are you going?" I asked.

"I'm going north to Saint Louis. I'm blind. I can stay between the lines and follow the car ahead of me, but I can't read the road signs."

The exit to St. Louis was just a few miles ahead.

"I'm continuing west," I said.

THE VISION

"That's okay; I just need to know what exit to take."

That wasn't much of a ride, but it worked well for both of us. I escaped the law, and he found his exit.

Again, I immediately caught another ride in the back of an old truck. This was another quickie with three teenagers. They took me to an on-ramp at Interstate 40.

It was a long walk carrying my heavy bag to the top of the ramp. Another hitchhiker was standing there. He was a strange, pink-faced young fellow, and we caught a ride with two long-haired men dressed in hippie-type clothing. We had a great discussion about left-wing politics before they dropped us off at the next truck stop.

Arriving after dark, I went in for a cup of coffee. I felt uncomfortable with the pink-faced guy and left him at that point. After a relaxing sit, I walked to an on-ramp and climbed to the top of a hill that had a small ledge under a freeway bridge. There was a half-moon. I spread my sleeping bag out and quickly dozed off. A couple of hours later, I woke up. The traffic had died off, and the moon had set. There were hundreds of tiny fireflies that looked like moving stars. I had never seen fireflies before. I watched them until I fell back asleep.

The following morning was a Sunday; you could tell by the quiet and lack of traffic. I stowed my sleeping bag and caught the first ride I thumbed. There were four people in the front of a pickup. They said they were going to California. "We'll give you a ride, but you need to get in the back."

That was fine with me. I tossed my duffle in the back and hopped in. Within ten minutes, I was shivering in the cold windy bed of that truck. I pulled out my sleeping bag and crawled inside. AAAH! That was much better—toasty but still bouncy.

A short time later, they pulled over again and picked up another hitchhiker. His name was John, and he was decked out in new, up-to-date hiking equipment. It wasn't long before he pulled out his sleeping bag and crawled in.

John was going west for now. Then he planned to go north along the Pacific Coast to Washington and then back to his home on the East Coast. His plan was to stop and spend a few days at each national park, hiking, and camping. The motivation for him was the difficult time he was having with his girlfriend back home. He had to get away and think things through. We got along great. He was easy to talk to, and we enjoyed each other's company.

We met the four travelers who rode up front when we pulled into a rest area. Don was the driver. He was around sixty years old and he only had five dollars to his name. He had just bought this new, 1976, baby-blue pickup and needed to make it to California, figuring that if he loaded up with hitchhikers, he could scrounge enough for the rest of the trip. The other three—two gals and a guy in their early twenties—were also hitching. All they had was the clothes on their back—no money. They were originally going to Florida until they met Don, who talked them into California.

John and I pitched in for gas. The three hitchers in front rotated riding in the back with us to give the others a little more room in the cramped cab. It was a great trip. John and I enjoyed the people we traveled with as we drove all day and that night through hail and a lightning storm, using John's and my gear for comfort. I had an air mattress that we all sat on to keep our tailbones from shattering.

Our money wasn't going to last long at this rate, so John and I left our ride at a truck stop just outside of Albuquerque, New Mexico. It was a friendly parting. The last we saw of them, they were trying to hock Don's spare tire for more gas money.

THE VISION

John looked at me and said, "Ready for a nice breakfast?"

"You bet," I said.

We headed to the truck-stop restaurant and had a more than enjoyable meal. We felt too guilty to eat in front of the others, so we had starved along with them.

After indulging ourselves with a fine American breakfast, we marched our way to the on-ramp. It was a bit of a walk. I, dragging my too-heavy duffle bag, and John, walking erectly with all his gear stowed neatly in his backpack.

It was getting hot—real hot. Thankfully, it only took thirty minutes before a blue van pulled next to us. We slid open the sliding door and piled in. AAAH! Air conditioning!

This guy looked military. He also had a couple of Air Force stickers on his van. The first thing he did was open a cooler and give us each a sandwich and a bottle of beer.

A radio was loudly spewing road chatter; he was really into his CB radio. You could hear all the happenings on that stretch of road—where the police were hiding, who was stuck on the side of the road, and their locations. Our driver was also talking. He was involved in the CB conversation, and from the contents of the van, it looked like he was ready for any emergency. There were a couple of first-aid kits, jugs of water, blankets, jumper cables, a tow rope, etc.

Mid to late afternoon, our driver dropped us off just outside of Flagstaff, Arizona. We walked into some thick woods and found a secluded camping spot. Well, it felt secluded, but you could still hear the freeway background noise. John pulled out his tent, and we collected wood to start a campfire. Through an opening in the woods, we could see a beautiful, snow-capped mountain.

John pulled out a couple of freeze-dried meals. He had bought these to prepare for his trip and finally had a chance to try them. It turned out to be a disaster. We were barely able to swallow the stuff, but he saved the day by pulling out a bag of snack food.

We sat back enjoying the woods and the campfire, smoked some weed, talked, laughed, and told stories.

"I think I'll hike up to that mountain tomorrow," he said, as we looked at the fading light and its beautiful effects on the environment. "Come with me. This is part of the reason I'm taking this trip. When we get back, we can go up the coast to Oregon and Washington."

I rested my head against my duffle and contemplated his proposal. My bag would be a major pain in the ass.

"No, I don't think so. I'm tempted, but I'm anxious to get back to San Diego."

We swapped addresses, prepared our sleeping bags, and quickly dozed off.

The next morning, we walked back to the freeway off-ramp and followed it into town. We found a Denny's restaurant and had another great breakfast. When we had cleaned our campsite, I had thrown my duffle bag in a deep hole. Carrying it into town would have been a pain.

After our meal, we walked outside, shook hands, and said our goodbyes. He started walking directly toward his mountain, and I walked back up the road to the freeway ramp to collect my bag.

Halfway up the ramp, I had an unexpected visitor. An Arizona Highway Patrol car pulled next to me.

"So, where are you going?" he yelled through the open passenger side window.

"I'm hitchhiking to San Diego."

"So, where's your bag?"

"I dropped it in a hole just up ahead."

"Bad idea!" he said. "There are transients all over this area. Go get your bag, and I'll take you to a good spot to catch a ride."

I walked into the woods, retrieved my bag—it was still there—and walked back out to the patrol car.

"Throw your bag in the back. You can sit up front with me."

He drove me to the beginning of a busier on-ramp.

"Good luck, buddy."

"Thanks! I appreciate it," I said, as I pulled my bag out of his back seat and shut the door.

Off he went, quickly blending with the traffic and disappearing. Now that was a different experience from the last run-in I had had in Memphis.

A young man in a jeep picked me up. He was checking out the university in Flagstaff and on his way back home to Kingman, Arizona. It was another great ride. Chicago, America, and The Eagles played loudly on his radio.

I got off in Kingman and was hit by a wall of heat. This was a huge difference from the cool mountain air of Flagstaff. Kingman was only seventy-five miles from Vegas. People who have visited the Vegas area know what the heat is like.

I glanced a block away and beheld a wondrous sight—a Greyhound bus station! No one had to twist my arm. I arrived in Vegas two hours later.

I found a payphone and called my parents. Mom answered and picked me up within twenty minutes. There is nothing like going home after an ordeal like mine. Actually, I had a wonderful trip—no problems and plenty of adventure.

I checked in with Sue and then called my roommates in San Diego to let them know I would be back in a couple of weeks. In the short time I was gone, they had received a notice that the owner was moving back into the house. They had to move.

Dad rented a U-Haul truck for me to make the trip to San Diego. My roommates could use some help moving out of the house. All I really had there were art supplies and lots of paintings that I loaded and drove back to Vegas.

While I was in San Diego, I checked on some paintings I had placed in a couple of galleries. I had sold one and received a purchase award for another.

When I returned to Vegas, Dad told me that the schools would let out for the summer in two weeks. At the time, he was teaching in the Clark County school district. My teaching certificate was still valid, so I stayed and substitute taught until the students were released for summer.

THE VISION

It was nice to see my parents even though it got old fast. I had tasted freedom, and they were stuck in the same mundane tasks and habits. That didn't matter. Their place always recharged my batteries, and they loved me; but in two weeks, I would be bouncing off the walls. In the meantime, I bought some Masonite, sanded it, and applied two coats of gesso to a 36" by 48" panel. I found a wall, pushed the furniture aside, and sat cross-legged in front of it with a brush in hand and oil paints on a palette next to me.

My parents would have been happy if I had stayed there and painted the rest of my life.

This was a point in my life when I had time to look at the whole picture and think about what I was doing. I was actually feeling pretty lost. I could hook up with John and hitch up to the Northwest; I missed Sue, but I had no idea if I would see her again, and Judy had a job offer for me at Vanderbilt University Hospital in Nashville.

Since I had last visited my parents, Barbara had sent photos of Kevin and Kim to them. She wouldn't send them to me, using the excuse that I wouldn't let her have my address. My brother and parents would have been happy to supply that information. I looked at the photos and cried.

It was really hard dealing with Barbara's passive-aggressive behavior. She made it a point to make sure she cozied up to my family and at the same time kept any communication between me and my son and daughter nonexistent. When I did attempt to contact them, she did what she could to degrade me and enjoyed denying me any access to them. She even drove to Vegas to visit my family. My brother Don, who taught structural engineering at UW, and his family were not spared either. Her whole point was to play the game of "poor me," deserted by Paul so he could run around having fun while using the excuse that he's an artist.

What she didn't understand was that she was treating my family as if they couldn't see through her manipulations. They would always love me and knew me better than that. They knew I wanted to see and be with my kids.

At one point, my mom called me. "I am *so* glad you divorced Barbara! I do not like that woman."

At least my parents had the opportunity to see my kids.

Substitute teaching was not an easy job in Vegas. There were students from many diverse ethnic groups, and there were also students with parents who had jobs in the entertainment industry or the casinos. They were all pretty transient. That was the complete opposite of what I had experienced in Wyoming.

When the school year ended, my dad was ready to travel. He loved seeing new places. The rest of the family couldn't stand traveling with him. I was different. I enjoyed traveling with my dad. I recalled the memories of living in Mountain View during grade school and traveling to Salt Lake City every two weeks to pick up supplies.

I had something the rest of the family didn't have with Dad—that was patience. So, Dad and I decided to take a trip. We began by driving north through Nevada, then turned west to Sacramento. We swapped driving, but when it was his turn, that's when the fun began—or "the terror" according to the rest of the family.

When it was Dad's turn to drive, he plopped in the driver's seat, started the car, and took off. The weaving back and forth could be a little scary, but it didn't bother me since this hadn't changed in ten years, and at least he stayed between the lines. He reached across the

THE VISION

seat to the glove box as he moved closer to the centerline of the two-lane road. He removed a map and dropped it in my lap, as he jerked the wheel back toward the center of the lane. That was a sure sign that I needed to open it; so, I did, spreading it out on my lap.

"There's a tablet and pen in there too," he said

"OK, I see it."

"Take down this number: 85301.4."

"OK, got it," I said, as I wrote down the numbers from his odometer.

"Can you find where we are on the map?

"Uhhh, yeah."

"Try our homemade pies."

"What?"

"That sign—it says try our homemade pies."

"Oh, OK, I found us on the map."

"What's the next town?"

"Uhhh, Coaldale."

"How do you know?"

"I just saw a sign."

"What was the name of the last town we just went through?"

"Tonopah," I said, as I placed my finger on the map and traced the road back to the previous dot.

"What town is after Coaldale?"

"Mount Montgomery. I'm not sure if it's a town or a mountain."

"Yosemite, 120 miles," he said, as he ducked his head to look at the mileage.

"Yeah, I found it."

"Write this down: 85312.9."

"There's a lake right before we enter Yosemite."

"What's the name of the lake?"

"Mono Lake."

"Food and gas next exit."

"What? Are we stopping there?"

"No. That's just what the sign said."

"Hey, Dad, could you pull over? I need to get something in the trunk."

"Sure," he said as he pulled off the road.

I climbed out, walked to the back, and opened the pull-up door on the Datsun. I pulled out my duffle, scrounged around, and pulled out the book I was reading. It was another Carl Jung book from his volume set. I knew I wouldn't get a chance to read. It was just an excuse for what I was really after.

THE VISION

I pulled out a bag that Melinda had given me when I was in San Diego. I reached in, pulled out a marijuana brownie, and gobbled it down. Then went back to the cab with my book.

"What book is that?" Dad asked.

"*Symbols of Transformation.*"

Dad took off down the road. "How far to Mono Lake? Can you figure it out?"

"UUHHH—about 118 miles. There is a road we need to take about eighteen miles past Mount Montgomery. There should be a sign."

"Best Italian Pizza—Wally's Family Restaurant—twenty miles."

"What?"

"That sign."

"Oh."

"Hey, remember when we lived in that trailer at Coal Mine?"

"I sure do, Dad."

"It was like being in a boat in the middle of a storm the way it rocked in the wind. I miss that. That was fun, wasn't it?"

"That is a great memory, Dad. I'll always remember it."

"Camping and recreation—five miles."

"What?"

"That's what the sign said. Oh, take down this number: 85331.2."

And so, the saga continued. Yosemite was our next stop. A close friend, Ron McCully whom I had met in San Diego, was working as a tour bus driver. We tracked him down and hopped on his bus.

Ron had been a part-time roommate at the Ocean Beach house. He was very adventurous—spur-of-the-moment adventurous. I came home from work one Friday, and the next thing I knew, we were on our way to the Grand Canyon for the weekend. He had some friends who worked at the restaurant and bunkhouse at the bottom of the canyon, right on the Colorado River. We had a great place to sleep, good food, and our own personal tour guides. We visited places ordinary tourists were never aware of.

Ron had also bought several of my paintings. He was very supportive of my art and my direction.

From Yosemite, Dad and I traveled to Sacramento and then north to Redding. We drove west to Eureka and spent the night. The next morning, we followed the coast down to the San Francisco Bay Area.

We arrived in San Francisco late in the afternoon. I was driving. It was the same crazy anthill I had run into when I left Wyoming, so I was better prepared this time. We entered from the north, crossing the Golden Gate Bridge.

"I'm starved!" said Dad. "Let's get something to eat. What do ya say?"

"Sounds good, Dad. What do you feel like?"

"Anything. Pullover and park. I see a lot of restaurants in this area."

I found a spot, and we got out, stretched, and walked down the sidewalk.

THE VISION

"Here's an Italian restaurant, Dad."

He walked up to a menu hanging in the window.

"Too expensive. Let's try that one over there."

"It's not that bad. You're used to getting deals in Vegas."

He walked two doors down to an old-looking café. "Mmmm. No menu in the window."

"Let's go in and sit down. They can't be that expensive."

We found a booth, and a middle-aged waitress came over with water and menus.

"Here you go, gentlemen. What would you like to drink?"

"Water's fine," said Dad as he scanned the menu. "God damn it! They charge an arm and a leg here! Let's go."

"Dad! This is what they charge in San Diego."

Too late. Dad's out the door.

"How about that one across the street?" We crossed the street. It had a window menu.

"God damn it to hell! They're even more expensive! Let's drive to another part of town."

So back to the car we went. Dad drove. Ten minutes later, we found another area that had a few restaurants.

The first window menu: "Damn it! They're thieves!"

After two more, I said, "Dad! I'd rather see the sights than go restaurant hopping!" He picked up that I was getting mad.

"OK, this one works." We sat down and finally had dinner.

We went through the same process when we looked for a motel to spend the night. After six attempts to pick an affordable room, we finally settled into a cheap dumpy place, but again, I had to put my foot down, or he would have compared prices until midnight.

Needing a break, I told Dad I needed to take a walk. San Francisco at night is beautiful. During my stroll, I accidentally ran into the San Francisco Art Institute. It was a beautiful building. The back of the building had a ladder leading to the roof, so I climbed it. Looking down through the skylights, I could see the individual art classrooms. At one point, a janitor looked up and saw me. He waved and motioned for me to come down. The building was completely empty except for him. He said I was welcome to check the place out. I wandered through the building, wishing that I could have gone to school there. Maybe I could do graduate work in this place.

The next morning, we headed south to Santa Cruz and turned inland. We had one more overnight at Bakersfield, then back to Vegas.

One thing I have failed to mention was my commitment to the National Guard. Through all of this activity, I was still required to attend monthly meetings and two weeks of summer camp for the six-year stint that was required.

I was in the Evanston, Wyoming National Guard when I had worked at the hospital. It was an artillery unit. Summer camps were in Utah. We had war games and practiced shooting live rounds from our eight-inch howitzers.

THE VISION

Then I transferred to the Vegas unit for one year and had the forgettable experience of summer camp at Death Valley in August.

The final three years—ending in 1976—were spent in a unit in El Cajon, California. We convoyed to Death Valley while I was in this unit as well. This was also in August, the hottest days of summer. The temperature soared to 120 degrees in the daytime. There were no air conditioners, and the only relief we got was after the sunset. After the evening mess, a group of us would walk out to an unused firing range and watch the sunset while smoking weed. We didn't need a joint to enjoy the sunsets. They were absolutely spectacular. The cooling began immediately. It even got to the point of being downright cold.

Living my life as a young adult and inserting a military commitment into it was like living two separate lives. At first, I was annoyed by the inconvenience. As time went on, I was more than capable of enjoying both realities. After all, I had no choice—might as well put my focus into whichever was happening at the time. It was good for my character. The Guard—as it turned out—was much better than the alternative.

Growing my hair to fit with the times would have been great, but all my friends were okay with it being short. They understood that the Guard required a military cut hairdo.

I will never understand why our country was involved in so many of the wars we fought in. Maybe so we would have a fit and prepared military. If our lives really were threatened, we would need a well-equipped military and seasoned veterans who knew the reality of the situation.

The scariest and most truthful reasons for going to war were what frightens me most—greed and power! Unfortunately, our country is teeming with both.

CHAPTER SIX

Hitchhiking became a usual thing for me. After Dad and I arrived back in Vegas, I had him drop me off on the strip so I could thumb a ride to San Diego.

There was no problem getting my job back at The Fine Art Store. I started driving the delivery truck the day after I returned.

Working at the art store, I met a guy named Martin. He worked in the molding department. Frame molding needed to be ordered and organized. He and his supervisor Dave cut and joined frames for the fitters.

Martin met a young gal named Mellissa, and they lived together in a small apartment in Pacific Beach.

As things always seem to work out, when I returned from my traveling experience, Martin and Mellissa took a two-week vacation. They needed someone to watch their place and take care of their cat. There I was, needing a place to stay until I found a place for myself. I had friends who said I could stay with them, but it is always better to have your privacy and not feel obligated.

While driving the delivery truck, I needed to stop at the other two stores to drop off and pick up supplies and framing. At the Pacific Beach store, Xavier asked me if I would come see him after work.

When I arrived that evening, we sat down, and he said:

"I'm laying you off. I'm doing this because I think you are a very talented artist and you need to spend time actually doing your work. You will receive unemployment benefits for a year. I will rehire you after that."

I sat back in surprise as he continued.

"I have an artist friend who just passed away. Before he died, he built a fabulous studio. His widow will only allow another artist to use it. She trusts me. This is the address; it's a couple of blocks from here. Go see her, and tell her Xavier sent you. Offer her 100 dollars a month."

That studio became my home for three years, and I did tons of work. I bought a bicycle and put some high-rise handlebars on it. The beach was a couple of blocks away, so I cruised the beach on my bike and did my surfing thing every morning. In the afternoon, I took a break from painting and rode down the Mission Beach boardwalk. I would peddle down the ocean side and peddle back on the bayside—three miles each way.

Once a week I biked to La Jolla, following the coast north past Windansea to watch the surfers, then on to the La Jolla Cove. On the way back, I would visit the Museum of Modern Art and make a stop at my favorite bookstore where I would browse or buy. It was a fabulous bookstore with a great environment.

The studio I rented was well equipped. It had a huge bookshelf that was packed with hundreds of art books. There were drawers filled with brushes, palette knives, and tubes of unopened paints. The only problem with the studio was that it had no shower or bath. It did have a toilet, a kitchen sink, and a refrigerator.

There was no problem finding a place to shower. My friends seemed more than happy to accommodate me. They gave me keys to their houses, so I could bathe when I wanted, even if they weren't there. They also had showers at the beach. After spending the morning surfing, I would shower to get the saltwater off before I returned to the studio.

While I lived in the Ocean Beach house, one of my roommates, Bob Thompson, began dating Melinda, the person who ran the order desk at the art store. It wasn't long before she moved in with him. We had several fun parties at their house.

During that time, I met Melinda's younger sister Karen. Karen was a gorgeous blond and began giving me attention after Sue moved to Long Island, New York.

A few days after I moved into the Pacific Beach studio, Karen showed up carrying two ferns in hanging pots. More plants followed, along with a small bar with stools. Every time she visited, more items and food were added to the studio. She cooked my meals, shared my bed, and modeled for me.

Karen was also a free spirit and disappeared for a few days every now and then. She was ambitious and landed well-paying jobs. We maintained a great relationship for the rest of the years that I lived in San Diego. I became close friends with her whole family, and we would go to her mom's house for fantastic meals and a shower every week or so.

Life was strange in Southern California. People didn't become attached to one another like they did in Wyoming. If I became

THE VISION

involved with another woman, Karen would back off and then start coming around again when the relationship had ended. She became a friend, a lover, and one of my best patrons. She bought several of my paintings at full price and eventually bought her own house. At one point, she either got married or lived with a guy who had a successful career. He also bought my work—a bronze sculpture. I am not sure how that relationship ended, but Karen and I still saw each other and spent time at her mom's house for dinner.

After I had been in the studio for about a year, I returned to work at The Fine Art Store.

That was also the time Sue returned from Long Island and showed up at my door.

"I told you I would come back."

I was taken aback. "I never expected to see you again. I haven't heard much from you since I left you in New York."

We had had some correspondence, but that had slowed the longer she was gone.

We went out for dinner, and the conversation immediately turned to my relationship with Karen. Sue had already talked to someone who had filled her in on the details.

Unfortunately, that was the last I saw of Sue. I could have—would have—stayed with her. We got along great! If only I could have known she really was coming back. She had been gone for two years. My relationship with Karen was one in which I could have easily gone back to Sue, but she was hurt that I didn't wait. It was over.

I also developed a closer friendship with Martin. You would need to know Martin to understand that he really *was* a character—not always in a good way. There were many snags in our relationship. He had a knack for causing trouble, but the good came with the bad.

We bought guitars at the same time and played music together. I would hang at his house often and shower there when I needed to. In 1977, he quit the art store and got a job at the Reuter Gallery in the Gaslamp Quarter on Fifth Avenue. A year later, he contacted me and said that David Reuter, the owner, was looking for more help. He said I should check the place out and meet him. Martin had already sold him on my abilities, so I had the job if I wanted it. I quit The Fine Art Store and started a few days later.

The Gaslamp was in the middle of downtown San Diego. It was the old part of town with beautiful buildings that were constructed in the late 1800s. It had never been completely renovated, and great studio spaces were available.

Gary Ghirardi was a major factor in and contributor to the energy of Fifth Avenue. He also held the lease to a ballroom I moved into and lived in for eight years. He was a great advocate of the arts and found spaces for many artists. Gary had been in the area for a while and was familiar with what was available.

His opening of Installation Gallery added an alternative to many existing galleries. This place provided many great shows and installations by Gaslamp artists. He was very liberal in his thinking, providing exposure and opportunities to many artists, many of whom other galleries were not willing to show.

I moved from my studio in Pacific Beach to Gary's 6,000 square-foot ballroom. It had beautiful two-foot-square tin tiles for the ceiling along with two huge skylights. There was a small stage in the corner and built-in benches along the walls. You could bang the edges of these benches with your fist, and little rocky shapes with tooth marks in them would fall to the floor. On closer inspection, I realized it was fossilized gum that was stuck under the bench during dances at the time of World War II. When I leaned down and looked under the edge, it was densely packed with these little antiques.

Two huge doors opened to the third-floor fire escape, and you could sit there and watch the activity on the street for hours. There was plenty of entertainment.

The fire escape ladder went one flight up to the roof. I often climbed it and sat next to one of the skylights. Tall buildings surrounded me. I would smoke a joint, drink wine, and enjoy the surrounding view, contemplating my place in this world and where my art was going. It stimulated my creative energy. The street activity and noise also inspired me. I loved that environment.

Fifth Avenue was filled with activity—the wrong kind perhaps, but it actually added to the character of the area. There were sailors, bums, hookers, tattoo parlors, and x-rated book and video stores.

I knew a few artists in the Gaslamp and quickly met more. As it turned out, the buildings were occupied by really good artists. Some were from New York and San Francisco. It seemed that only an elite few knew about this place. Because of the reputation and condition of the buildings, no normal person wanted to move downtown.

There were performance artists, too. Diamanda Galás, a well-known performance singer living in New York, often visited her brother, Philip-Dimitri Galás, who performed in the Gaslamp; and Whoopi Goldberg was there before making it big. There were painters, sculptors, actors, photographers, and musicians, all on the cutting edge of their art.

I had always felt left out by not having experienced the historically popular impressionist movement of Europe in the late 1800s and the abstract expressionist movement of New York in the early to mid-1900s. I was born too late. Reading about the artists and the art scenes of those times was a favorite pastime of mine. Their stories seemed familiar like I had lived them myself. Maybe I had— in another life.

The Gaslamp was vibrant with that same energy, and it made me think of those past art movements.

I bought 300 feet of one-inch by two-inch pine and a roll of canvas. Within a couple of weeks, I stretched and applied gesso to fifteen canvases that ranged from four feet square to eight feet by twelve feet. I dove in and painted day and night, breaking only to work at the gallery and socialize with other artists.

I also attended figure-drawing workshops. This evolved into my providing weekly figure-drawing classes in my studio. I used the same models that the local universities and colleges used. After paying the models, I had a little cash left over—not a lot.

These models were always dependable and experienced. I had friends who asked me if they could model. It would never work out. I always said yes, but I called my regular models anyway. The friends who wanted to pose would never show up. The classes were three hours long, the same as I had always been used to. Not only would I teach but I would also sit with the group and draw.

I didn't just make art. The history and origins of art have always fascinated me, from cave paintings to the present. I loved art history and read about artists and art movements on a continual basis. I had a subscription to *Artforum International Magazine* and kept up with activities across the globe.

THE VISION

I had focused on Salvador Dali when I was a young man. His deformation, coupled with his realistic style, brought his paintings to life in the form of dreams and imagination. I moved on to the impressionists by reading *Lust for Life* by Irving Stone and continued to biographies of Monet, Degas, Cezanne, and many more. I read about the artists and styles of the Renaissance with its Christian influence.

An artist friend was obsessed with the hyperrealism of the Pre-Raphaelites, so I bought a book he suggested. I read about Asian art, Egyptian art, and symbols. I also enjoyed reading about the Incan, Mayan, and Aztec art and their symbolism. Modern art fascinated me with New York abstract expressionists and minimalists. All of these countless styles and civilizations—Wow!

I also read historical novels that weren't art-related, so I could intertwine them with the lives of these many artists I had studied.

The society we live in today seems to push the arts aside. The education system has cut funding for the arts and encourages the sciences, math, and history. Sports have become a highly funded direction in some schools.

What about the individual? How can a person feel unique and special without personal expression? I believe that a lot of the problems we have today are a result of this lopsided philosophy.

Thinking back on my school days, when I went to UW, I would go home to Grainger for the holidays and spring break. My dad asked me on one occasion if I would teach an art class to his junior high students. I jumped at the chance.

When I walked into the classroom, I handed out a blank piece of paper to each student.

"OK, everyone, draw a horse," I said.

A couple of students dove in, and a few started drawing with hesitation, not so confident or sure of what they were doing. A few sat in stunned silence, and one said, "I can't draw."

"Everyone needs to draw," I said. "You have forty-five minutes."

After the time had expired, I collected the drawings and placed them around the room.

"OK. Which drawing is the best?"

Immediately, the students pointed to a couple of drawings that were actually very well done.

"Those are really good drawings!" I said after spending few moments pondering their choice. I also wanted to give attention to the students who really could draw horses well.

"So how about this one?" I pointed to one that was closer to a stick figure with legs that were much too long.

The students were silent.

I had prepared some visual aids that consisted of art done by well-known artists.

I pulled out a work by Salvador Dali and asked if anyone had heard of the artist, and most had. His horse also had extreme, exaggerated, long legs with a tiny horse body on the top.

"Or how about this one?" I held up a drawing of a horse by Pablo Picasso. "Look how deformed and exaggerated this one is!"

I glanced around the room. "When you look at all of these drawings, what stands out? What is consistent with all these drawings?"

"They're all horses," announced a bright young student.

"Right! But the point I want to make is that every horse is different. No two are the same." The students scanned the room as if that wasn't obvious.

"Everyone in this room is unique and different. Each person has his own way of depicting a horse. That's a good thing."

My dad talked to me after I returned to school. After I left Grainger, every time they had an art class, his students were completely focused and excited about their work. They even ran around showing each other what they had done.

I also had fun with my non-artist friends in San Diego. A few would invite me to dinner on occasion or let me use their shower.

On one occasion, I was sitting in a friend's living room talking, I scoped their place out and was surprised that they had absolutely nothing on their walls.

"So," I said, "I am working on a painting that is really bothering me. It just doesn't seem finished, or maybe I'm using the wrong colors. Would you mind if I brought it over here for a month? I'm really tired of looking at it. We can hang it on your wall, and I can take a break and work on another one without being distracted."

"Sure!" they said with excitement.

The next time I visited, I brought a somewhat large canvas, and we hung it on their biggest living room wall.

"Thanks!" I said, "I need this break."

A month later, I visited them again. I thanked them and took the painting back to my studio. The next time I showed up—lo and behold—their walls were filled with art, posters, or hangings of some sort.

With a smile and a bit of embarrassment, they said, "After you took the painting back, we couldn't stand looking at empty walls."

"Mission accomplished."

Every artist I met had a unique vision and a philosophy. Mine was more like a learning experience that would last a lifetime. It wasn't so much about my artwork; it was what I had learned and how I could use that experience on my next painting.

I had been told a few times that an artist should not put white in all his colors. My response to that was to spend a year putting white in all my colors. What they said made sense, but I had to understand it through experience.

So, what did I learn? It's not a good idea to put white in all my colors! Actually, mixing white with a color was fine; it just read better if it was next to a color with no white.

I also became aware of what happens while you mix white with a color. Cerulean blue, for instance, gains in value and intensity, but there is a peak to the intensity. At a certain point, the intensity drops off as the value increases.

THE VISION

Every color has its own range. I learned to recognize that and use it the way I wanted—with understanding.

The importance of maintaining my skill level has always been a priority. To do this, I continually worked from the human figure and painted landscapes.

My figurative work always seemed like an exercise rather than an attempt to do a finished piece. Capturing the feeling and expression of the model's pose was a priority. This translated to anything else I drew, even non-figurative work. Speed was important, not to see how fast I could draw, but to keep the liveliness in the shapes and the overall composition. To draw slowly and meticulously resulted in the image being stiff and boring. The portrait always interested me. I have done many drawings and paintings of friends, people in public places, and self-portraits.

The landscapes were a little more finished and executed with water-based paints or oils. I would go to some location that interested me and paint the world around me.

I had an aversion to working from photographs. I wanted my eye, my mind, and my hand to translate the scene in front of me. Drawing from the world around me, however, was not only from nature, but also included cityscapes, buildings, and inanimate objects—like a chair next to a window or a still life.

The paintings that interested me the most were from my imagination. These paintings seemed to include all the work I did from life—figure drawing and landscape painting. But they were integrated with the internal expression of my thoughts and imagination.

I did not want to control the work so that it turned out exactly as I expected. If I did this, my energy would be drained and the work would become hard to finish and lifeless.

After stretching and priming a canvas, I had a basic idea of the direction I wanted to go. I also kept in mind a composition or imagery that I wanted to include.

Starting with a Jackson Pollock-type attack, I laid the canvas on the floor and applied paint with lots of turpentine. I would sop up the paints with rags, splatter the canvas with more thinner, and add random brush strokes.

When this had dried, I would place the canvas on the wall and pick out unplanned images and shapes. I then defined these images and added the pre-planned thoughts that I originated with. As a result, the painting became a living thing. It was like a relationship. If you tried to control it too much, it seemed to die and suck energy from me. If I saw what the painting was offering me, I would allow its influence to control certain aspects of my direction.

By doing this, I had plenty of natural energy flowing through me. The painting always turned out better than I could have imagined. It was also fun to look at and contemplate after it was finished.

If people asked me why I painted certain images, what it all meant, or what I was trying to say, I would scratch my head and say that I didn't know, but it must mean something.

This was an effect Carl Jung's teachings had on me. His descriptions of symbolism and shapes that naturally formed in the minds and dreams of people from all civilizations fascinated me. This was the common surfacing of religious icons that could be found in all forms of beliefs and were expressed by humanity from every area of the earth—a common bond we all have.

THE VISION

I regularly went to bars that artists favored and met friends for happy hour. You could get a glass of beer and all the tacos you could eat for two bucks. We sat around and talked about art. We were all curious to know what everyone was doing—their philosophy and their medium, what shows and performances were happening, and who the people were to talk to for exposure.

One of my favorite bars was just around the corner from my studio. It was owned by a couple of ex-cons. There were some shady people there, but I never witnessed any problems. One evening, I was sitting at a booth with two other artists. Allan was talking about abstract expressionism. That was his chosen direction. I interrupted him in the middle of his passionate speech.

"So, did you go to school at San Diego State?"

"Yes, I did. How did you know?"

"Every artist I know that paints that way, in this area, majored in art at San Diego State. I took a couple of graduate courses there, and it seemed that everyone had the same philosophy. I don't think a school should teach one style or philosophy. A school should expose students to many styles and philosophies. As they mature as artists, they can develop their own unique visions and reasons for making art."

Allan continued to make his point. "Abstract expressionism is the only legitimate way left," he said. "Since the camera was invented, there is no way an artist can compete. The images are better than any artist is capable of. Every other style has already been done."

"I can't agree with that. Just because you do images doesn't mean your goal is to paint in a photo-realistic manner. Natural distortion actually adds character."

"Not just realism—surrealism, cubism, impressionism. It's all been explored; it has been done," said Allan.

"I think of all other styles as something a true artist should explore," I said. "The more, the merrier. You're just adding more tools to your toolbox. When you eventually evolve into your own style, you can visually accomplish a unique vision."

Janet, a minimalist landscape artist, put her two bits in. "I don't think you evolve into a style. You need to find a common thread so you can do consistent work. When you show in a gallery, people need to see your style, and it becomes your label. To vary your style can be suicide for your career."

"The hell with styles!" I countered. "That's if you look at your art as a product in a commercial society."

"Of course!" she replied. "You have to make a living."

"My art is an internal exploration into the unknown. It's like a scientist in a laboratory, a poet, or a philosopher. Like seeking the Holy Grail. I don't want to be nailed down to a specific style. I would work side jobs in order to continue my journey."

Etc., etc. Yada, yada, yada. Ad infinitum …

We would then go to one of the artists' studios, drink wine or vodka, and discuss that particular artist's work.

There were continual shows and performances as well. The local theater populated a local bar when there wasn't a performance or practice. Uncle Bill's was packed with actors and actresses, as well as with some of the audience during show nights. The walls were filled with photos of the many performers that frequented the place or had been there in the past.

The Reuter Gallery was on the third floor of a five-story warehouse. David hung a new show every month, and we framed the whole show accompanied by his stereo system blasting out the newest music—The Police, The B-52s.

During breaks and lunch, we took the elevator to the roof and smoked weed. It was common for David to bring artisan bread that we would break up and slather with Brie cheese.

We framed art and posters for his regular customers. Artists would come in to have their work framed for their shows in addition to other galleries who needed this work done.

The first Sunday of every month, we met at David's house. He made omelets and served freshly brewed coffee as we addressed and stamped invitations for the next show. David was also a painter and would have a show of his work on occasion. He was popular with his patrons, and he sold his work regularly.

David was an "out of the closet" gay man, and his boyfriend would show up to chat and joke as we worked. He was also the best boss I have ever had. Not only did we work our butts off but he also treated us better than I have ever been treated in a work environment

In 1982, the gallery moved to a ground-level storefront on Fifth Avenue. It was two blocks from my studio. I eventually asked if I could work part-time, so I could have more days to focus on my work. That was fine with David, but if he ever had more work than he could handle, I would be there for him and work full-time until things slowed.

David was an early victim of AIDS. At the time, he didn't know what it was. We were clueless. We saw less of him as time went on and missed him at the gallery. What a loss.

There were a few times when I was selling more of my artwork, as well as teaching figure drawing. That put me in a position to just paint without needing to work a side job. The odd thing about this was that I didn't accomplish much when I had all my free time to just paint. I would sleep in after painting all night and during the day found that I wasn't as focused and productive as I used to be when I worked at the gallery. However, I realized that part of being an artist was experiencing life around me and taking in information. This gave me more energy and determination when I did paint.

The ideal situation was working at the gallery three days a week. By framing for shows, I was around quality artwork while I prepared them for display. I met the artists, and we would have instructive and fun conversations. We became close enough to joke around and develop friendships. That all translated into my artistic energy building to the point of bursting. I was so excited to get back to my work that I was twice as productive as when I had all the time to myself.

The artists in the area had a special relationship with the street people. We actually got along great and respected each other's space.

One evening when I worked late at the gallery, I walked the two blocks to my studio. Two huge black men were walking toward me. As we began to pass, one of them took a firm grip on my collar and pulled me to the side between two parked cars. His friend immediately grabbed his collar from the back and pulled him off.

"Hey, man, he's one of the artists."

The man immediately released his grip, threw his hands up in the air, and backed off. "Sorry, man."

The bums and transients sleeping in the doorways never asked me for money. They always greeted me with a smile and asked how my day was going. It was the same with the hookers and pimps. I was greeted with a smile, a tip of the hat, or a wink.

Speaking of the street people, my fire escape that looked down on Fifth Avenue was ideal for observing their activity. You could see the intricate dances they performed with their various professions.

A car would drive up to a prostitute, and she would lean into the window, then back off and continue walking. The car would drive off. Five minutes later, as the prostitute strolled down the sidewalk or talked with her friends, the same car would drive around the corner and pull next to her. You would hear a voice from the car yell out.

"Hey, Sue! Where have you been?"

She would feign surprise and smile. "Johnny, it's been a long time!" and she would open the passenger door and hop in.

Taxicabs were involved in the well-rehearsed charade as well.

There were drug deals and discreet hand-offs of items as two people passed each other—money, drugs, covert exchanges with spies, or the CIA?

The artists worked well with the available spaces and the property owners. I had amassed a large quantity of work. There were juried shows and galleries that showed local work, and there were large open spaces where the performance artists could do their thing and make it available to the public.

Across the street from my studio was one of the most beautiful buildings on Fifth Avenue. The first floor was massive with high ceilings. I contacted the owner, and he allowed me to arrange a one-man show in this space. Having the experience of the Reuter Gallery, I made invitations and sent press releases to the local newspapers and publications. The show worked in coordination with the monthly art walk and drew massive crowds. The shows in this area were covered and reported by *San Diego Magazine* and *The San Diego Union-Tribune,* as well as art and event publications.

I offered performance artists the use of my stage for no charge. Phillip-Dimitri Galás performed there. The ballroom space was also ideal for one-man and group shows, which we took advantage of.

Anyway, it wasn't Paris in the late 1800s or New York in the first half of the 1900s, but it was damn close.

CHAPTER SEVEN

During an opening at my ballroom studio, Bob Thompson, my former roommate at Ocean Beach and co-worker at The Fine Art Store, showed up. I hadn't seen him for years since I moved downtown.

Bob looked a little less hippie and more corporate as he strolled around the gallery checking out the work.

I walked up and shook his hand. "Hey, Bob! Nice to see you. What have you been up to?"

"Hey, nice show!" he said, as he gazed around the ballroom. "I see you've been busy."

"I have!"

"This is your studio?"

"Yes, pretty amazing, huh? I work part-time at a gallery a couple of blocks away."

"Nice!" Bob countered. "I landed a great job! I'm the art director of Robert Keith & Company."

"Sounds impressive, what's that?"

"We make giant inflatables—like huge balloons."

I became a little less impressed when he said the word "balloons."

"We have some big jobs coming up," he said. "I wanted to see what you were doing. We need help. We're looking for someone to make clay sculpture. That's how we start each project."

"Sounds cool, but I'm actually enjoying my situation at the moment."

"I think you should come check us out. You can drop by anytime. I'll introduce you to everyone. I think you'll be impressed."

I smiled and gave him a semi-enthusiastic reply, "Yeah, I think I can do that."

I showed Bob around and introduced him to a few people. As usual, the opening was during the monthly art walk. There was a great turnout. Bob stayed through the opening, and we went to Uncle Bill's for a few drinks afterward.

"When he left, he put his arm around my shoulder and said, "Really. Come see what we do."

I like Bob. He was a great friend. At first, I didn't follow up with a visit, but he didn't give up. I received a call about ten days later.

"So do I need to twist your arm?"

"OK. Where is this place again?"

"Kearny Mesa."

During the opening, Bob had handed me a Robert Keith & Company card confirming its location with his title Art Director prominently displayed.

"I gave you a card. Do you still have it?"

"Yes, I do."

"How about tomorrow?" Bob said. "I've already built you up, and they are anxious to meet you."

The next day, I hopped in my old Econoline and headed to Bob's workplace.

As it turned out, it was much more than a balloon factory. At the time, there were about fifty employees. Bob introduced me to the owners—Robert Keith himself and his wife Ann Wawer. They had a great sales staff, but what really impressed me was the warehouse. It was filled with twenty-foot and larger inflatables—characters, beer cans, and numerous other projects. Huge sewing tables lined the walls. Painters did the artwork from tall ladders, and silk screeners worked on twenty-foot screens.

For me, this was the beginning of a thirty-three-year involvement that included owning my own inflatable company by the early nineties. I had no intention of starting a company. It just happened that way. I had to get a business license since I needed to hire help. I was also determined to continue my painting.

The good thing about making inflatables was that it used all of my art skills, as well as refining my algebra and geometry abilities. The people at Robert Keith loved my work. I met some super people.

Not only did I make the original sculpture for each project but I was also asked to do a technical drawing on grid velum, showing all views. I had little experience with technical drawings. (This was before personal computers and design software were common.) I not only picked it up fast but I also enjoyed hanging over a drawing table, doing detailed work, and figuring out mathematical solutions for the shapes.

This first visit from Bob was in 1982. There were few—if any—inflatable companies other than Robert Keith then.

Robert Keith grew to over 100 employees and was smothered by clients wanting inflatables. We made giant product samples and did work for world expos, sports events, and theater—just as a start. The list grew much larger.

When I started at Robert Keith, everyone was gearing up to make a seventy-foot-high King Kong that would be placed on the Empire State Building in 1983 for the fiftieth anniversary of the movie.

When it came time to install King Kong in New York, we found ourselves working late nights to iron out the final details. The winds were expected to be high, and we had a webbing system that crossed his back in several places. The inflatable needed to be firmly attached to the building.

The Robert Keith crew took the inflatable as far up in the Empire State Building as possible via the elevator. Then it had to be spread out and rolled into a long thin shape to be snaked up the final stairs to the appropriate spot.

Now, how do we get it outside the building? The solution: break a window. From this point, it was the riggers' responsibility. The process was well planned, but, of course, there is always the unexpected. To begin with, the inflatable needed to be stretched out and tied down before inflation. A five-horsepower blower was standing by, awaiting its grand entry to inflate King Kong to his final shape.

THE VISION

That is one aspect of this business: continually running blowers were used for inflation. The seams are not sealed.

When King Kong was secured to the building and ready to inflate, the blower was attached and turned on.

Oops! It twisted. The inflatable had to be detached, brought back inside, and untwisted. The winds made it all but impossible to do this outside the building.

The second try went much better. King Kong was spread out and attached securely to the building.

OK, now for the second snag in the operation. It was time for lunch, and the riggers were required to come back inside—union rules. When they returned, the fabric had ripped from the intense winds. Once inflated, that wouldn't be a problem. The strapped-down, inflated shape would be much more stable and secure.

So, for the second time, the King needed to be unstrapped and brought back inside. Great forethought then prevailed. A sewing machine had already been made available, and the sewing was done within a couple of hours.

Keep in mind that struggling with this inflation, along with the high winds, took days—maybe even a week—I really don't recall. News crews and helicopters were at the ready to report the inflation when it happened—if it happened. Nationwide, the news channels were continually updating the progress.

Ta-da! Finally, King Kong stood out in its full glory, and the images were splashed across the world. It was only up for a couple of hours—enough time for the photo ops—and then was removed. Why tempt fate any longer?

This was a great coup for Robert Keith. The problems installing the King didn't matter; the exposure did. The daily struggle actually kept it in the news cycle longer than was anticipated. Robert Keith enjoyed the flood of orders that poured in as a result.

The company moved to a huge facility. This building was referred to as Darth Vader's Castle by the employees because of its size, black windows, and structure. It had twice the space that was necessary. More employees were hired, and the company began producing on a massive scale.

As I grew up, I was always involved in sports, and I now missed playing on teams. I went to the San Diego County recreation building and found out they had softball leagues—co-ed and all-male or all-female teams.

Since I hadn't played in a while, I signed up for any team that was looking for another player. I received a call a couple of weeks later with the disappointing news that the teams were full, but I could start my own team and join their league.

When I went back to work the next day, I talked to Robert Keith and asked if he would sponsor a co-ed team. I would find the players and manage the team if he would buy the shirts and pay the fees. He thought it was a tremendous idea. I posted the "looking for players to be in a company softball team" memo and had a great turnout. More than enough names to form a team was on the list.

Thus began my twenty-five-year stint of managing and playing on great softball teams with fun people.

Our co-ed team was really good—especially the women. We always made the playoffs, including a couple of first places. The team had several trophies.

After the games, we would go to a bar in the area, order pitchers of beer, and have a hilarious time making fun of each other and talking about great plays. The feminine influence on the team made the game much better. Egos were in check. The women made many of the game-winning plays.

Hanging out in the Robert Keith warehouse with the production crew was a blast. They all seemed excited to see me. They asked questions about the projects they were working on. We joked around, and—all in all—we felt comfortable around each other. I wasn't the boss or the manager; I was the guy who got the process going. They treated me like I was one of them. Best of all, they really respected my opinion.

I was very interested in the process of making inflatables. The sewing machine operators taught me to sew on their double-needle industrial machines. I learned how to wind and replace a bobbin. They taught me how to thread the needle, how to pass the thread through the machine to create the proper tension, and then how to actually sew.

The painters had a character of their own. They were also open to putting a brush in my hand, showing me how they mixed the paints and cluing me in on the techniques and tools they used. This included airbrush and Binks air guns.

Suzy and Buzz were the two goofballs that pretty much ran the art department. Not just because of their abilities and knowledge but their characters as well. They worked well with their crew—always willing to help—with big smiles and lots of entertainment.

Unfortunately, the paint shop was the last stop on the production schedule. The one or two weeks that they were given to paint the inflatables were usually cut to a couple of days. This meant painting day and night until the work was done

The employees in the wood and metal shop were also amazingly talented. Nobody manufactured blowers for inflatables at the time. Grainger was a company that supplied us with different motors and fan blades. The shop workers would experiment with these, and when they found one that worked, they would build a box around it with a hole for the intake and the exhaust. They were custom-made depending on the inflatable and how it was being used.

Finally, there was the silkscreen shop. The screens themselves were twenty feet long and over five feet wide. The drying racks were the same size. Everything was on a huge scale.

All in all, Robert Keith was an exciting place to work. Everyone was happy with their jobs and showed it. We could see our work evolve to its final shape. When we inflated each project, it brought huge smiles to our faces. It was a great sense of accomplishment.

The company treated its crews well. There must have been well over 100 employees at the time. The owners had parties at their house, and at Christmas, everyone received a nice gift. One year, we all were given nice, quality sweaters.

I had no problem keeping up with my work even though there was plenty to do. King Kong was rented out to fairs and events. They hired someone to drive it around to each location, install it, and babysit it until it was time to pack it up. Then I would head to the next installation site.

THE VISION

One day, one of the office managers approached me at my workstation.

"Want a fun job for the rest of this week?"

"Sure!" I said. "What's up?"

"A storm blew through LA and ripped King Kong. The venue called and couldn't get hold of the caretaker so they called us. They finally found the guy. He was passed out drunk in his motel room. We need you to go repair King Kong and keep an eye on him until next Monday."

"Sure, I'll do that!" I was always up for trips and challenges.

When I arrived that evening, the King was deflated and still hanging from the support beam it was tethered to. There was a fifteen-foot rip in his arm. It was a bit difficult to install, so the grounds crew asked if I could sew it up without taking it down.

They already had a ladder available to climb up the structure. I crawled out on a beam, reached down, and pulled the arm up to a position that I could manage.

Several hours later, I finished the repair job. My legs were wrapped around the beam with one free arm and partial use of my other arm to accomplish the sewing. I finished about two in the morning.

After a short night's sleep, I went back to the site as the sun was rising and turned on the blower. It popped up with no problem. I took myself and my sore muscles back to my room and grabbed a couple more hours of sleep.

From then on, they sent me on most of the other King Kong installs. I also helped install other jobs. One was at the New Orleans World Fair.

All in all, Robert Keith provided me with the knowledge and experience that no school could provide.

As an artist, it introduced a medium that I would be absorbed in for the next thirty-five years.

After three years, I had saved enough money to move to Seattle. I had taken my two-week vacations in the Northwest, spending some time in the city, but most of the time camping and exploring in the Olympic Mountains. This beautiful area met all my expectations—plus, it was beautiful! I felt like I fit in like a long-lost puzzle piece.

My move to Seattle wasn't to be—**yet.** I craved moving there but needed to take advantage of a few opportunities first. The ballroom studio was still my home, and I needed to wrap up some projects.

Putting in my notice at Robert Keith was a sad ordeal since I had grown so close to my co-workers.

Then came a proposal that would keep me in San Diego a little longer. Andy, the Robert Keith accountant, and Mark, the production manager, asked me if I could meet with them. We got together after work that day.

"So, I see that you put in your notice to leave the company," Andy said as we settled into our booth.

"Yeah, I've been planning this for years. I really want to move to Seattle."

Not beating around the bush, Mark chimed in.

THE VISION

"We're starting a new inflatable company. Do you want to be part-owner? You're the only one who understands all of the production aspects of the business and can do the whole process."

This was all a surprise to me. I liked Andy a lot. I wasn't sure about Mark. He was pretty young. The employees seemed to like him. I worked well with him—or so I thought.

My thoughts were on Seattle, but it would be an adventure to be on the ground floor of a new company.

"Are you asking me to be part-owner because of my merits, or do you need money?"

Andy replied, "We know your abilities and need them, but we also need funding. Can you raise any money? Any amount would work; your investment would get you a percentage of ownership, depending on what you are able to contribute."

"I'm not your guy," I said. "I don't have access to large funds."

"Any rich relatives? Can you get a loan? This will work; I know it will."

"The money I could contribute would be a drop in the bucket compared to what you would need."

Andy looked a little bit disappointed.

"We're just hesitant, not knowing the real risks of our other options. We understand your position. It would be nice if the owners were actually participating in the company and not just investors."

"So, could you still help us get started? We can make you art director and give you more than you're making now."

I really did like the opportunity to see how this would go. It would be no risk on my part. I could leave at any time.

"OK, this is what I can do. I gave my two-week notice. When I leave, I will take a good three-week vacation in Seattle. That will get it temporarily out of my system. If you get your funding figured out by the time I return, I will work a couple of years. We can see how things look at that time."

"Fair enough," said Andy. "Could you make a list of who you think would be the best people to hire? It was easy to approach you since you were leaving anyway."

"Sure, I can do that."

I decided to move out of the Gaslamp studio. For me, it was a productive eight-year stint that I will always remember.

The fact was that, if I could have stayed longer, I would have. A year before I left, the artistic energy was forced out of the Gaslamp area. The City of San Diego decided it was time to renovate their old town district. They offered the building owners a proposal they couldn't refuse. The city would pay for half of their renovation costs to improve the structures and bring them up to code.

The artists did their part as they have done in other cities around the country. The brilliant work and the presence of so many talented artists provided art, performances, and music on a scale that the whole area became aware of.

San Diego Magazine, the newspapers, and many other publications wrote about the activities. People attended these shows in vast numbers. What was a dream come true for the artists eventually wooed the populace into wide-eyed excitement for businesses, condos, and lofts for the well-to-do. They saw the spaces and coveted them. If only they could live and work in such unique spaces.

I squeezed an extra year out of this opportunity because I was on the top floor of San Diego Hardware, an established and popular store that had been there since the area first flourished. They didn't have the pressure to renovate like the others.

Finally, an architect wandered up the stairs to the ballroom. The next thing I knew, I was packing my art supplies and paintings to begin a new phase in my life.

By this time, I wasn't as obsessed with surfing as I used to be, but I still loved it and found time every now and then.

Before I left on my Seattle trip, I grabbed my surfboard and drove to Ocean Beach. The waves were perfect—about six feet. This was the type of day that drew a lot of surfers.

The white water had a lot of force as I paddled out toward the swells. That was a part of surfing I enjoyed. It was not just riding waves. You had to respect the strength of the white water on your board and body. It forced you back a few feet as you fought through the turbulence.

I had my own technique to get through the white water. I waxed the tip of my board so I could grip it tightly. Just before the white water hit, I grabbed the nose of the board and pulled it down to my crotch. At the same time, I curled up in a ball. Just as I felt the force of the white water, I would quickly stretch out, forcing the nose of the board ahead of me. This would squirt me through the turbulence and prevent the wave from pushing me back so far. I could usually make it to the swells while other surfers were still battling the white water.

When I was among the swells, I jammed the board between my legs, and it lifted me out of the water in a sitting position—my legs dangling on either side.

What a great feeling—the rise and fall of the swells passing under you while watching the flat horizon of the ocean. Then dark strips would appear. You could tell the size of the swell by the height of these dark waves.

Huge swells were approaching, getting larger every second. I turned the board around, laid on it, and began to paddle. As the wave began to lift me, I put more energy into my paddling.

Looking to the side, I saw flecks of foam on the wave's crest as it began to break. The next thing I knew, I was dropping down the wall of the wave. My knees bent in a comfortable squat as I turned away from the curl. The momentum I had when I hit the bottom took me back up to the top where the wave was just breaking.

I dropped in again, but this time, I reversed my direction and hit the full force of the wave as it was throwing the water ahead of it. This force threw me back in the other direction. I dropped to the bottom again, and, on my way up the wall, I tucked myself into the curl as deep as I could. At that point, the edge of my board dug into the wall, and I rode the increasing speed of the wave while moving up and down to keep me tucked into the curl.

At this point, I need to explain the etiquette of the surfing world. When surfers catch a wave, the one closest to where the wave first breaks is the person who owns the wave. Everyone else politely pulls out and allows him or her to take charge.

THE VISION

If you continue surfing, knowing there is someone right behind you, there are grounds for the surfer closest to the curl to be righteously pissed. This leads to name-calling, bird-flipping, and even fights on the beach afterward.

Back to my ride: that was a perfect first wave to catch, and a thrill ran through my body as I pulled out of the wave, using my momentum to fling myself and my board several feet in the air—landing on the backside of the wave.

Oh my God!

As I pulled out, I noticed that there was a surfer who pulled out right behind me; he had the inside position.

"Sorry, man," I said. "I really didn't know you were behind me."

"No problem, I did that on purpose," he said with a smile.

It was Luis, the person who had taught me to surf ten years before, the guy who had several trophies from surfing competitively, the guy who backed and wired frames at The Fine Art Store.

"I snuck in behind you. I was a couple of feet behind the whole way, mimicking your every move. I wanted to see if I taught you right. You're doing damn good!" he said with a huge grin.

We greeted each other with a high five and a grip of each other's forearm. I loved those days learning to surf with Luis. I will always remember the magic.

CHAPTER EIGHT

I had a great trip up the coast to Seattle. This was my third trip to this wonderful place. I have a friend from The Fine Art Store who had moved up there a couple of years earlier.

Mark Zingarelli is an exceptional cartoonist. He knew the route he needed to pursue, and by the time I got there, he was well underway with jobs and great clients. He showed me around the city for a couple of days before I headed for the Olympic Peninsula.

I spent two weeks camping and exploring—mostly thinking and reflecting on where I had been and where I was going. I had dreams, too. Things I wanted to do and things I wanted to experience.

Mark suggested a place I will always remember—Shi Shi Beach.

During my past trips to the Olympic Peninsula, I had visited Lake Ozette, a large natural body of water with nice campsites on the northern end. There are two trailheads at that location. Each trail is three miles long and terminates at different beaches on the Pacific Ocean. The northern route goes to Cape Alava and has a rocky coastline. The southern trail ends at Sand Point—a sandy beach. Each trail is three miles long.

Both trails are raised just above ground level and made from wood slats so the natural growth is not disturbed.

THE VISION

The hike is long enough to make it an accomplishment. As you walk toward the ocean, you slowly become aware of a roaring sound. At first, I thought there was a freeway close by. It was actually the roar of breaking waves.

These are popular trails, and they are used regularly. Beware of winter; the rains can be discouraging, so go prepared.

Shi Shi Beach is north of Cape Alava, about six miles—no trail, but I found an old logging road.

If you follow the coast, because of the rocky terrain, it takes a while. Don't take that route at high tide.

You can approach it from the north. Drive to Neah Bay, and work your way southwest until you reach the ocean. The trailhead to Shi Shi Beach starts there. It's about six miles.

This area is on an Indian reservation, and they have closed the trail on several occasions. It is a sacred beach. All you need to do is visit, and you can feel the magic. It is common to be alone when you arrive. Camping is also a sacred experience. In the sixties and early seventies, people made hand-built cabins just inside the woods. They have been torn down and removed since then.

The beach itself is a crescent about a mile long. It is a beautiful beach with iconic rock formations at each end. The stars at night are vivid and astonishing. There is no light pollution.

Seattle is the most beautiful city I have ever experienced. There are several volcanoes in the snow-capped Cascade Range to the east and the Olympics loom large toward the west. These mountains are forever changing due to the weather and the mystical lighting of the Pacific Northwest. Puget Sound is filled with islands and peninsulas with ferries crossing its expanse. The city skyline rises as high as seventy-six stories, and the buildings are all condensed into a beautiful city with the silhouette of the Space Needle standing out to the north.

Countless local breweries with hundreds of unique ales are scattered around the city and in the rural areas. Coffee is big, and the arts are a major factor in its character. This includes musicians and novelists, as well as the visual arts.

After three weeks, I followed the coastline back down to San Diego. When I arrived, I called Andy and found out that he had "backed out" from being involved with a new company. They did find their investors, but that was the problem. Andy did not want to be partners with the two other people providing the funding. One was Dick who was a salesman at Robert Keith. If I remember correctly, he was head of their sales team at one time. The second person who invested was from Mexico. Rumor had it that he was involved in the illegal drug market or at least had been. This connection provided clients in Mexico.

My living situation was in a confused state since I had left my Gaslamp studio. I had lived there for eight years. When I returned from Seattle, I lived in my van for a couple of months. Joann, a secretary from Robert Keith, had just bought an orange orchard by Escondido with a funky house, and she needed a roommate. She was a bit older than me—I am sure that had a lot of people talking. Joann was a good person and involved in the new company conspiracy. She was a great source of information.

There was a fairly large room in the house that was used for crating oranges. I used it as a studio and began an orange orchard series. All of these paintings sold.

Joann kept up on the progress of the new company. I contacted Mark Bachman and he was glad to hear from me. I did some concept art for the new sales staff for some potential jobs. Since my focus was more on the production art side, they asked me if I knew anyone else who could do concept art. My immediate response was to remind them of a very good artist named George, who did the same job for Robert Keith. He had quit there before the breakup, so he was fair game. They wouldn't be stealing him. There were already legal issues arising, so why complicate matters?

"Oh, yeah!" Mark said. "I forgot about George."

The owners of the new company had decided on a name: Bigger Than Life. They contacted me when they found a facility in El Cajon. It was a little small but would work for starters. They wanted me to show up for work as soon as I could.

I drove to El Cajon and was amazed at how many employees had transferred over from Robert Keith. I knew Dick and met with Mark and the other owner of the company.

The one thing that I realized at Robert Keith was the importance of a great sales staff. Within three months, Bigger Than Life had a million dollars in sales, and they grew from there. Within six months, the company found a new and much larger facility.

I began work immediately. Everyone was glad to see me and they all brought their happy faces with them. I had a list of clay sculptures that needed to be done and I began each project with a technical drawing. The rumors about the owners didn't bother me, and I was treated well. They appreciated my work and the artistic ability I put into it. That changed after a couple of years.

I also started a new co-ed softball team, and the company happily chipped in for the fees and bought the tee shirts. The name of the new team was—of course—"Bigger Than Life."

The sales staff decided they wanted to start an all-male team. I signed up without hesitation.

In case you haven't already figured it out, salespeople are an unusual breed. This was especially true with the sales staff for this inflatable company. They had clients with major businesses or organizations and were landing high-profile jobs. The egos were huge!

They all thought they were God's gift to softball.

"I'm pitching," said Brian, the person who started the team.

The rest of the sales staff all wanted the positions they said they were excellent at.

"Where should I play?" I asked.

"Well, I'm not sure. You play with girls, so I'm not sure you can play on an all-men's team. We can sub you in—or maybe catcher?"

Actually, the team really sucked. It was a circus. They struck out and looked like they had never played before. Outfielders would dance around under a fly ball, and then it would fall to the ground at their feet. Brian kept walking batters. Throws to first went wide and rolled to the fence while the hitter waltzed into third. Our players took their snorts of cocaine when we finally made it to the dugout to bat, and it changed them back into superhumans.

We lost the first four games.

Many of the salesmen were better talkers than players. There were a few who were damn good, but you didn't hear a peep from them. When you're good, you don't need to prove anything.

Bruce, silk screener extraordinaire, and I, who played with girls, kicked butt. I finally became the pitcher, and we won almost every game after that. We both had great on-base percentages. Mine was around 700. I had an inside-out swing that would pop over third base and hit the ground with a spin. It would land inbounds and then squirt out of bounds until it hit the fence. They were all two or three baggers. When the other team figured it out and covered that spot, I would hit line drives to the vacant areas. The rest of the team finally improved after they fought through their egos and started having fun.

After the games, the all-male team would go to the local 7-Eleven store and buy a case of beer. We would go to the back of the building, hang out by the dumpster, and talk bullshit. It was convenient to crush a can of beer when finished and toss it in the trash. Half the tosses missed—close enough.

OK—I am not giving the sales staff the credit they deserve. Even though they were a little deprived of softball abilities, they made the company the success it became. Not just any salesman could work there. Their sales abilities were way beyond any used car salesmen. They couldn't con anyone. They were dealing with savvy, intelligent clients that wouldn't put up with any bullshit.

When they started work at Bigger Than Life, they got twelve dollars an hour for three months. After that, it was just commission. If they didn't have their act together by then, it was goodbye. They made million-dollar sales, and a talented salesperson made damn good money at ten percent commission.

As salesmen, they wanted potential buyers to understand the advantages of using inflatables for advertising and events. It was common for them to call me to their office to talk with the clients who wanted to know the details. How were inflatables made? What were the advantages of using inflatables over solid work? What special effects could we offer that other 3D materials could not?

The differences between Robert Keith and Bigger Than Life quickly became apparent.

Robert and Ann, the owners of Robert Keith, had built their business around unique energy and artistic ability. They were on the ground floor of developing the technology and materials needed to make a quality product. They also liked having a good relationship with their employees, and our meetings were designed to encourage working together, doing our parts, and helping each other.

When they created a high-profile job, they contacted the hometown media of each employee, giving them credit for the work they did.

Just wanting to accept the highest-paying jobs was a mistake. Becoming successful so quickly added to their illusion that the cornucopia of riches pouring into the company was endless. This, along with their national (and in many cases international) popularity, did go to their heads. That wasn't surprising, since the jobs they landed were the best clients you could imagine.

Bigger Than Life was a company run by salesmen. They saw the potential in what Robert Keith offered. The problem was that, if the employees disappeared, they would have no idea how to build an inflatable. Well, that's not exactly true. I should say that they knew how to make an inflatable, but none of them had the talent or artistic ability to create one. They lacked artistic input—you know—creative thinking. They depended on the employees to supply that aspect of the business.

My transition from Robert Keith to BTL was seamless. I immediately bonded with the owners, the salesmen, and the employees.

The jobs were plentiful and high profile. The most exciting job was the half-time show for Super Bowl XX in New Orleans. We made a futuristic city that was 100 feet in diameter. Along with this, we made a fifty-foot diameter Earth and other giant planets ranging from twenty to forty feet in diameter.

BTL made hundreds of product samples ranging from twenty-foot beer bottles and cans, as well as Pepsi and Coke products, to potato chip bags and packages of chewing tobacco—all ranging from twenty to forty feet in diameter. These were huge quantity orders and also moneymakers; we made hundreds of each if not more.

Absorbed in my daily routines, I would follow each project down the production line. The sewing machine operators liked my interest in their work and enjoyed it when I visited them. They were proud of the part they played in the projects. Many of the pieces were huge. It was hard to know what part to sew first—where it started and where it ended. Having designed the project, I would take one end and pin it at the starting point. They were impressed at how much I knew about the project they were working on.

Suzie and Buzz were there, and it was fun to visit the painting department. They were good at what they did, and they maintained the humor they had had at Robert Keith. It always brought a smile to my face.

Suzie became my favorite sushi buddy. I took her to my favorite sushi bar, and she was immediately hooked. The chefs loved her. Suzie had the whole restaurant laughing uncontrollably at times. It helped that she actually did stand-up comedy on the side. She told me of one successful performance but didn't show much enthusiasm for continuing. It was just a daily thing for her. She entertained whoever was around her at the time.

One of her claims to fame—and she had many—was a Halloween costume she made. It was a huge sandwich with a bite out of the corner. Her face poked out in the middle and her long perfect legs stuck out the bottom. She had recently won first place in a local Halloween contest.

The costume was one of the connections we shared. We weren't sexually or romantically involved, but we did develop a good friendship. I actually felt that she was too good for me.

A couple of years earlier when I was in the Gaslamp studio, I became tired of improvising last-minute costumes for Halloween. The artist community came up with amazing parties, so I finally decided to make something that took a little effort.

Finding a tall, thin cardboard box, I turned it into an outhouse. It had no door. I pulled it over my head so that my real legs stuck out the bottom while fake legs were positioned to look as if I were sitting on the crapper.

The fake legs were made out of Styrofoam, and I dressed them in old jeans and underwear. I nailed a pair of tennis shoes on the floor of the outhouse and fit the legs into them.

Pulling out a black magic marker, I drew a wood grain with knotholes on the outside. For ventilation, I cut a crescent moon above the door and made a stovepipe with a cone head coming out the top.

This costume was hilarious. I equipped it with a *Penthouse* magazine and a roll of toilet paper. The party I went to that year was not a contest, but the costume blew people's minds. It actually was embarrassing to look at—like you were invading someone's privacy. It produced endless remarks and jokes.

"What a crappy costume!"

"Where does the line start?"

"Are you constipated? You've been sitting there for a long time." The remarks were continual.

Several people made the same comment: "What are you doing here? You should be at a Halloween contest. That's a sure winner!"

The following year, I went to my next party. This one wasn't a contest either. It was a Robert Keith company party.

Lo and behold—there was Suzie in her sandwich costume.

She came up to me and said, "Hey, I'm going to two contests tonight. Want to join me?"

"Sure!" I said.

That Friday, we loaded our costumes in my van and went to two Halloween contests. I got first place at the first party—a trip for two to Mazatlan—and Suzie got second prize.

At the next party, I got first again—$500—and Suzie got third.

The next night, Saturday, I went to another by myself and won again. This was the beginning of a ten-year run that netted me sixteen first places. After a while, it wasn't so fun. It was like going to work, and the way the costume hung around my hips made me fart all night after I took it off.

Other than my Halloween party successes, my life at this time was a bit unsettled—like something was missing. I was anxious to get back into my painting and was tired of living in my van or at Joann's.

An artist friend of mine told me about an old building that was being rented by a group of artists. It was an old church on Broadway and Eighth Avenue. I moved my paintings and art supplies to a large corner studio and began painting.

My euphoria over my great job and friends didn't continue for the full three years I worked at BTL. As it turned out, Mark was having difficulty with me. I didn't pick up on that at first, but it began sinking in as the years progressed. He was really young—somewhere in his early twenties.

At Robert Keith, we got along great, but as an owner of BTL, he seemed to act strangely toward me. The rest of the company respected what I had to offer. The employees saw me as the person who made things happen since I started each project. I didn't think I was different from anyone else. We all had our duties. A couple of other employees asked me why I didn't start my own company. It was because I wasn't a businessman, and I really loved my job. I didn't have to deal with the problems that the owners and managers had. Mark still perceived me as a threat.

I thought I was on his side—helping him make a quality product.

Management decided that they needed to choose an actual "Production Manager." I'm not sure what that exactly meant, except maybe being able to boss employees around and getting a pay raise.

A company meeting was called after a few days of this subject's floating in the air. There must have been over 100 employees at the time. The big announcement came during the special meeting that Dave Rodriquez was to be the new production manager. The employees just sat there with maybe a couple of claps from a couple of people. When I looked at Dave, he was looking at me with a big smile on his face.

It seemed that each department ran itself pretty well, and we had production meetings to discuss everyone's part and what could or couldn't be done. However, I did understand that the company was getting bigger, and there probably was a need for that position.

After the meeting, Dave came to my workroom.

"Hey, man," he said. "I know you really wanted to be production manager. I just wanted to say good try, but I think my qualifications are better."

I looked at him in astonishment. "What?"

"I know, I know. You thought you worked well with everyone, and they would listen to you."

"Sorry to disappoint you, Dave, but the last job I want is production manager. The reason I'm here is that I love to design and make inflatables. I couldn't do that if I had to manage people. To your credit, they need someone who can organize and manage people. That's not me."

"Oh," he said with a confused look on his face. "I just thought you really wanted to be production manager."

"Nope. I'm happy where I'm at."

Dave turned and walked out.

Little did I realize how this would affect my job.

I was excited about a new project for Honda. They wanted a thirty-foot-high inflatable of a Honda Four-Wheeler. At the production meeting, I was given the concept art and a brochure. There was also a spec sheet of the four-wheeler. It showed the sizes and different views.

Taking the info to my drafting table, I did a to-scale drawing showing all sides and a view from the top. I drew out the lettering and art that needed to be projected. This included the tread for the tires. I drew a section of the tread that, when placed end to end, provided a continual tread around the circumference. This would be silk-screened in about six pieces per tire. When sewn, the ends would match up to make a continual tread.

I also did a clay sculpture to scale. To create most of the patterns, there was no need for the clay, but for certain areas like the handlebars and other details, the clay was easier to work from. I kept an eye on the production and helped where I could.

THE VISION

Several weeks later, one of the production people came to my workspace and told me they were doing the first inflation.

Alright, we finally get to see this monster! It wasn't painted yet, but if there were to be changes, they needed to be done before the painting department got to it.

When I walked into the painting area, the blowers were turned on, and the inflatable was starting to rise. Employees were arriving from the different departments to see the first inflation. It was always fun to get the first glimpse of a new project.

As it took shape, there were *oohs* and *ahhs*. Mark and Dave walked in and stood next to it.

"Beautiful job, gang. Boy, that bugger is big!" said Dave. "What do you think, Mark?"

"I like it. Looks like we're ready to paint."

"Ah, excuse me," I said. "I see a big problem."

"Huh? What's that?" asked Dave.

I pointed at the tires. "The front tires are touching the back tires."

Dave looked at the tires. "I think it looks good that way. The patterners and I decided to move them in. It will be more stable."

"There is a whole engine that fits between them," I said. "How can you leave out the engine? The client will flip out."

Dave looked around and yelled, "Hey, Buzz, come here."

Buzz walked over and Dave said, "Do you think we need to show the engine?"

"Uh, yeah?"

"Do you think you can paint it above the tires?"

"I'll do whatever you want, Dave."

"Just a minute," I said as I left for my drawing table. I grabbed my technical drawing along with the client's art and brochure.

When I returned, I put a photo of the Honda in front of them. "Look—engine—between the two tires. I figured this out to scale; it is exact. You need eight feet between the tires so there is room to paint the engine."

Buzz looked at us and rolled his eyes. "Whatever you say, guys."

Mark was standing behind us as we talked.

"So, Mark, what do you think?" Dave asked.

"I'll tell you what, let's compromise. Make it four feet apart."

"Hey, Buzz, could you put that engine in a four-foot space?"

"Sure, we can do anything. We can paint it on top of the tires if you want." He shook his head and walked off.

"Four feet it is," said Dave as everyone filed back to their stations.

I really couldn't understand what had just happened there. As time went on, I realized that they wanted to be involved in some of the decisions. I was game for that, but why make it different from what the client wanted?

A couple of months later, Mark called me to his office.

When I walked in, Mark was sitting at his desk with a young woman sitting across from him. Dick was also there.

"Have a seat, Paul," Dick said. "This is Ann. She's an artist from New York and needs to have an inflatable built. She's looking for someone to fabricate it."

"Hello, Ann," I said as I sat down.

"Hi, Paul. So, what is your job here?" Her tone was a little uptight—almost angry.

"I start with artwork provided by the client. The first thing I do is make a technical drawing, followed by making an armature for the clay. I scale the drawing to the size of the clay to make sure it is the exact size. We then pattern it, so it can be projected to the correct size for the cutters."

"What kind of clay do you use?"

"Plastaline. It's clay with an oil and wax base."

Ann glared at Mark and Dick. "Was that so hard? Why didn't you ask him to come in here in the first place?"

She stood up and added. "Can I go see where he works? I would like to see his process."

Mark and Dick looked peevishly at each other and said, "Sure."

I took Ann to my drawing table first and showed her the drawings I was working on and then to the sculpture room that was filled with old cut-up clays and one that was almost finished for a new project.

I explained the process I used. She calmed down from her Mark and Dick experience.

"I don't care much for the owners of this place."

"Why, what happened?"

"Can we have dinner tonight? We can talk then."

"Sure," I said. "Do you like sushi?"

"I sure do."

I gave her the address.

"Great. See you at 6:00?"

"I'll be there."

That evening, Ann was waiting at the door of my favorite sushi bar. The one Suzie and I went to.

We were seated at the bar, and she began her dialog.

"I need a giant pair of legs to put on a theater in New York. I've searched the country. Robert Keith and BTL are the only ones I found who can make what I want."

"Sooo," she said. "Who should make it, BTL or Robert Keith?"

I took a drink of sake to wash down the *uni* I had just devoured.

"Well, I would say that the patterning is better at Robert Keith and the art department is better at BTL."

Ann gripped a piece of yellowtail sashimi with her chopsticks. As she brought it to her mouth, she glanced at me. "Why don't you start your own company?"

I was a little taken aback. I had never really thought about it.

"I don't consider myself a businessman. I like what I'm doing, and it's fun to make inflatables. I would enjoy doing what you're doing more, I guess."

I continued with my diatribe, "I've been painting most of my life, and I want to pursue that. I could probably do the same with inflatables—make things that come from my own mind and heart. I like making these projects for the company; it's a challenge. I guess it would be nicer to actually build an inflatable the way I would prefer to make it. Especially when I know I can do it better without all the bad decisions from people who don't know what they're talking about."

Changing the subject, I asked her, "So, what happened in Mark's office?"

With a slight expression of disgust, she said, "I already visited Robert Keith, and it was a good experience. I called and made an appointment with BTL to compare and decide which company I would prefer.

When I walked into Mark's office, he called Dick in. I sat down and asked if I could speak to the artist who designs the inflatables. Mark said he was the guy. I asked a couple of simple questions like: How do you make these? What kind of clay do you use? Did you go to school in art? I could tell immediately that he wasn't the one doing the design or artwork. So, I said, 'Who really designs these?'

He stammered and picked up the phone. A short while later, a guy named Dave walked in. I asked what his job was, and he said he was the production manager. I told him I wanted to see the person who designs the inflatables.

He said that he did. I asked him similar questions and got similar responses.

I started getting mad and asked them why I couldn't talk to the person who *really* designs the inflatables. That's when they called you in."

Ann later contacted me and said that she had Robert Keith pattern and sew her project. She designed it and did the painting.

That's the way things were changing. I thought it was time to move on. My stint at BTL was just short of three years. Not being the impulsive type, I began planning my move to Seattle. I had saved some money and could concentrate on saving more.

It was the end of October 1987. I was looking for one final Halloween party before quitting BTL and moving to Seattle.

In the previous few years, I had gone to parties with contests sponsored by radio stations. They had the best prizes. Hearing that there was a huge one every year, alternating locations from Sea World to the Del Mar Fairgrounds, I decided to go for it. This was the year for Del Mar.

THE VISION

When I arrived at the fairground facility, I was blown away. The building was huge and the crowd packed the place. Three popular bands played that night. I don't recall who; I was totally focused on other matters.

Halfway through the event, someone came over and gave me a number.

"You're one of the finalists," she yelled over the music, the whooping, and the hollering. "When the band finishes its set, they will ask you to come up on stage."

There were some amazing costumes. One guy was in a huge and ultra-realistic shell. It was covered with thousands of beads. The beads were iridescent, and the whole shell shimmered with changing colors depending on how the light hit it.

One prize was the "People's Choice Award." We each stepped forward one at a time. As they worked down the line, the applause was moderate, and in some cases, quiet. When I stepped forward, the whole place erupted.

So, that's the prize I got.

Then there were first, second, and third prizes. First was a motorcycle. I can't remember the other prizes—something like a weekend at a resort or dinner for two at an expensive restaurant?

Anyway, I received a ten-day round trip for two to London at a five-star hotel (next to Hyde Park) and two tickets to a theater to see the production of *Cats* in the round. That meant the production was on a huge disc that rotated during the performance.

When I returned to work on Monday, the phone in my sculpture area rang. It was Mark.

"Did you go to a contest over the weekend?"

"Yes, I did," wondering why he was interested. "I went to the Del Mar Fairgrounds."

"How did you do?" he asked.

"Great! I got the People's Choice Award," I explained the details.

"Darn!" he said. "I went to one and was picked as a finalist."

"What costume did you wear?"

"I used an inflatable elephant costume we made for a client. When they called us to select the winners, the battery died so they excluded me."

"Wow! Sorry, Mark. You probably would have placed first." I was honored that he chose to share that with me.

I set a date for my London trip—March 1—four months away.

I spent those months doing my regular duties at BTL while trying to organize my thoughts on preparing for the trip.

I needed someone to watch my studio.

Doug Anderson was one of the painters in the art department. Doug was excited about starting a picture-framing business. I knew the trade and wanted to help Doug learn the process. At the same time, I was thinking I should keep up on my ability to frame artwork. Not wanting that knowledge to be wasted, I showed him the ropes, and he loved it.

He also said he would stay in my studio while I was gone.

THE VISION

I finally came to the ultimate decision concerning my trip. I had money saved for my move to Seattle, but I just couldn't resist the idea of using the money to travel Europe—for three months. I would be broke when I came back, but so what? I had been in that situation before. Things always worked out, and I could move to the Northwest when I returned.

The next decision was who to take with me for the first ten days. I wanted to travel alone for the remainder of my trip.

I had a couple of options, but one became an obvious choice. Karen at the time had married, and she had lined me up with a friend of hers a couple of months earlier. Her name was Anellina, and we had dated a few times.

Anellina was really excited about going and offered to store my van in her garage. I was comfortable around Anellina. She was a therapist and had a nice home in the Mount Helix area. The trip would give me a chance to know her better. I felt that she was interested in a long-term relationship. I'm not sure I was, but it seemed like a relationship that could work out. It was a matter of learning more about each other. I was dead set on moving to the Northwest, and she had just settled into a new house in a nice area. I wasn't sure she would give that up.

Halfway through February, I did the deed and put in my notice at BTL. More than a few co-workers seemed concerned about the importance of my job and didn't think I could be replaced. I told them that I didn't think the owners felt that way. They didn't seem to care about the quality end of things—just the profits. To them, everyone was replaceable—like the pieces of a machine that, if something broke, you just picked up a catalog and ordered a new one.

On the last day of work, I wanted to get together with a couple of close friends at a local bar to celebrate. I cleaned out my personal items and made the rounds to say my goodbyes. There were lots of hugs. I would miss them, and I also would miss my job. I loved what I was able to do there, but I felt that I needed to control my own life and get back into the arts.

When I arrived at the bar, a few other employees were already waiting for me. There also seemed to be a continual flow of co-workers coming through the door until it seemed that the whole company was there. The owners didn't show up. Dave was there and that surprised me. He actually sat in a seat next to me.

My friends from the art department walked over carrying a large poster board. They had cut around the edges to shape it into a huge artist's palette. They had made large shapes of colored construction paper that looked like blobs of paint. There was one color for each of the departments, and they had all signed their name, wishing me luck and saying they would miss me. Green was the painting department; blue was the silk screeners; and on it went—the sewing department, the wood and metal shop, the sales staff, the office workers, the shipping department, etc.

I looked over at Dave, and there were tears in his eyes—actually flowing. He picked up his napkin to wipe his face.

"How sweet," I thought. I didn't think he cared.

I heard that after I left, the owners gave each employee a $500 bonus, thinking that would keep them from deserting. Since they had taken the employees from Robert Keith, they were sure that I was doing the same to them.

That was not my motivation at all. I was really excited to travel Europe, see great art, and move to Seattle. The business life was not appealing to me. I really enjoyed designing and making inflatables. I did have some ideas in that direction that I was interested in pursuing. Other than that, I had no goals after Europe except to pursue my passion for the fine arts.

CHAPTER NINE

Since I finally had Bigger Than Life behind me, I began preparing for my trip to London by making lists and thinking about what I wanted to do and where I wanted to go when I traveled Europe.

I had three objectives:

- Do watercolors of the trip.
  I bought two watercolor blocks—one twelve inches by sixteen inches and one eight inches by twelve inches.

- Go to the major cities and spend a week to ten days seeing the great art museums of each of these cities.

  I wanted to go to each museum more than once and, of course, see the sights and meet the people. I felt I needed to stay at each location a while, so I could relax and get the feel of each place.

- Eat well!
  Each country had its own unique menu and flavor. I wanted to experience each country through its food.

Anellina and I met for dinner and spent the night together on several occasions talking about the trip. She had a sister who was going to be in London at the same time we were, and Anellina wanted to see her. We also wanted to rent a car and drive around southern England.

I had a close friend, Betty Rose, the best salesperson Robert Keith ever had. Unfortunately, she was so good that the company wanted to reduce her commission. Betty was making more than they were, and the owners couldn't allow that. She quit and decided to do real estate sales.

We went out for sushi often. She took me out in exchange for giving her son drum lessons.

Her family had traveled Europe often, and she did a great job helping me prepare for the trip. One thing I needed to get was a Dolt bag. It was easy to carry with shoulder and waist straps. It held a lot of stuff. She had me get a line with clamps on each end to hang clothes to dry. Dramamine was high on her list. The list went on. Her advice and recommendations all turned out to be useful. Unfortunately, I did not take some of her advice but wish I had, now that I look back on it.

Doug Anderson, who was going to stay in my studio while I was gone, asked me if I would call our favorite sushi bar from London at midnight on his birthday. He said a lot of our friends would be there. I told him I would.

There were a few minor hassles before I left. I was driving my van into Anellina's garage and found that it was one inch too high to fit in the door. This was an easy fix. I let the air out of the tires, not completely though, just enough to lower it and not be riding on the rims.

LONDON

Anellina and I flew out of San Diego at five o'clock in the evening on February 29. We connected with a flight at LAX airport and took a 747 jet to London. It was an eleven-hour flight. The movie *Surrender* passed some of the time, but other than that, I didn't get much sleep.

Arriving in London at noon on March 1, we went through customs and then exchanged our money for English currency—$1.86 for one pound.

We took the underground to the Marble Arch in Central London, next to Hyde Park, and found our hotel a block away—the Mount Royal.

Needless to say, we took a nap for a couple of hours.

Anellina contacted her sister Marina and arranged for us to meet her and her boss Fred at their hotel for a drink.

That evening, we went out to a high-class French restaurant. The meal cost over 140 pounds for the two of us but was excellent. I am not a white-wine drinker, but the bottle we had was the best wine I have ever tasted. We had escargots and duck, and the desserts were amazing. We each had our own waiter who served us in unison, lifting the lids on the dishes at the same time, revealing the courses they were serving at the time. This was a great way to kick off our vacation.

The following morning, we had a continental breakfast in our room, then walked to the Tate gallery.

I was finally seeing the great works of the old artists—in real life—for the first time. Even before arriving, I was anxious to see Joseph

THE VISION

Turner's paintings. I was not disappointed. They were large pieces that could never be properly represented in the photos I had seen. They were borderline abstract with amazing colors. He was definitely an influence on the impressionist movement.

We took a lunch break at one-thirty at an English pub, and then it was back to the Tate to see the work of another artist, David Hockney, who did work beyond what any book could represent.

When we returned to the hotel, Anellina freshened up and left to visit her sister.

Anellina must have had a great time since she didn't arrive back at the hotel until 2:00 in the morning. After confirming her fantastic night with her sister, she immediately fell into a deep sleep.

We slept until noon. Anellina was not feeling well at all when she woke. She asked if I was upset with her.

"No, of course not. Why would I be upset?"

"We didn't have sex last night. I just thought you were mad."

"I didn't think you were up for it."

I let her go back to sleep while I went out. I went to the same English tavern we were at the day before and then went back to the Tate Museum to see the rest of what I had missed.

Seeing this artwork was like an injection of energy. I was in a contemplative mood when I left the museum and walked north along the Thames River. When I reached the House of Commons and Big Ben—lo and behold—there was Rodin's *Burghers of Calais*! I had seen photos of it as well as detailed shots. It was magnificent!

When I returned to the hotel, Anellina was feeling better. We dressed up and went to our appointed time to see *Cats*.

As it turned out, we didn't have tickets to *Cats*, I called Mr. R Miller of RCA when we returned. Oops! It was actually the production of *Chess*. He arranged seats for us the following night at the Prince Edward Theatre. By that time, it was getting late, so we went to the hotel bar and drowned our sorrows in a couple of drinks. I didn't disappoint Anellina that night.

The next morning, I had the usual continental breakfast. Anellina had still not completely recovered from two nights ago, so she slept in. I went to Hyde Park in the early morning and painted. The clear air was a bit nippy, but it felt good. It felt good to be in London, and it felt good to paint.

Anellina was much better when I got back and she was ready to do something. We walked through the park to the Victoria and Albert Museum and spent a lot of time viewing paintings by Constable. Then it was back to the hotel to nap and prepare ourselves for the theater that evening. The napping was not all because of drinking. We were wrestling with a bit of jet lag.

There were tickets waiting at the door this time. *Chess* was a wonderful play—great sets, singing, and acting.

Italian food was next on our agenda. The restaurant was in the Soho district, and we both loved that part of town. Not only were there interesting places to eat but there were also more theaters, galleries, and pubs. The streets were narrow, adding to the old European atmosphere.

Getting up a little later than usual the following morning, we took the Underground back to the Soho district. I took my thirty-five-millimeter camera and shot some black and white photos. My friend

Doug wanted a tee shirt at the London Hard Rock Cafe, so that was the next thing we did.

We were both disappointed that we didn't see *Cats* the other night, so we decided to see if we could get tickets at the door—no problem! The scenery awed me with its detail, and I fantasized about actually making a set like that.

Later in life, I realized that when I wanted to do something, I needed to take it seriously. Dreams like this often became a reality for me. A decade later, I did just that—I made a *Cats* set.

On our last day at the hotel, we split up so we could do the things we each wanted to do before leaving London. Anellina wanted to go to Harrods department store. I wanted to explore parts of the city I hadn't yet seen and to shoot some black and white photography. There were also more museums that I was interested in. I walked towards Trafalgar Square and spent some time at London's National Gallery. I didn't come close to seeing it all—maybe on my return trip.

According to our plans, it was time to find a car to rent so we could explore southern England. The best tactic was to take a cab to Heathrow Airport and rent one there. When we returned, I would take Anellina straight to the airport, turn in the car, and start my solo trip to mainland Europe.

We headed west from London. It felt odd driving on the opposite side of the road than I was used to. I had a latent fear that I might space out and just start driving in the wrong lane. Finally, l got used to it. The cars on the freeway zoomed past us at what seemed like incredible speeds. I accelerated and got in the flow.

There were things we wanted to see, but for the time being, we just relaxed and drove. We would hit those places on the way back. Somewhere along the way, I took a wrong turn and we ended up in Wales.

It was starting to get late. Anellina brought a book on bed and breakfasts, and she began taking notice of our location. She was checking to see what was in the area.

We found a place in a small town—Newport—just as the sun was setting. Climbing the stairs, we knocked on the door only to find out that they were full. They were pleasant people, and they referred us to the house next door.

We climbed the stairs to the neighbor's house and knocked on the door. A woman answered with a big smile.

"We're looking for a place to stay tonight," Anellina said. "Your neighbors suggested we see if you have a vacancy."

"Yes, we do," she said in some sort of British accent. "They just called us and said you were coming over. Come in."

"Go ahead," I told Anellina. "I'll grab our bags and be right back."

The same lady was at the door when I returned.

"Your wife is waiting in the living room. Make yourself at home."

I guess it's not surprising she assumed that we were married. We figured we would play along to avoid confusion. She showed us to our room. "Dinner will be in about forty-five minutes."

We deposited our bags and walked down to the living room to chat. Suddenly, the front door swung open, and the man of the house walked in. He was dressed in his work clothes with scuffed boots, and from the looks of it, he had a physical job. His shirt was a little worn and a bit dirty from whatever he did.

He darted upstairs as he said, "I'll be back down in a few minutes."

Our hostess herded us into the dining room and showed us to our seats. A few minutes later, her children came down and joined us.

The table was set, and she started bringing in plates of food.

Her husband—I am assuming he was her husband—came back downstairs. He looked to be about sixty-five years old and had changed his clothes to an elaborate suit with a vest and cufflinks. He sat at the head of the table.

"Wonderful, we have company!" He seemed delighted. There was a smile on his face as he introduced himself and his family. He looked like a very proud man and seemed much respected by his wife and children.

We introduced ourselves and told him where we lived.

The food was tasty, and there was plenty more food if we wanted seconds.

After dinner, he stood and said, "Please excuse Paul and me. We have business to attend to."

He motioned for me to follow him as he opened the front door. We walked down the stairs, across the street, and through the door of a tavern. We found a table and sat down. He waved at a waitress while holding up two fingers. The waitress brought us two pints of beer. We had a fun conversation comparing our two countries and chatting about Anellina's and my trip and where we were going.

As we drank our beers, I realized he had already finished his. He waved at the waitress and along came two more beers. He looked at me with a dour look on his face. I was sipping mine and had barely started.

"Drink that beer," he said. "Don't sip it."

He was talking to the right man as I recalled my fraternity days and downed the pint in five seconds.

"There you go!" he said. "You know how to do it!"

Being in a bar across the street from his house, I realized that he was proud to show me off to his bar buddies.

For as fast as we downed the beers, a bit of time had expired because the waitress had been pacing us with about twenty minutes between the last two beers. We were so involved in our conversation that we didn't notice the gaps.

After four pints each, we staggered back across the street, up his stairs, and through the door. It had been a fun conversation, and my host was a hell of a nice guy.

The next morning, we had a filling breakfast, hopped in the car, and headed back into England. Anellina had her own stories to tell about the night before. She had had a good time, too. This visit had given us a little insight into how these people live. We were part of their family from the moment we arrived until the moment we left.

On the drive back, we stopped at the town of Bath and saw the remnants of the Roman-built bathhouses.

Stonehenge was our next stop. We spent a couple of hours there and had a little picnic from the sandwiches we bought in a small store as we left Newport.

These huge, monumental stones really captured the feelings of an epic history that is still not fully understood. I took photos, and we walked between the stones feeling the power in them and the history.

Anellina and I spent one more night together at a Holiday Inn. We tried to find a little British inn or a place with a little atmosphere but failed. It was getting dark, and we were tired. Leaving each other was a bit sad, and we sat at the bar that evening talking about our trip. She wanted me to call her every week. I agreed. "Well, maybe two times a week," she said.

I was a little reluctant but agreed. I really cared for Anellina, but the calls turned out to be a mistake. I need to stick up for what I want. I'm bad that way. As it later turned out, I began to resent the two times a week calls. I really wanted to immerse myself in Europe, and after a while, I felt like I was reporting home to Mom. I explained that to her over the phone, but it came out like I had met someone else. I hadn't.

Early the next morning, we went straight to the airport and returned the car. Anellina had an early flight, so the hotel we stayed at was intended to be as close to Heathrow as possible. I took her as far to the departure gate as I could, and we said our goodbyes.

I took the Underground to Central London. It was still early morning. I bought a train ticket to Harwich from British Rail for that evening and made a boat reservation to the Hook of Holland. There were still about eight hours to kill. I took the Tube (Londoners' affectionate term for the Underground) to our usual pub next to the Tate Gallery for an early lunch and then went to the National

Gallery again. After getting my fill, I walked to the National Portrait Gallery and spent the rest of my time there.

AMSTERDAM

I caught the train at 7:08 p.m., and by midnight, I was in the middle of the English Channel on the boat to Holland.

That night, I took short catnaps anywhere I could find to be comfortable, but I didn't get much sleep. The boat arrived at the Hook of Holland just before sunup. I activated my Eurail pass and rode first class into Amsterdam.

The one thing that stamped the biggest impression on my mind was how flat Holland was. Also, the number of people on bicycles was unexpected, even though I had heard about it. Seeing it looked to me like a cartoon. There were also a lot of canals, even before reaching Amsterdam.

When the train arrived, I took a tram to the Heineken brewery. This place must have been a tourist attraction more than a local hangout. Everyone there seemed to be an American. Having only one beer, I walked the short distance to the Hotel de Moor.

I stayed in room number fourteen. It is supposed to have a history of famous people of the past staying there (as it was touted in travel brochures). It was a tiny, quaint little room overlooking the Prinsengracht Canal. Throughout my stay, I worked on a painting of the view out the window, framed by curtains and the sill with a heater below it. The buildings across the canal were very detailed. They also reminded me of cartoons. A few days later, I did another "quicker" painting of a bridge going over a canal with a boat moored to the sidewall.

I loved those arched pedestrian bridges! The brick and stone environment with the walkways and canals had an eerie but wonderful feeling—also like a cartoon—no disrespect meant.

I've talked before about the artists that influenced me in my youth. One was Salvador Dali. The other was Vincent van Gogh.

I would like to think that I like all artists since each has a unique view. Real artists learn from other artists, from creative thinking and from experimentation. These are the tools needed to build their own styles.

There are several artists that have influenced me more than others. I saw things in their work that were eye-opening and that transcended typical views of art. I will bring these artists to your attention as I progress with my tale.

Vincent affected me because of his colors—more so than other artists. Seeing his work in books did not do him justice; seeing his work in real life was astonishing.

I liked him when I first saw the photos of his work, but the real paintings took the surface of the canvas away and his colors wove in and out of space as if alive. To top that off, there was his brushstroke. His paintings were alive.

Hence, when I first walked into my room, I threw my bag on the bed and left immediately to see the Van Gogh Museum. It was still early.

The Van Gogh Museum was like being in a candy store for the eyes. I spent the morning and early afternoon enjoying each painting.

Finally, after scouring books about his life and his work, I was seeing them in real life. When I was in London, I saw his work in an impressionism exhibit—I think it was at the Tate. Here, the walls were filled with his work.

I did have a favorite. I liked one particular self-portrait of the several that I had seen. My earlier description of his work was fully embodied in this painting. I did not see a surface, just the colors and brush strokes dancing around in space, like a portal into a three-dimensional world.

This wasn't the last of the Van Goghs I would see. Paris had some of his best paintings. The Musée d'Orsay had a remarkable permanent collection of the impressionist period.

Before going back to the hotel, I stopped at a grocery store for cheese, sausage, and bread. Back in the room, I had a snack and took a long nap. I hadn't slept well since I left England.

That evening, I walked around the area with my camera and ended up in Rembrandt Square (Rembrandtplein) and had a couple of beers. I felt a little handicapped because of the language barrier. That didn't last long. When I talked to or responded to someone who spoke to me in Dutch, they all responded in perfect English with a delightful Dutch accent. All in all, we had fluent and fun conversations.

When I arrived back at the hotel, I heard a lot of talking and giggling. The owner was at the reception desk and told me there was a TV in the lounge. "My daughter is in there with her friends, but don't mind them. They are used to our guests relaxing in there."

That wasn't my original plan, but I walked in and seated myself in the back of the room anyway. The TV was high enough to see over the head of the group of girls. There were about ten of them, and they were chatting in Dutch and laughing. They seemed to be playing some game. They took turns standing and talking to the group. The TV was boring, but the girls were animated and having a blast. They were too young for my interests—maybe thirteenish. They ignored me for a while. Then one girl who was talking looked over at me, turned red (obvious with her pale skin), and giggled. All of their heads turned to me, and they burst out laughing. They said a few things that sounded like an apology and then continued. Just the atmosphere they created made me want to laugh.

I stood and walked up to my room. Before leaving, they all waved goodbye with their happy faces and said something that I didn't understand, but it sounded friendly.

I woke up fresh the following morning and walked downstairs to try their breakfast. It was tasty and filling. Returning to my room, I worked on the painting from my window overlooking the Prinsengracht Canal. Then it was off to the Rijksmuseum.

Wow! This was a huge step into the past with beautiful paintings by Rembrandt, Rubens, and Vermeer. I was lost in the names, the portraiture, the landscapes, and the human bodies. The paintings were really dark, but it allowed the light that was in them to come out strong.

In the afternoon, I went back to my room overlooking the canal and took a long nap. I was hungry when I awoke and kept thinking of a food vendor who parked close to the bridge, just down the street. I wanted to try it since they served herring, eel, and other exotic Dutch treats. I had an eel sandwich. It was pretty good.

OK, time for a little bar hopping!

I spruced myself up, which meant trimming my mustache and putting on my last clean set of clothes. I then walked to a square called Leidseplein.

The first bar I walked into had a friendly owner who actually sat next to me. We began talking of general topics that are common when you first meet someone. It then evolved into the reality around us.

"So, what can I get you?" he asked, as he casually stood up and moved behind the bar.

"I'll have a Kioki Coffee."

"OK. What's a Kioki Coffee?" he asked with a tilt of the head and a crooked look to his mouth.

"It's Kahlua, brandy, and coffee. You top it with whipped cream and a cherry then pour a bit of crème de cocoa over it."

"We don't have coffee—just espresso," he said.

"Sounds intense, but I'll try it."

The other patrons were listening and chimed in with "Me, too!" and "Hey, I'll try that." The bartender served us, and—yes—it was pretty intense. It was like a thick desert with alcohol. A regular Kioki Coffee was intense just as it is. I thought it best to only have one.

I said my goodbyes. Everyone chimed in with "Enjoy your trip" and "Stop in again" remarks.

I wandered around until I found a packed tavern. There didn't seem to be a place to sit until I spied a few seats at the end of the bar. As soon as I sat down, three gorgeous Dutch women came over and joined me. They greeted me and switched to English as soon as they realized I had no idea what they were saying.

They lived north of Amsterdam, and they came here to drink and party. They kept plying me with drinks. As soon as I finished one, another appeared in front of me. They were regulars and knew a lot of others who frequented the place. They introduced me to their friends who also asked if they could buy me a drink.

I was drinking brandy. It was a Dutch brandy that was very smooth (meaning that it was a little too easy to drink). It was also half the price of the French equivalent. I realized that I needed to refuse their generous offers before I fell on the floor.

On the way back to the hotel, I walked by the first bar where I had stopped earlier. I poked my head in the door and said "hi," only to be coaxed in for another espresso Kioki Coffee. The bartender refused to charge me. I got into bed around two-thirty that morning.

"Oh my God" was all I could mutter that morning when I finally awoke. I went downstairs and had breakfast. It helped to get something in my stomach.

For most of the day, I stayed in my room recovering from the night before. I slept a lot but was still productive. I washed my clothes in the sink then stretched my laundry cord across the room. The clothes were dry enough to wear in a couple of hours.

I worked on the painting of the view out my window between the napping. Feeling hungry, I finally got out in the fresh air at five o'clock in the evening. I went back to Leidseplein and had a nice meal at an Indian restaurant, then went to bed early.

The following morning, there was a light rain that lasted all day. I painted and then wandered around with my camera to areas I hadn't yet seen. During this trip of discovery, I found myself on Zeedijk Street. It was Sunday, and the streets were deserted, but I read about this place—high crime rate, hookers, and drug dealers. It reminded me of my studio in the Gaslamp. I also saw the windows where women displayed their goods. The streets were narrow—my vision of what most of Europe must be like.

One thing on my agenda was to stop at the train station. I was leaving for Paris on Tuesday. I took the tram back to the hotel but had an odd experience. The driver kept looking at me in his mirror, and his expression seemed angry. When I was getting close to the Prinsengracht, I stood and walked to the front, as I did the time before, taking my lead from what other passengers did. The driver drove past my stop while still glaring at me in the mirror. Immediately, a tiny elderly lady got up from her seat, walked upfront with her cane, and stood in front of me. She was glaring at the driver who immediately stopped the tram and opened the door. She moved aside and motioned that I could leave. She smiled at me, and I thanked her.

Anne Frank's house was my last stop.

On my walk back to my room I found a telehouse (as telephone booths are called in Holland). I made my first call to Anellina.

I woke to my last day in Amsterdam and finished my paintings, grabbed my thirty-five-millimeter camera, and went in a direction I hadn't been—up the Amstel Canal. It was great, but it seemed that I was experiencing more of the same. I had several gilders left. Hmmm, what shall I do?

THE VISION

There was a restaurant on the corner across from the canal that I liked, but a woman I met at the hotel breakfast said I should try the one on our side of the canal.

It was downstairs from street level, and I enjoyed a fantastic plate of ribs. It had a wonderful brick interior, and they played Cat Stevens music the whole time. I was in heaven.

I walked to Leidseplein—again. I must have liked that place. There was a lot going on that day. After priming myself with a couple of beers, I walked to the center of the square. There were people playing ice hockey and a four-piece band doing their thing.

I realized that I hadn't had a single cup of coffee since I arrived. I was in the mood to just sit down and have a cup. I looked around and saw a sign that said "coffee," so I walked in that direction. The coffee shop was down about five steps. I walked into a wide entrance and hit a wall of smoke.

"Whoa! That smells like marijuana!" I thought—and it was.

I had always heard that weed was legal here. I wondered why I hadn't seen any signs of it since I arrived. Now I knew—coffee shops.

I walked up to the bar, and a woman with heavy eyelids casually strolled in my direction.

"I'll have a latte, please."

"Got it," she said. "The marijuana is over there." She motioned with her eyes to the corner of the café.

I looked in the direction she nodded and saw a man with several mini bags of pot from "everywhere." I walked over to see his goods.

"Wow," I said. "I'm from the States, and you never see anything like this!"

"I feel sorry for you, man. Land of the free?"

"Someday," I said. "They're working on it. Oh, yeah. I'll have some of this 'Tiberian numb tongue.'" (OK, I made that up, but the real names were just as good.)

I bought a small baggy for half what it costs in the States.

I walked back to the counter, and my latte was waiting for me. I sat down and had a sip.

There was an elbow nudge in my left rib. It was the guy sitting next to me trying to get my attention. He passed me a lit joint.

"Thanks!" I gripped it with my thumb and index finger then took a puff. I almost fell off my stool. Whatever that was, it was strong. I held on to my barstool to make sure I wasn't going to tip over and then focused on my coffee.

I looked down the length of the bar and saw people rolling joints with little piles of weed poured out on the bar.

So, the stories were true: pot was legal, but the smoking was contained and not anything you experienced in public.

CHAPTER TEN

PARIS

Crawling out of bed earlier than normal, I packed my gear in my Dolt bag, had breakfast, and made my way to the train station. I caught the 8:53 a.m. train to Paris.

I had to toss the rest of the weed I bought yesterday. I heard that if you were busted in France, they would send you to the guillotine, and I really didn't want to lose my head over such a small purchase.

On the train, I sat next to an Australian man named Barry. Actually, he was born in Yugoslavia. That was his destination; he was going home to see family.

There were big troubles in that country at the time. Well, actually the troubles were just beginning as it became evident in the news after returning to the States.

When we arrived in Paris, we hung together until we figured out the Metro subway system and found our hotels. Mine was the Grand Hotel de Lima—175 francs per night.

Barry's hotel was three blocks away, and we met for a beer and dinner. We sat next to three young women and tried to have a conversation, but the language barrier stymied it. It began pouring rain while we were there, so I dug in my pack and pulled out a poncho. I loaned it to Barry; he had further to go.

Initially, there was a lot on my agenda. Betty Rose had a friend named Rivian whom she had introduced me to in San Diego.

Rivian was now in Paris and lived right next door to the Musée d'Orsay. I called her and took the Metro to her place. We made plans and chatted until late. I walked back along the Seine to my hotel arriving at twelve-thirty that night.

Barry met me at my hotel the following morning. We walked to the Notre Dame Cathedral and had coffee while we waited for the Louvre Museum to open.

We entered the Louvre together but quickly realized that we needed to part and go the direction we each wanted to go—such a vast museum! Viewing artwork is a personal experience between an individual and the artist. We made plans to meet that evening.

I walked around, again being overwhelmed by the size, the history, and the painting techniques. I had plans to meet Rivian a couple of hours later at a café next to the opera. As it turned out, my watch was off by an hour. I somehow had it on Cairo time. I was there an hour early. I didn't realize it at the time, so I decided to check out some more museums.

The next item on my list was the George Pompidou Center. At the time, I was running around like a mad animal. I spent most of the afternoon at the National Museum of Modern Art. Then it was a Picasso show at the Grand Gallery.

Barry was at my hotel at eight-thirty that evening. We went out to dinner and then went bar hopping. I returned to my room at two-thirty in the morning.

THE VISION

The next morning was Barry's last day in Paris. He was going to Nice for a couple of days before moving on. We had breakfast, exchanged addresses, and said our goodbyes. He left me with an invitation to travel with him. I considered the offer but preferred my own agenda.

Boy! I had hit the ground running when I arrived in Paris. I seemed to be constantly occupied—meeting people, dining with others, and visiting museums. Amsterdam was slow and mellow compared to what I ran into here. My whole visit continued at this pace until I caught the train out of town.

Rivian called and asked what had happened to our meeting the day before. I had finally realized the evening before that my watch had been wrong, and I explained it to her. She had been there when she was supposed to be.

We planned to meet for dinner that evening with two Frenchmen she knew.

I finally treated myself to a long nap that afternoon. When I woke, I grabbed my camera and went to the Pompidou Center. I took detailed black and white photos of the architecture. The shots I enjoyed most were taken from the top of the building. The view was amazing. I took panoramic shots of the skyline and rooftops.

That evening, I caught the Metro to Rivian's house. Her two friends were there, and we went out for Italian food.

Jean Paul, one of her friends, lived in a small town named Angouleme—not real small—about 40,000 people. He wanted me to come visit him and his family; not just visit—he said I should stay a while. I was excited about that opportunity.

He was in Paris for his work. If I remember correctly, he did theater sets, trade show booths, and exhibitions. It was a fun evening.

Knowing I liked Van Gogh, Rivian informed me that the Musée d'Orsay was having a special exhibit that focused on him. There were also samples of other impressionist artists in the show. Lines to get in stretched around the corner. Rivian knew that, so we went early.

Up until now, this was the most awesome show I had seen yet. It was a "best of" selection of work. It even outshined the Van Gogh Museum in Amsterdam.

After a snack on the top floor, Rivian and I parted. I decided to stay and see the other exhibits.

What an awesome museum the Musée d'Orsay is. It used to be a train station. It was built in 1897, and after a period of decline and disuse, the museum was founded. That was in 1986—two years before my visit. The center of the museum is completely open, and the ceiling is made of glass that arches over the huge space. The sides of the building have smaller galleries showing both their permanent shows and their special exhibits. These galleries continue up in tiers until they reach the ceiling. To top it all off, the open center is filled with sculpture.

The sculpture needs to be commented on since it is such a major presence in the museum. The detailed and ultra-lifelike work almost seems to breathe.

Alexandre Schoenewerk sculpted a marble figure—*Young Tarantine*—a reclining nude who was stretching and twisting over a box shape that was covered in fabric.

There was a sculpture that appeared as a large wall with figures and animals, larger than life, standing out from the wall in full three dimensions while the wall itself had shapes carved in deep relief. Jean-Baptiste Carpeaux sculpted the piece I am referring to in marble.

THE VISION

Finally, one of my favorites was the marble version of *The Gates of Hell* by Rodin. I saw the bronze the next day at the Rodin Museum.

Just a few months before, I had read a biography of Rodin. I was glued to that book until I finished it. Seeing his work in Europe was special since it was so fresh in my memory. Rodin worked on *The Gates of Hell* for thirty-seven years, and it is still said to be unfinished. He did multiple sculptures of the individual parts, and he made them in marble and cast bronze.

Rodin was commissioned to do *The Gates of Hell* in 1880 for a decorative arts museum that never opened. Some of Rodin's most known works, such as *The Kiss* and *The Thinker,* were originally sculpted into *The Gates of Hell*.

The sculptor died in 1917. *The Gates of Hell* was later cast in bronze, in full for the first time, eight years later.

The museum had a vast variety of European paintings, sculptures, etchings, and drawings from the distant pre-Renaissance period until now. The countries of Europe were all so different with their many unique artists and styles—from the time of dominant influence by Christianity to the modern individual artists expressing their unique visions.

I returned to the hotel and decided to go to an outdoor café that was close by. It was deserted but open. A waiter walked over, and like an idiot, I ask for red wine in French—or what I thought was French. I massacred it. After pointing to the menu, he stomped off. Five minutes later, he brought the wine and I never saw him the rest of the evening. I rocked back on my chair, rested my legs on the table, and read my book for two hours. I then put some francs on the table and went home.

I've heard that some French people are totally insulted if you pronounce the words in their language wrong. I guess I found out, but it was the only time it happened.

THE PARTY

I had breakfast at the hotel, and Rivian called while I was eating. She wanted to invite me later that afternoon for a little get-together. I had a full day ahead of me.

I gathered my art supplies and camera then took the Metro to the Eiffel Tower. The tower was huge. Standing at a distance and seeing it on the horizon doesn't do it justice. Standing next to or under it makes you realize its size. You feel downright puny.

From there, I walked to the Musée Rodin. The grounds weren't open until two o'clock, and it was noon, so I found a small park with a wonderful view. The Eiffel Tower was in the distance, and the park had a white figurative sculpture in the middle of it. I removed my art supplies from my bag and painted for two hours.

Just after two o'clock, I returned to the grounds of the Musée Rodin. I say grounds because that is what it was. Inside the gates, there was a whole city block of grass, trees, and magnificent sculpture. There was a small but beautiful stone manor in the middle that housed Rodin's smaller works with descriptions of his process and history.

The large bronze sculptures were exhibited on the grounds—perfect for the presentation of his work.

THE VISION

I took the Metro to meet Rivian. She informed me that there was a party at the place where she lived.

This place was an immaculate building and was owned by a prince. Entering the building, I walked up the stairs and into a large room where several groups of people were scattered about. I wandered around listening in on the conversations. They were all talking in the language they were familiar with.

There was a large table filled with fruits, vegetables, and cheese, all arranged artistically by someone with an eye for interior decoration.

As was pointed out to me later in the evening, the people who were invited were artists: visual artists, dancers, performing artists, musicians, and writers.

"Excuse me," said a voice, as a woman laid a friendly hand on my shoulder. "There is a group over there." She pointed to a group of nine people. "They are speaking English."

"Thank you," I said, and I walked over—sidling my way in a covert manner, trying to pick up bits of their conversation.

A woman was talking passionately about South Africa. She lived there—or did once. The people listening were enrapt in her words. They were all sitting comfortably on the floor next to a window. I sat just at the edge of their group.

At the first lull in the conversation, I chimed in as if I were knowledgeable on the subject.

"So, if I am correct, I have heard that the area has three factions: the Boers, who are Dutch; the Zulus and associated native tribes; and the English. There is no possibility of their working together, and tensions are always high, correct?"

The group—all women—looked at me. The speaker confirmed my remarks.

"Yes, that is correct." And she changed her dialog to describe in more detail what I had contributed.

I was relieved and proud of myself to be able to contribute and take my place in the group. My tactic from that point on was to say as little as possible and to listen to the conversation. I tried to avoid any untamed ego from baring itself, resulting in my coming across as a "know it all" asshole. I actually didn't know much more than what I had said, so I was truly interested in her dialog.

It was nice to sit with intelligent people talking of interesting things in a light and casual interchange.

After a while, some of the group got up and mingled with others, or other guests joined us. I also needed to stand up and stretch my legs.

I walked over to the huge balcony doors that were wide open revealing the courtyard of the Musee d'Orsay with the Seine flowing in the background.

Even though I could have stood there enjoying the view, my eyes kept wandering to the ornate arrangement of cheeses, salads, and fruits. I was starving, and I had a great desire to walk over, pick up one of the conveniently placed knives, and politely slice off a piece of cheese. So, I did just that.

I felt that soft tender touch on my shoulder from the same woman who had pointed my way to the English-speaking group.

"I'm sorry, but the cheese table is for after the meal."

"Oh, shoot," I responded. "I feel awful."

THE VISION

"It's no problem. Everyone now knows you're from the States where the appetizers and salads come first. They understand."

The problem was that I still had to look at the cheese with the slice out of the middle for the next hour. That's when dinner was served.

The variety of people at the party was truly amazing. I didn't see Rivian. I met a couple from the American Embassy, two Germans—one who had just returned from South Africa—a woman from Sweden, and an English actress.

The list continued. There was a Frenchman who spoke good English and talked a lot about painting. Carolyn Belko was a dancer from America and was living in Paris.

It made me wonder why I was invited. I'm sure it was through Rivian. She later explained to me that she had moved out of her room at this house to spend time in Southern California. That was when Betty introduced us. Her room was opening up again at the end of the month. She definitely had connections.

Carolyn, the American dancer, expressed an interest in doing something with me before I left Paris. I was leaving early on Tuesday. Monday was the only available day. Unfortunately, Sarah, the English actress, had already called and invited me to accompany her to the Picasso Museum on Monday.

On Sunday morning, I focused on the painting I was working on. I painted until four in the afternoon then went out to dinner. When I returned to the hotel, I talked to Anellina on the phone. Doug called me right after. It made me miss home. They sounded like they really missed me.

It was Monday morning. I rose early and went down to the lower level of the Seine. I walked along the river until Notre Dame was visible. Finding a comfortable spot, I did a painting of the building with the river in the foreground. I then ascended the stairs of the cathedral and took photos from the top.

Returning to my room, I received a phone call from Sarah. She couldn't meet me for our Picasso tour but wanted me to go with her to meet friends for dinner at a Jewish restaurant. Again, typical of most restaurants during my travels, the food was fantastic. We decided to go to a movie—*House of Games,* an American movie with French subtitles. We went out for a beer afterward then said our goodbyes.

I had a restless night trying to sleep—thinking of my next day's train ride.

THE LONG TRAIN RIDE

The rail system in Europe is pretty amazing compared to what we have in the States. I had bought a Eurail pass, and I was quickly getting used to the ins and outs of the process. It was required that I travel first class since I was over twenty-one. Travelers under that age had to travel second class.

To this point, I had only traveled in northern Europe, and the trains were modern, clean, and on time. The pass was for three months and cost 300 dollars.

It was a short walk to the train station. I took the train to Bordeaux. This route went through Angoulême where Jean-Paul lived. His return from Paris was a day later, but I thought I could stay in a hotel for the night.

THE VISION

I rethought this as the train approached that area. He would probably appreciate a few days' rest when he returned home, and, according to my plans, I would pass through Angoulême at least once more. When I arrived at Bordeaux, I had a choice to make—east to Italy or south to Spain.

I had a good friend in Spain. Linda had been a waitress at Yakitori II, my favorite sushi bar in San Diego. Her major in school was Spanish. It was her senior year and she had to spend a full school year living in Spain. She also had to take classes at a local university.

We had talked about my best arrival time to visit her. It didn't matter much to her, but we did settle on a date, and I would be arriving about a month early.

So, east to Italy it was.

I had a five-hour layover in Bordeaux, so I strolled through the city looking for a good restaurant. The skyline of the town encompassed a huge old church with a spire reaching to the sky in a sharp point. I headed straight toward the church but the roads wouldn't cooperate. The character of the place was intriguing, even though it seemed gray and drab. The roads were thin and wound around in what seemed to be directionless curves. The stone walls seemed to close in on you. There were no signs or lights. It was mid-day, so I wasn't sure how lit up it would be at night. I didn't see a soul.

I finally found what my psychic self thought was a good restaurant.

The food I could only describe as strange, but the red wine was excellent. I wonder what I ordered.

As I was finishing, a young lady came in asking for an English menu. This was met by a dumbfounded response from the staff. She sat at the table next to me, and we fell into an instant conversation.

I joined her at her table until I had to catch the train. She was from New Orleans, had worked in London for six months, and was doing a quick tour of Europe with a friend before she went home.

The first-class sleeping car I had reserved was a welcome sight. I had it all to myself.

When I awoke, I was in Lyon. It was early, and I had four eggs and ham breakfast in the train station. Then it was back on board to Geneva.

The countryside was changing from the beautiful French country to the foothills of the mountains. The Alps were gorgeous with turquoise lakes at their base.

From Geneva, the train traveled to Lausanne, then on to Bern, and from Bern to Interlaken.

Interlaken was a place I picked out on the map to take a break from the train and find a hotel. It turned out to be pretty touristy. The weather was rainy, and the trains going to the high Alps weren't running. I decided to leave the next day. My original plan had been to stay a while.

I had a fantastic Swiss dinner and slept in a comfortable bed without the motion of the train underneath me.

I called Anellina. Checking in—it was nice to hear a voice from home.

In the morning, I did a painting of the scene out my window. I had a beautiful view. It seemed like it was manicured too much as if gardeners worked full time to maintain its pristine condition.

The train I originally wanted to catch was going to Florence, but it had been canceled because of avalanches between Interlaken and Milan. Instead, I trained it to Lucerne, a gorgeous town. We then headed south through beautiful snow-covered mountains.

KB, a salesman at BTL, had told me to stay at Lugano. He said it was the best time he ever had. When we arrived, it didn't look like much, so I decided not to stop. As the train continued, the view of the town revealed a steep drop with tiers of houses and buildings dropping down to a beautiful lake at its foot. I think I made a mistake by not stopping.

Instead, I continued on to Milan and immediately transferred to a train to Florence, arriving at eleven that night.

FLORENCE

The Hotel Fedora was the place I had planned to stay, but they were full. All the other places I tried were full also, but I finally found one dingy *pensione* for that night.

I hadn't had a chance to exchange my money for Italian lira. Trying to communicate with the elderly man behind the desk was difficult. We finally agreed that I would give him my passport and pay him the next day. He was a very sweet man and took his time trying to communicate.

Early the next morning, I went to a bank to change my Swiss francs to Italian lira. I wandered the streets looking for a place to stay, but all the *pensiones* were filled with groups. I found one that would take a credit card, but it was hectic with people running all over the place. I wasn't ready for the craziness. So, I left and found a hotel with a large, quiet room and a big bed. It was also clean. A bit more expensive, but at the moment, I had no choice.

I retrieved my bags and passport from the previous night's *pensione* and paid the bill.

The number of people packing the city confused me, but I suddenly realized it was Easter week—a big thing in Florence. This whole week would be crazy. If I had figured that out sooner—or realized it was such a big deal—I would have stayed in Lugano for that week.

I took a couple of hours to relax in my room at the Hotel Arianna and then started wandering around Florence. I had pizza and beer for lunch, then bought a map and some postcards. The streets were typically "old European," being narrow and made of stone.

My camera was with me, and that made it too easy to view the scenery with it attached to my eye. Sometimes, I purposely don't take my camera with me, so I can just look and let my brain flow and absorb the images. Tourists were everywhere, crowding the shops and alleyways.

When I returned to my room, I addressed postcards and marked all the museums on the map for the next day's schedule.

I spent the rest of the evening finishing the Swiss "out the window" painting.

That night, I had a dream. When I dream, I usually remember them, but this one was especially ultra-vivid and realistic.

THE DREAM

I'm in San Diego. The last I remembered, I was in Florence. I didn't know what happened in between or how I got back to San Diego. I thought this should be a dream but it seemed too real—like I had completely lost my memory of what happened on the rest of my Europe tour.

I asked people if they could fill me in on what had happened to the rest of my trip, but no one responded.

I see several people lying in a bed.

There is a huge wheel with a large dowel sticking out of it. I begin to climb the dowel and that makes the wheel turn. I'm going nowhere, but not trying very hard to get anywhere.

Then I found myself sitting at a sushi bar. Two chefs are talking to each other. One glanced in my direction and said, "He's too nice."

When I woke, I had no idea where I was. It shocked me to see the strange room surrounding me as if this were the dream. It actually took about a minute to realize that I was in my hotel room in Florence. A minute can be a long time.

The epitome of the craziness of the masses of people in Florence during Easter was during my visit the next day to the Uffizi Gallery. Even though I went early, the lines were long. They were so long, they were worse than a security check on a busy day at the airport.

You know—roped off in a zigzag, covering the whole courtyard in front of the entrance.

I waited an hour as Italians continually crowded in front of the tourists. The line wasn't moving at all. I was still close to the back of the line. There was an older American couple in front of me.

The good thing was that there were two huge muscle-bound Italian guards in tight tee shirts at the entrance to the museum. They were also smart and aware of what was happening. When a person who had crowded in was at the entrance, they muscled him to the side to let others pass. He eventually gave up and left.

There was a shrill whistle, and I looked around until I saw that one of the entrance guards was pointing at me.

"How many?" he yelled.

"Who me?" I yelled back.

"Yes. How many?"

I held up three fingers to include the couple I was standing with, and he waved us up to the door.

"Enjoy," he said, as he opened the door for us.

The amazing thing was that each gallery inside the Uffizi had only three or four people in it. When people left, the guard allowed the same number to enter. I could relax and view at my own pace without fighting the crowds.

The work at the Uffizi mostly ranged from the thirteenth century to the seventeenth century.

The earlier paintings were done with tempera on wood panels. You can see the use of oil paint on canvas growing in the next two centuries.

A well-known painting there—for those who have any interest in art history—is *The Birth of Venus*, painted in the 1480s by Sandro Botticelli. This was done with tempera on canvas. Venus is depicted nude and standing on a shell.

There was a wonderful collection of works painted by Leonardo da Vinci in the late fifteenth and early sixteenth century. This included his *Annunciation* that has received some attention because of the type of paint he used on the kneeling angel. This figure of the angel disappeared when it was x-rayed.

The Adoration of the Magi was also housed at the Uffizi. This painting was left unfinished but is totally awesome in its sketched-out form. It was done in sepia colors.

Titian's work of a controversial nude, *Venus of Urbino*, has been shown in many art history books. It is beautiful in real life.

But most of all, I loved the work of Rembrandt van Rijn. Two of his portraits—*Portrait of the Artist as a Young Man* and *Portrait of an Old Man*—were my favorites.

Leaving the museum, I walked around the area and found myself behind the Pitti Palace. I was in the middle of a huge, lush garden—well-tended and immaculate.

From there, I climbed to Forte Belvedere. When I reached the top, I was looking at a fabulous view of the city. This place was ideal for my next painting. It was quiet and shaded. I planned to do that the next day, along with taking photos.

Searching for a place with as few people as possible, I walked through a back street and found a nice small restaurant and had another fantastic meal.

When I returned to my room, I requested another two nights—no problem.

I called Anellina. The hotel did not have a phone, so I walked to the train station and called from there. We talked for a long time.

After breakfast the next morning, I made the walk to Forte Belvedere and began painting, then ran around taking photos.

Returning to the hotel, I read up on Rome and took a long nap. It was Sunday, and the museums were all closed. I painted until late.

I also found the time to do my laundry. I hoped it would dry by the next morning.

ROME

I paid my hotel bill and walked directly to the train station. It took a little over two hours to get to Rome. The train was packed.

I imagined Rome to be filled with beautiful art and architecture, and it had been one of my long-awaited cities to visit.

I said "had been" because frankly I was fed up with Italians and Italy. A little too harsh, I suppose. I hadn't seen southern Italy, and I hadn't yet seen Rome—so why jump to conclusions? I would stay and learn, but instead of lingering to feel the character of the place, I planned to see what I came to see and do a painting or two. My plan was to do it all in two days.

I already felt the character.

THE VISION

To begin this process, I grabbed the first hotel I saw, close to the train station.

I immediately took my watercolors and camera to the Colosseum and the Roman Forum and started painting.

Wow! What an empire this must have been. Imagine what it would be like to live in ancient Rome as a citizen, as a soldier, or as an artist. How about a gladiator, an actor, or a politician? I imagined wearing a toga and seeing beautiful women in tunics with belts around their waists or just loose folds of fabric.

I admired Rome's innovative water system. What was it like to be the conquerors of the known world? How about soaking in the baths in Britain like the ones I saw a month ago, or what was it like to march into ancient Egypt?

Did the common citizen go to work like we do today? Go to bars and dine on foods imported from ancient lands? What was it like going to the theater or watching the Christians being thrown to the lions and ripped apart in front of roaring crowds?

All of this history, and then I watched—disheartened—as an Italian took a pee on a beautiful marble column.

I stopped at a small restaurant and had lasagna and a salad. The rest of the evening, I worked on the painting I had started while at the Colosseum.

All of these revelations, and I was still calling Anellina regularly. Oh yeah, she is Italian.

When I crawled out of bed the next morning, I felt like I had a cold. I packed my bag to ready myself for a full day's jaunt through the city.

The bank was the first thing on my agenda. I cashed some travelers' checks and went back to the Colosseum. Instead of thinking about the glories of Rome, I was saddened—almost disgusted—by the degradation of society. What internal politics or strife lead to the rotting away—the falling apart—of such an empire?

There is plenty of literature on all of these thoughts and concerns. I have read about it as many students have, but did they feel it? Could we, the people of today's world, feel and understand? Did we learn the lessons that came out of the downfall of Rome and the demise of this once-great society?

The streets were confusing and going every which way; they seemed like utter chaos. I was looking for the Pantheon, and I finally found it after finding Piazza Navona.

The Pantheon was quite the sight. At first glance, it seemed small and unimpressive. When I moved closer and entered, it was pretty amazing. The dome was huge, spanning 142 feet, and made of concrete. It was built in 27 to 25 BC and later burned down. It was rebuilt in 125 AD. I was definitely transfixed; the whole interior was beautiful.

Next stop: the Vatican. On my way there, I decided I needed a friend for the rest of the trip. I walked into a store and bought a Sony Walkman. I also bought two tapes: Cat Sevens and Jarre.

The Vatican was inundated with decoration and art: frescos, sculptures, and fantastic murals. I walked around enjoying the ornate place. I went downstairs and saw the tombs.

The Sistine Chapel was a must-see. The art was the best I had seen in Vatican City, with the ceiling and wall fresco of *The Last Judgment* by Michelangelo. There were also works by Botticelli and tapestries by Raphael. The ceiling was being restored, so it had scaffolding covering a large section. You could see the difference between the older dark areas and the section that had been cleaned.

THE VISION

The sculpture of the Pietà was also on view, but you couldn't get close because of the time it had been attacked with a hammer. I was close enough to see how well the restoration was going, however. The statue was so lifelike it seemed to breathe.

I moved on to the Vatican Museum. The modern art was not impressive, but the busts and statues were very impressive—dating from before Christ.

Not being Catholic, I don't really understand the rituals or the riches, but the religion has lasted through the centuries and is still strong and powerful in countries throughout the world.

Having been born and raised in the LDS church, I just could not understand the guilt thing or the confession.

If I understand this correctly, the Catholics are born guilty. You confess and ask for forgiveness for the rest of your life.

The Mormons are born innocent. You become ultimately responsible for your actions at the age of eight when you are baptized.

When I left, I had pizza and a beer across the street and then followed the Tiber River to an island. I crossed the river and found that I was completely lost. I didn't care. I walked for hours. I finally asked someone for directions to the train station. Once there, I found my bearings; my hotel was within a block.

By that time, it was six-thirty in the evening. I found a bookstore with books in English and bought *Poland* by Michener. I found a place where I could relax and have a beer, and then I retired to my hotel room.

I filled out postcards, kicked back, and prepared for my long trip. Beginning the next day, I was going to Greece.

CHAPTER ELEVEN

THE LONG TRAIN AND FERRY RIDE

The train left at 9:05 AM for Bari, Italy.

I decided to stop depending on the scheduled times for departures and arrivals.

The trains in Italy were not like those in northern Europe. They could be late—sometimes hours late. The trains were older and not as comfortable as the trains I had experienced to this point. There was no first-class, and we were all crammed together in a rickety coach.

The train ride seemed to take forever. The good part was the view of the southern Italian countryside. The landscape was lush with olives, grapes, and other crops.

The Sony Walkman and I became fast friends—as I thought we would.

When we finally arrived at Bari after a half day's travel, we had a two-hour layover. I was really thirsty and walked to a little shop that had food items.

THE VISION

There was no one in the shop—I thought—until a high-pitched voice said something in Italian.

A young boy's head popped above the counter and repeated what he said before.

I asked in English, "What do you have to drink?"

He couldn't understand me.

I looked on the counter and saw some juice cans—obviously warm. I picked one up and said, "How much?" I had no idea what the exchange rate was.

I took out my Italian lire and showed them to him. He pointed at a couple of coins, so I picked them up and reached out to pay.

Suddenly, the door to the backroom swung open, and an older lady charged in, ranting in Italian.

I showed her the juice can and the lire.

The woman glared at me with angry eyes, grabbed the lire I was holding out, and reached down and grabbed a few more that I had put on the counter. She gripped the boy roughly by the upper arm and marched him back through the door with an angry glance back at me as she was exiting.

Wow! What was that about? I walked out, opened my small can of warm juice, and downed it in a couple of gulps.

That was three times now that someone had shown me such livid anger: the tram driver in Amsterdam, the waiter in Paris, and now the elderly lady in her shop in Bari.

It seemed they were responding to my being from America. I wondered if this was latent anger from World War II. Out of all the people I had talked to or met, only three responded that way. Big deal? It shouldn't be, but something hurt inside me with each encounter; I had done nothing to deserve it.

I caught an even older train to Brindisi.

When we arrived, I walked a little less than a mile to the port, got my boarding pass, and reserved a seat on the ferry to Greece. By the end of this boat ride, I regretted not reserving a cabin. The seats were comfortable—like being in a movie theater—but after a night of windy rough seas, they became increasingly uncomfortable, to the point of not being able to sleep.

The good part was the people I met on either side of me. One was a Mormon missionary from Provo, Utah. He had just served his mission in Italy, so he spoke the language quite well. He was also a painter; he had majored in art at Brigham Young University.

To the right of me was a young student named Michelle. She was on spring break from a school in Germany. After a night of traveling through the Strait of Otranto, we arrived at the island of Corfu in Greece. It was a beautiful early morning. The missionary disembarked at this point.

As we followed the west coast of Greece, I couldn't help being awed by the beauty of the islands and the snow-capped mountains. There was a bitter wind, but I sat on the deck and enjoyed a break from the stuffy, packed interior.

We traveled all day and arrived at Patras at seven-thirty that evening.

I checked out the train station and found that the next train was leaving at two the next morning.

Patras was crazy with people, but Michelle and I managed to find a quiet authentic Greek restaurant. We had an amazing and inexpensive fish dinner—two beers each. We had difficulty communicating with the waitress until we found out that she spoke German. Michelle carried on from there. They were both fluent in German, enough so that they could joke and carry on about our travels and tell stories. I was a little left out but was caught up with the ease and happiness of the moment. Michelle translated as we went along.

We returned to the train station and watched an old American Western movie with Greek subtitles. It was still too early for our departure, so we played rummy until it was time to leave. She kicked my butt.

ATHENS

We arrived in Athens at 7:30 a.m., April 1, 1988.

Being a little bit on the hungry side, we found a small café for coffee and a donut. Michelle accompanied me until I found my hotel close to the Greek ruins—The Attalos Hotel, room 310.

I stayed with her until she caught a taxi. She was lucky to have a friend there and her friend's family to stay with. She would be able to experience the Greek side of life.

I went to my room, took a nice hot bath, and slept until two in the afternoon—the first real sleep I had had for three days. Just being horizontal was nice.

When I recovered from my stupor, I walked the streets. From my first impression, I liked Athens. I had a gyros and a beer and then continued scouting around. I found a store where I could buy some art supplies. The streets were open markets with fruit, meats, vegetables, clothes, cheese, etc. A lot of the vendors used carts so that by the end of the day, they could wheel their goods home.

The negative side was that it reminded me of Tijuana, Mexico, meaning it seemed unclean with flies buzzing all around the stands.

Returning to my hotel, I climbed to the roof and took photos of the view—fantastic!

It was time to call Anellina. I walked back down to my room and called her, looked over my info on places to visit in Athens, then hit the sack.

When I went to the lobby the next morning, I asked if I could stay more nights, and they said that all of their bookings had arrived. They recommended a hotel that was close by, the Hotel Carolina. When I found the place, I was not that excited about staying there. The room was very small and didn't feel clean. The bed was lumpy. What bothered me most were the other guests. I didn't trust them. They seemed shady and would look at me in weird ways that made my skin crawl.

I hadn't checked out of the first hotel yet, so I returned and packed the rest of my stuff. While I was there, Michelle called, and we met a couple of blocks away.

We dropped my pack off at my new digs and then walked to the Acropolis. The crowds were horrible—almost bad enough to go home and come back later, but we persevered and finally hiked to the top.

THE VISION

It was worth the visit. The Parthenon was more amazing than I thought. Again, my mind ran wild imagining how it must have looked and what life must have been like. I didn't realize there were also other ancient structures at the Acropolis: the temple of Athena Nike, the Propylaia, and the Erechtheion. There wasn't a lot to see other than that. However, what we did see was beautiful with the columns and sculpture. Oh, yeah. The view of Athens was spectacular!

We descended from the Acropolis and found a place for lunch. Michelle suggested we take the Metro to Piraeus—a port not far from the center of Athens.

We made the trip and strolled around gazing at the harbor and the yachts. There were also fishing boats and large ships anchored in the bay. Mostly, we talked about the fact that there wasn't much else to see.

From what I had heard, when you come to Athens, taking a week or two tours of the islands makes it all worth it. One such company was selling a tour on a large yacht. It could take up to twenty people. The tour was for two weeks, and they would stop at each island for the passengers to see the sights, party, and sleep in a comfortable bed.

On our return, I kept my eyes open for a better hotel. When we did arrive at the dive, Michelle pulled out a book *Let's Go Europe*, and we went through it pointing out the interesting and not so interesting parts.

Michelle returned to her friend's place, but not for long. Within an hour, she called and wanted to go to a late movie, so I took the Metro to the other side of Athens and met her. After the movie, we had a midnight meal and parted. The Metro wasn't running, so I walked back. It took about an hour.

I'll have to admit, I had been a little standoffish that night. Sitting together at the movie would have been an ideal time to put an arm around Michelle. She would have responded. It would then be hard to not continue; I would have gone with it.

I was beginning to feel a little troubled about Michelle. She had suggested we travel together and wanted to have a closer relationship.

I was actually enjoying having her around. What was wrong with me? I should have been taking advantage of this. What man wouldn't want to travel Europe and meet a young woman to travel with, to make love with, and to support each other?

When I think of past opportunities to get involved with women, my record isn't very good. I have actually shunned a large majority of women who opened up to me, even though I liked them and felt comfortable around them.

I really don't know what it is. I'm a loner and probably always will be.

When I asked Anellina to go with me to London, it was mainly because I had tickets for two and was prompted by Karen. I wasn't sure if we were going to be an item. I know she liked me and was willing to get involved. I cared for her, too, and she was a great traveling companion. I did feel comfortable with her. We had gone out several times before we left for London.

It bothered me that I was expected to check in with her at least once a week. I wanted to immerse myself in Europe. It had nothing to do with Anellina. Even though I had enjoyed London with her, I couldn't wait to get away and be by myself.

That is how I was feeling about Michelle.

THE VISION

Another thing I know about myself is that I have never had a one-night stand or picked anyone up at a bar. I always became involved with women after a long period of being with them in a work environment or in school or after hanging with them through groups of friends. That allowed us to flirt and joke with each other. It allowed time to understand what the other person was really like—a little mating dance, as it were.

It was a quiet Sunday morning when I awoke. The electricity went out for an hour. I packed, went down to the lobby, and checked out. I searched the area for a better place to stay and ran across a more modern touristy place called Hotel Electra.

I got a super room. I read, relaxed, and watched TV. It was a bit expensive, but I deserved it.

That afternoon, I walked around Athens for a while and picked a quiet restaurant where I could eat and read my book. When I returned, I called Anellina, and we had a long talk. Then Doug called and filled me in on the continuing drama and farce of Bigger Than Life.

I worked on an Athens painting and then called Michelle. She had asked me to call her earlier, but I kept putting it off. By the time I did call, she had left to do something with her friend. Just as well.

Greek food is *so* good! I found another great restaurant for dinner and then tried the hotel bar when I returned to the Electra. It was dead.

I soaked in a hot bubble bath and dried myself off after spending too long reading *Poland*—too long because the hot bath drained my energy and turned me into a prune. Before I retired, I booked a full-day cruise to three islands for Tuesday.

The next morning, my sinuses were killing me. I crawled out of bed and went downstairs for breakfast.

I started a new painting—another "view out the window."

Where should I go next? I was thinking of taking the train through Yugoslavia, so I caught the Metro to the train station. Maybe I wasn't paying attention when I arrived, because it seemed like a different station. It was small and dirty with dry sand around it as if it were sitting in the middle of the desert. I saw two characters that were borderline bums with old clothes, baggier than normal, and unshaven. One was leaning against the wall of the station, hands in his pockets glaring at me. The other one—dressed the same—was next to the tracks, pacing back and forth. His head hung down, but I saw his glances toward me every few seconds.

For some reason, I felt like I was entering a Stephen King novel. Continuing on this path would lead to horror and insane confusion.

I turned around, went to the hotel, and booked a flight to Vienna for Wednesday.

A trip through Yugoslavia to Austria by train takes about three days. It was supposed to be a beautiful trip. More than one person had warned me about traveling alone through this country. There would be a good chance of losing my passport. Passports were in high demand, so I had heard. Who knows what else I could have lost? It felt wrong.

I painted until I received a call from Michelle. She was in the lobby. We walked together to the docks to pick up my island tour ticket.

I had failed to ask her to come with me. We went out to dinner followed by dessert and coffee at a different restaurant.

We said our goodbyes with a hug, wished each other well and parted.

Returning to my room, I dove back into my paintings, finishing my Athens work and then did some final retouches on my Interlaken and Rome paintings. Finally, I spread all of my paintings around the room to see how they looked as a group.

The tour boat left the next morning as the sun was rising. It was a comfortable and relaxing cruise. The islands were absolutely beautiful!

What was I thinking about spending so much time hanging in Athens? That two-week tour on a yacht would have been heaven.

We stopped at Paros first and then on to Hydra—beautiful! I walked up a steep winding road through white-washed homes. The higher I walked, the more beautiful was the view—looking out across the Aegean Sea, dotted with islands among the turquoise water. I could live the rest of my life here.

Our final stop was the island of Aegina. It was more populated and flat compared to the other two.

We arrived back in Athens as the sun was setting.

I met some people from San Diego at the end of our tour, and we had dinner together that night.

VIENNA

It was still a little early to go to the airport, so I took my time packing, but I felt anxious to move on. The taxi I had called would be there in fifteen minutes. I could have relaxed in my room another hour—maybe two.

I arrived at the airport three hours before my flight, and the time in the air would take two hours. I hadn't flown in Europe, so being early would relieve the stress of rushing through ticketing and security.

The most remarkable thing about this flight was the meal. Flights in the States were pretty lame in the food department. Sometimes, it was only a snack. If you had a meal, it would be on a much longer flight. It was usually a quick meal in a box.

The meal on my flight to Vienna was like being in a restaurant. I had a three-course meal—served one at a time on actual plates and real silverware. The food was excellent.

The skies were clear, and the view below was of the mountains I probably would have traversed if I had taken a train. It was beautiful and rugged. I'm sure I would have had stories to tell if I had traveled by rail. I wonder if I would have made it alive.

Maybe I would have been abducted into a rebel army and given a uniform and a rifle.

This was more of a reality than I realized at the time. After returning to the States, I read about the turmoil Yugoslavia would be burdened with. Maybe if I had traveled with companions, it could have worked.

When we arrived at the Vienna airport, I took the bus to the city center and found a peaceful park. I felt good vibes in this place. Everyone I talked to spoke English fluently.

THE VISION

What a shock Vienna was after southern Italy and Athens.

The city was spit-shine clean with architecture that impressed me more than the United States or many parts of Europe. It had that European feel with cobblestone streets and narrow alleyways but also had the wider, more modern roads and buildings.

The strangest thing was that I didn't see many people out on the streets. Maybe it was the time of day. Or maybe this was the old historical part of the city, and the mad rush was in other more commercial areas.

Anyway, this is all conjecture and first impressions. My main goal was to find a hotel. I eventually came upon Hotel Pension Nossek. They had no single rooms, so I took a room with two beds for one night. The room was huge with high ceilings.

I walked around the city to see if I could find a good room that wasn't so expensive and found one. I would change hotels the next day.

When I returned to my hotel, I was gearing up for a late meal and a little bar hopping but didn't make it. I flopped on the bed and was out for the night.

A good night's sleep was all I needed. After packing my bag, I moved to the new hotel. It was really nice—Hotel Post, room 311.

I took a stroll to the Museum of Fine Art. It was definitely on par with the better museums I had seen thus far. I recognized the paintings of several masters—Rembrandt, Titian, Peter Bruegel, etc. It was smaller than most museums but was a good size to wander through and not feel worn out when finished.

I spent the rest of the evening eating good food and checking out a few pubs, then retired to my hotel and made my phone calls.

Anellina had another friend of a friend—Diane and her family—who lived in Heidelberg, Germany. They were expecting me.

Gathering my painting supplies, I walked to the park I had originally seen when I first arrived. I did a detailed painting. On the way back to the hotel, I had a yummy fish sandwich.

My subway experience was odd. It was like stepping into the future. The station was empty, modern, and—again—spit-shined. I went to a machine, bought ten tickets, and waited for my ride. When the train quietly zoomed into the station, I noticed that it was ultra-modern. It was sleek and futuristic.

The doors hissed open; there was no one inside. I was looking around for someone to take my ticket; there was no one.

Stepping cautiously inside a car, in case alarm bells sounded, I took my seat next to nobody—heading for a destination, I knew not where, on an empty train.

Am I in that damn Stephen King novel again?

I took the subway to the river Danube. When I disembarked, I was still waving my ticket around, expecting someone to say, "Hey, idiot, over here!"

Finding myself across the river from UNO City, I sat under a bridge and did the second painting of the day, then returned to my neck of the woods and had another great meal.

In the hotel, I had to pay to take a bath; it was worth it.

THE VISION

The next day was spent focusing on finishing the two paintings I had started the day before. It was enjoyable walking the streets of this city. The shops were closed— strange for a Saturday. There were things I wanted to buy as souvenirs, and I also wanted to get something for Anellina. Instead, I relaxed over some lasagna, a glass of red wine, and read my book.

Venice was high on my list to visit. When I was going through the Swiss Alps, I had checked the route and was thinking seriously about making that my next stay. It turned out there was a railroad strike.

Thinking the strike would be over by now, I hopped on the subway— destination: train station. A sleeper car sounded really good for this leg of my journey. When I arrived, I found out that the railroad employees in Venice were still on strike.

I called Anellina's friend Diane to see if I could arrive at her place early the next night. She agreed.

Heidelberg

I checked out of the hotel and took the subway to the train station. Unfortunately, this station had connections to Venice but not to Germany. There was another train station that went to Germany. I caught a taxi and found the right one.

There was a first-class cabin available—thank God.

Shortly after departure, it started to snow. What can I say other than it was beautiful and contemplative?

It reminded me of that small snow cave when I was a child—sneaking out of my window in a snowstorm to escape going to church.

It was a pleasant trip.

I changed trains in Munich and arrived in Heidelberg at 5:15 p.m. Diane and a young German fellow, Frank, were waiting for me. We went to Diane's house, played cards, drank, and watched TV. She didn't actually live in Heidelberg. Her house was next to a military base a few miles away. They gave me some tourist info, and I retired to a nice room with a huge bed and three skylights.

It's not often that I sleep in, but I did that morning. Shuffling into the living room, I ran into Richard, Diane's son, who was watching TV and studying the bible. He had the day off from school. Diane showed up at eleven-thirty and escorted me on base to cash a travelers' check.

From there, I caught the OEG (the local train) to Heidelberg.

Wow! What a neat place. It was in a valley with the Neckar River running through it. There were locks for barges or small ships to pass. I stood on the bridge for a while, watching cargo boats enter and depart one of the locks. A small building that I supposed was a little energy plant stood on one side.

I crossed the locks, walked around town, and climbed a hill to the town's historic castle that was perched on top of the hill overlooking the whole magical scene; then back down to a restaurant and feasted on German food and red wine. The waitress was friendly, and I must have stayed there for at least two hours.

I caught the OEG back to Diane's with a little difficulty since I wasn't that familiar with the trains. It was nine-thirty that evening by the time I walked in the front door. I talked with Diane a little and went to bed.

The next morning, I took a shower, scarfed down some Raisin Bran, and caught the OEG back to Heidelberg.

I crossed the locks, climbed back up to the castle, and did a painting.

It was a cloudy drizzly day, but Heidelberg maintained its charm.

Back in town, I found another restaurant and spent a couple of hours reading, eating, and drinking wine. When finished, I crossed back over the river and climbed up to the Philosopher's Walk—a long paved trail high on a hill overlooking Heidelberg—a breathtaking view! The walk up to this trail was a narrow cobblestone passageway with eight-foot rock walls on either side.

The Philosopher's Walk extended the length of the town and followed the valley, high above the river.

I returned somewhat early at six that evening. Diane and Richard arrived shortly afterward. We kicked back, watched the Oscars, and went to bed.

The next day was rainy and stormy. I finished my castle painting and took the train to Mannheim. It was about twelve miles away. I had to see the Kunsthalle Mannheim Museum—small but nice—with paintings by Francis Bacon, Manet, Cezanne, Van Gogh, Lieberman, etc.

Noticing a needle-like structure—it was called the Fernmeldeturm—I took the elevator to its rotating restaurant and had a nice meal, taking in the view. It was created as a concrete telecommunications tower.

I returned to Diane's and met Gary, an old friend of hers. We had a fun social evening. Gary did a good job of talking me into going to Berlin—well, almost a good job, anyway. I was a little confused as to my next destination, and Berlin sounded like an adventure. I should experience Berlin.

There was something nagging at me though. It was called Venice. I really wanted to go there. When I was in Mannheim earlier in the day, I asked at the rail station if the strike was still on. They didn't know anything about it.

Thinking that was a good sign, I packed up and set out for Venice.

My time at Diane's had been comfortable, and I had thoughts of using her place as a home base. I could do a tour of Germany and hit a list of cities with nice museums. It was a list that Gary had given me.

However, there were too many places other than his list that I wanted to experience, so I decided to exit Germany.

I barely caught the train to Munich. I could travel on to Venice from there. When I arrived, I tried to transfer to the train to Venice but was met with the usual news.

Damn! Still on strike.

I thought of going back to Diane's.

Nah, I needed to move on.

So, north to Sweden or west to Spain? I decided to get a room in a hotel, relax, and make some decisions.

THE VISION

After dumping my pack in a hotel across the street from the train station, I wandered the city. Munich looked like a gigantic shopping mall—both at ground level and underground.

I escaped the area and ran into a fabulous museum. It made the stop worth it. The Alte Pinakothek was loaded with world-famous paintings from all the old masters.

Instead of running down the list of painters whose work I had already seen a lot of during this trip, there is one in particular I need to mention: Peter Paul Rubens.

Rubens was a Flemish painter with a Baroque style. His work is noted for its movement, color, and sensuality. It's his color I want to talk about.

I had seen a lot of his work in the Louvre and the Uffizi. They seemed different. As I found out, old paintings cannot be stripped of their varnish or restored because of the risk of damage. Everything in the paintings was dark. The Vatican was an exception. There was restoration work going on there.

It's different in Germany. The painting of a large nude by Rubens had intense colors—I mean *really* intense.

Could they have embellished it? I don't think so. It would be a sin to have changed this painting to something that it had never been. It was absolutely brilliant. It gave me more of an understanding and appreciation of the work of the old masters.

After I returned from Europe, they were beginning to restore work in Italy and France. There must have recently been some great inroads made in restoration techniques.

The decision was made. Spain it would be.

The view out the train window was absolutely gorgeous as I traveled through Switzerland—a beautiful fairy-tale land of Alpine peaks covered in snow with turquoise lakes and quaint villages.

I changed trains in Zurich and proceeded on to Geneva. After a five-hour layover, I took a *couchette* to Barcelona, sharing it with a German man who worked for the railroad. He was a very funny and animated man.

He made sure that my head was next to the window and my feet next to the door. It was common for thieves to quietly slide the door open and render the passenger unconscious from a nitrous-oxide-soaked cloth. The passenger would wake up with a headache and the absence of his money and travel documents—if he woke up.

Then came the stories in his heavy Germanic accent—while he occasionally hung his head over the side of his top bunk—smiling to see how I responded to his unusual tales.

We had a lengthy stop at the Spanish border. He explained that they had to change the wheels on the train since the track size in Spain was different than the rest of Europe.

Barcelona

Experiencing the Spanish railway system took a lot of patience. Compared to the rest of Europe, this system was a disaster. Forget times of arrival or departure. Since crossing the border into Spain at five in the morning, the train continually broke down for hours at a time.

Once it was a two-hour stoppage inside a tunnel. Many passengers grabbed their luggage and got off to look for other modes of transportation. One group of young travelers asked me if I wanted to join them. I politely refused, deciding to curl up in my seat—read and take naps—putting the thought of actually reaching a destination out of my mind. I think that is called the art of Zen.

The train finally arrived in Barcelona at 11:45 a.m. I found a locker for my belongings and found a place to stay—Hotel Transient. Finding the main street, I hailed a cab and had the driver take me to the Picasso Museum.

Picasso was a painter so known for his cubistic style that few have really understood where cubism came from. In most of his exhibits, you see his style in full force—the colors, deformed shapes, and the use of the flat surface with the depth of space. Analytic cubism began with little color but later developed into a more colorful abstract style.

But could he draw? Did he learn the basics? Could he paint a landscape or realistic figure?

The answer is "yes"—and the Picasso Museum showed the artist's progression from the age of ten (as a child prodigy) to his death.

At the age of fifteen, his work was amazing and realistic.

The Picasso paintings I love the most don't depict his known styles. These are paintings of doves on a windowsill. My memory sees them as around four- or five-foot square. They are wonderfully realistic and painterly. I've looked for reproductions of these paintings and have yet to find them.

Walking out into a beautiful plaza with the museum behind, I felt elation and excitement about my work. The energy inside me wanted to be back in a studio.

My reverie was shattered as I looked across the plaza. A middle-aged woman was walking with elderly women, who seemed up in years. She was a bit frail, gauging from her guarded walk across the cobblestones.

My eye caught a movement on the side of the open space. A man was sprinting across the plaza toward the women, whose backs were turned.

I comprehended the gist of the situation and yelled as I started running toward them. One moment later, the man grabbed the elderly lady's purse and was off running.

The woman wouldn't let go and went immediately horizontal, hit the cobblestones, and was being dragged while she still maintained a fierce grip on her purse.

The man looked at me; I still had about twenty yards to go. He released the purse and darted through an alley. You could hear the crashes and bangs as he upended everything in his path; he was out of sight—gone.

I knelt down to check on the woman, as did her daughter (the middle-aged woman). We checked her condition and asked if she could stand.

"Yes, I'm OK," she said as she began to get up.

"I can't believe you held on to your purse," I said, as her daughter and I held each arm as she rose.

"Oh, there's nothing in my purse. My money and my passport are on my belt. I just didn't want him to get away with it."

The daughter thanked me and introduced her mother and herself. They were from the States. Waving goodbye with smiles, tempered by the shock of the situation, we wished each other a wonderful rest of the day.

"What a feisty woman!"

Barcelona was a one-night stand.

Before retiring, I noticed a modern structure on a hill that overlooked the city. I asked a vendor in the plaza what it was.

He said it was the Joan Miró museum.

Off I went. I climbed the hill. It was a beautiful structure, reflective of his work. It didn't look very busy. "Oh, shoot! It's closed."

I did have the opportunity to look in the windows.

I was happy with my decision to go to Spain.

There was so much to see in Europe. I'm sure that Berlin would have been more than a great experience. The wall would be torn down a little over a year from when I was there. I didn't know that at the time.

My name and the large majority of my heritage is Swedish—twenty-five percent, I believe. I felt an obligation to go there and was also curious.

Then there was the elusive Venice. I would visit there one day, but not this trip.

There was another reason for being in Spain. I was counting my days until departure, and I wanted to make sure there was time to spend with Linda in Granada. Everyone who knew her from Yakitori II was sad to see her leave for her required schooling as a Spanish major. Linda spent a lot of time convincing me to visit her. I really didn't need convincing.

There was also Jean-Paul in Angoulême, France. His invitation to stay was an opportunity I did not want to pass up.

Oh, yeah! I had to see Ireland, too.

My path to Granada was not straight. Madrid had to be my next stop. How could I not see the Prado Museum?

Before I left Barcelona, I walked to the corner bakery and purchased a few items for my train trip. I also wandered around the train station and bought food and liquids for my trek to Madrid.

It was a lovely trip through the Spanish countryside. Most impressive were the ruins of castles I saw along the way. They must be scattered throughout the whole country. They were all on the top of hills for obvious reasons. They seemed to be left as they were. There was no attempt to reconstruct them. I think that was great. Let them be what they are and don't touch them. Just learn from them.

Some of these castles had small towns at their base. The little I know of Spanish history was tripled from this visit—so much to learn!

Learning from my experiences on this trip was a good thing. Having sparked my interest to know more was even better.

The train to Madrid actually had TV sets. They showed two movies as well as shorts—all in Spanish.

Arriving in Madrid, I headed straight for the Prado. It was closed. It was also closed the next day. Damn!

I had to come back this way. I needed to see this museum, so I would visit it when I returned.

I decided to catch a night train to Granada.

CHAPTER TWELVE

GRANADA

I made a reservation for a *couchette* and then took an underground train to another station for my connection to Granada.

I shared the sleeper car with a Spanish man, but I also met two young Boston women. They invited me to their cabin, and we talked until three in the morning.

I arrived in Granada at eight that morning and called Linda. She was excited to hear from me. I took a taxi to Plaza Bib-Rambla where we would meet. I just love European plazas. This one had a real Spanish feel to it with a beautifully sculpted fountain. The plaza was covered with cobblestones.

When Linda arrived, she was "all smiles." Actually, from the time I met her, she was always "all smiles"—a great way to start a day.

She escorted me to her apartment, and I unloaded my pack on the fold-out couch—my bed.

Linda decided to miss her first class. Instead, she took me on a tour of the Alhambra. The Arabs built this castle in the thirteenth and fourteenth centuries. It was their last stronghold in Spain before they lost it in 1492.

THE VISION

We had lunch in the Arab section, found an outside table, and talked.

There was plenty to talk about. She had worked at the sushi bar in San Diego for years as she toiled her way through school. We had clicked immediately, and my sushi experience was made more delightful with jokes, flirts, and her smile. I had eaten there often.

Linda then had to go to her afternoon class. I went back to her place, showered, and slept.

When Linda returned, she was scheduled to give English lessons to a nine-year-old Spanish boy. She didn't want him distracted, so I went down to the plaza and read my book.

When Linda came down to get me, she had a friend with her. She introduced me to Jana. They took me bar hopping—I should say tapas bar hopping or tapas hopping.

This was a new one for me. In the States, we have happy hours—half-priced drinks and appetizers. In Spain, it's tapas.

It goes like this: you order a drink, and they give you a little token appetizer. Order another drink, and you get an even better appetizer. Several drinks into the evening, you are getting ten-inch slabs of fried squid.

They also serve your food on paper plates and your drinks in plastic cups. They don't bus your tables; they push everything off on the floor.

TA-DA! Your table or the bar is cleared off and clean, ready to order more. At the end of the night, you wade through knee-deep trash to get outside.

When the place is closed, the staff gets a large push broom, piles everything in a heap, and dumps it.

OK, back to Linda and Jana who were determined that I have a good time. You know it when you are around good positive people.

We had fun. We had amazing conversations as we drank and stumbled around Granada. They filled me in on what they were experiencing, and I told them about my travels and dreams.

I also got them hooked on my blabbering about Carl Jung. They understood exactly what I was talking about.

To me, he had opened up a door that allowed me to see the world in a different way. It applies to everything that happens every day—internally and externally.

OK, back to Linda and Jana. We walked Jana home and said our slurred goodbyes. Linda and I still weren't finished. We went to yet another bar with a pleasant atmosphere. Linda wanted me to experience the differences between red sweet sherry and dry clear sherry.

Come morning, Linda and I went out for coffee before she went to school. When she returned, she gave me a tour of the things that might come in handy—the bank, the telephone house, and a place where I could buy stamps (a tobacco stand).

Linda's private lesson didn't happen. Her student didn't show up.

Instead, she took me to an upscale, expensive, Arab restaurant. We had to wait until two in the afternoon—that's when lunch starts and the siestas are over.

THE VISION

Yes, siestas are a real thing in Spain. I think honoring that time is brilliant. It follows human nature.

Hanging seven-year-old dead pigs in the doorway of food establishments is a real thing, too. It's supposed to be a delicacy. There is a little tin cup below its snout that catches the oils; the soon-to-be carcass is continually sliced and salted. You seriously had to turn sideways and squeeze yourself between the pig and the doorjamb to enter the establishment.

After our sumptuous meal, Linda and I parted for the afternoon. I grabbed my painting supplies and went looking for a magical place to paint. I found one at a local cemetery. The cemetery had white-washed walls and housed urns that were placed on shelves inside. This was merely my background. In front of the walls was an olive tree orchard. The red soil had been furrowed, and yellow flowers covered the foreground. This was one of those paintings that just fell together.

I walked back to Linda's and met two friends of hers—Yens from Sweden and Steve from Los Angeles. We hit the bar-hopping scene—again—until two in the morning. Jana and her boyfriend showed up for a while. I am having a blast with these people!

Linda had trouble getting out of bed that morning and missed her first class. We did our usual morning coffee. She went to her next class, and I decided to explore the Alhambra.

I spent most of the day there and started a new painting. It was a view of Granada and the surrounding terrain from the top of the castle. The parapets inside the wall were in the foreground. I worked on it for the next few days. I think I captured the feeling and details. The perspective bothered me. I made some adjustments, but it never has seemed right.

Linda and I were planning to have lunch at a favorite place of hers when I returned. But when we met, she said she couldn't go. She needed to meet with a friend. She told me where the restaurant was and said she would meet me there later. I took my time, read my book, and placed my order, savoring every bite. I relaxed, ate slowly, and continued reading before I paid the tab.

After a while, I left. I went to a park and read. We later met at the plaza in front of her house. She said she did show up at the restaurant, but it was after I left.

She filled me in on what had happened with her friend and explained that she was having a relationship with this person. It sounded like it was over.

We did the usual tapas thing that evening but retired from the bar scene earlier than normal. Yens and I played chess. We all had chicken soup and stayed up talking. It was a great discussion that had me laughing most of the evening. I needed that. I think Linda did, too.

There was something different about our evening routine as we prepared for bed. The previous nights, Linda had said good night and shut her door. This night, she left the door wide open. I could see her as she slept.

It felt like an invitation, but I didn't want to take anything for granted. After all, I was a guest in her home.

That is one thing that I have experienced a lot with people of the female persuasion. They seem to hint at what they want but never make the actual move. That is left up to the guy. I can't say that all women do that. Just the ones I meet. OK, there have been a couple of exceptions, but not Linda.

OK, scenario time. You know, like the time I met a bobcat during a trek through the Wyoming high desert.

Scenario one:

I walk into her room

"Linda, are you awake?"

Linda turns toward me, reaches out, and pulls me toward her.

"Oh my God, Paul. It's about time!"

She smothers me in kisses, and we fumble with each other's pajamas, breaking a few buttons in the process.

I smother her large breasts with kisses as she reaches down and strokes my stiffness.

We passionately consume each other, thrashing wildly about. As we climax violently together, we fall off the side of her bed and onto the floor. We are so utterly exhausted that we pass out in each other's arms. We find ourselves in the same position the following morning.

Scenario two:

I silently walk into her room and pull back the covers. I crawl in beside her.

Her back is toward me. She moves back snuggling close as she reaches back and grabs my hand; she then places my arm around her.

I can feel the fullness of her breasts as I slide my hand between the buttons of her pajamas. Tenderly, I kiss the back of her neck.

I slide my hand lower and feel her moistness.

She turns toward me, and we kiss passionately.

Slowly mounting her, I gently slide into her wetness.

We kiss and hold each other tight as our movement brings us to an early climax.

We settle into a passionate embrace and fall into a deep undisturbed sleep.

Scenario three:

I walk into Linda's bedroom and lean down to kiss her.

Her eyes pop open in complete surprise.

"Oh my God! I invite you into my home, the next thing I know you barge into my bedroom and try to rape me!"

As I draw away from the kiss, she violently bites me on the neck and rips out my aorta.

She spits out my flesh as I spew blood over her walls and ceiling.

She runs down her stairs to escape as she screams for the police.

"Help! Help! I'm being raped!"

THE VISION

Goodbye Europe vacation.

"OK," I thought to myself. How about as she retires to her room, she looks back and says, "You can join me if you want."

That would work for me. She would commit herself, and I could join her with a clear conscience.

During our coffee the following morning, Linda placed her elbow on the table, her chin on her hand, and asked, "Can you stay longer? Like until I'm finished with school. We can travel together before we go back to the States."

Gazing back at her, I said, "I would enjoy that. The problem is that I have some commitments. My flight leaves in a couple of weeks. My van is stored in a friend's garage. I'm sure it is a big inconvenience to them."

Linda stated the obvious. "You can change your return flight. Call a friend to move your van?"

I adored that about Linda. She had solutions for problems, and she was up-front about wanting to be with me. We could travel together—spend time together, understand each other, and develop a real relationship. She was up for that.

"I need to think about it," I said.

"For now, I would like to visit a family in France. They are expecting me. I also want to visit Ireland. How about you concentrate on finishing school? I will call you. I'll use this travel time to think."

Linda actually went to all her classes. When she returned, she asked me if I would join her for a couple of errands.

The first stop was to her bank to make a deposit. The second stop was a travel agent. We found that it would cost me 100 dollars to change my departure date. The agent also said that if I miss the flight—even if I don't notify them—it would still only be 100 dollars.

So, I didn't really need to worry about leaving on my departure date.

"There's a place I want to take you," Linda said, as she grabbed my hand and led me up a thin, winding road.

It was like walking through an alley—a street made from cobblestones. The walls on either side were about ten feet high, made of stone and brick. Occasionally, I saw plastered and painted areas. There were few doors and no windows. I didn't see any numbers or signs.

Linda stopped at a large dark metal door that was highlighted with reddish-brown rust.

She opened the door for me.

Walking in, I immediately stopped in astonishment. "What a cool place!"

It was a large rectangular room made of stone and brick. Stairs led down to the floor from the doorway—about four feet. A few dark brown, varnished, picnic tables were arranged in order. Against the wall, kegs were stacked atop each other with spigots protruding from them.

"Have a seat," she said. "This is my favorite place."

Linda and I were the only ones there.

She walked over to the kegs. Picking up two small glasses, she filled them to the rim and returned to our table.

THE VISION

"This is the best sherry you'll find in Granada," she said, as we clanked glasses in a toast. "Here's to your canceling your flight."

"Now just a minute," I said. "I do like your proposal, but I still need to decide. Things are a little more complicated."

"I really do understand—just hoping out loud. I won't pressure you."

Our conversation wandered. She talked of school and missing Yakitori II. I was excited about the next couple of weeks. I've had a great trip. It was all going so fast. I could visualize being a constant traveler, seeing new things, and meeting more people.

Linda took my glass, walked back to the keg, and refilled both of our glasses.

We continued our conversation. She stood again and refilled our glasses for the third time. "Are you hungry?"

"Yes, I am!" I looked around at the empty cavern.

She set both full glasses on the table and disappeared into a back room.

A few moments later, she returned with a smile on her face.

"It'll be about twenty minutes."

The conversation continued as if we were bottomless pits of information, humor, and trivia.

Twenty minutes later, Linda walked into the back room and reappeared with two salads. She placed them on the table, disappeared again, and returned with an unbelievable pizza—the best I've ever had, *really*!

One sherry refill later, Linda grabbed my hand and pulled me into her secret hidden room. There stood a little old man with a huge smile on his face. Linda introduced us and gave him a list of what we had consumed. We paid him.

I added a super tip, but he refused.

It was Saturday, and Linda had the day off. We strolled around Granada. She took me to places I hadn't seen.

I pulled out my Walkman and let her listen to it.

"Oh, man! I need to get one of these."

We found a place that sold them. They were pretty expensive so she put them on her wish list.

I bought a Suzanne Vega tape, and we returned to Linda's place.

I walked to the telephone house and called Anellina. I felt depressed after we talked. If I didn't have my truck in her garage, I might decide to stay with Linda or pursue other options that would allow me to stay here longer. I was also concerned about Anellina's feelings.

Anellina and I hadn't known each other that long—just a few months before going to London. I mentioned to her that the calls every week were becoming more of a distraction than an attempt to stay in touch. She was a little disturbed by that. She's a therapist, for Christ's sake. She should have understood and appreciated my honesty.

THE VISION

I had felt this way for over a month; it wasn't about Linda.

All that day, I wrestled with my options. Come evening, I was close to convincing myself that I should stay in Granada for three months, learn Spanish, and develop my relationship with Linda. I could still go to France and Ireland.

Sunday. I spent most of the day carousing around town with Linda. Her friend Steve came by, and we went to a café and had more coffee—with orange liqueur.

I guess Sergio wasn't completely out of the picture like I originally thought. He didn't want to let go, so he arranged English lessons with Linda.

I felt a responsibility for Anellina; Linda was feeling the same toward Sergio. We were both burdened by being caring people. We couldn't be cruel.

It was Monday and my last day in Granada. I took my camera and walked around taking photos. I spent a lot of time in the Arab districts, relaxed in a couple of parks, and read my book. I was still reading *Poland* by Michener. It was a big book. I'm not a fast reader but I am a continual one. I read at the same speed I talk. I don't like speed-reading.

Back in the apartment, I packed my bags. The train was leaving for Madrid that night. Linda made pasta with asparagus and mushrooms, and we drank wine.

Steve met us at ten that evening. We walked over and picked up Yens and made our way to the train station.

These three wonderful people were not into quick goodbyes. They got on the train with me and sat down in my *couchette*. We talked and joked. I told them I just might come back in a couple of weeks; I needed time to think. I really wanted to return.

They stayed until the train lurched; we quickly hugged and said our goodbyes. I looked out the window as we were leaving the station. They were still there waving and blowing me kisses.

MADRID

Arriving early in Madrid, I found a café close to the Prado, munched on rolls, drank coffee, and waited for the museum to open. I wanted to be there before the crowds.

I expected a museum the size of the Louvre; it was not even close but most impressive. Most of the work was Spanish—as I would expect—realistic, figurative, and landscapes. There were lots of works by El Greco, Goya, and Hieronymus Bosch with a smattering of other Spanish painters.

Then came Picasso's *Guernica*! Wow! What a history there is in this piece. It depicted the ruthless slaughter of the people in this Spanish town by the Germans—practicing their aerial bombing for the war to come. It was painted in black and white.

The work was placed behind bulletproof glass, displayed alongside many original sketches done before and during the painting's creation.

It was also extremely political. This work was moved out of the country until the death of Francisco Franco in 1975. The painting was then moved back to Madrid. It had to be protected. There were still strong political feelings about it that remained alive.

I especially enjoyed the beautiful portraits by Madrazo. I had not heard of him until then.

The Prado was the only place I wanted to go while in Madrid, so afterward, I caught the subway to Chamartin, the other major railway station in the city.

I wanted to time my trip so I could see the Pyrenees Mountain range during the day and still have time to make it to Angoulême, France before nightfall.

The train route didn't accommodate me as I hoped. The destination took us to Hendaye, a port on the southwest coast of France on the Spanish border. We skirted the western edge of the mountains.

Just prior to reaching Hendaye, the train came to a stop—for hours.

Someone said the Spanish railway workers were on strike. They were responsible for changing the gauge of the Spanish wheels to fit the French tracks.

I'm not sure what that means, but it was a time-consuming process. I recently checked the system they have now to the system in the late eighties, and it's much improved.

Because of the delay, we made it to Angoulême at three-thirty in the morning. I was dead tired and didn't want to wake up Jean-Paul's family at that hour. Instead, I stretched out over three seats and slept, arriving in Paris as the sun rose. My idea was to sleep until I got to Paris and then take the train back to Angoulême so I would arrive at a decent hour.

When I arrived in Paris, the train had worn out its welcome. The thought of going back to Angoulême didn't entice me anymore.

I decided to move on.

It's a quick two-hour train ride to Le Havre from Paris. From there, I could board a ferry to Ireland. At first, the information I received said the boat was leaving that day, but when I arrived at Le Havre, I found out that it would leave the next day at six in the evening. I found a comfortable hotel and retired early.

When I made my ferry reservation, I thought ahead and reserved a cabin.

IRELAND

It was ten in the morning when I awoke.

As I was wandering around Le Havre, I found a grocery store. I bought French wine (two dollars a bottle), bread, cheese, and French mustard.

When the checker finished tallying up the total, I paid and stood at the check stand like an idiot. We stood there looking at each other as other shoppers stood waiting behind me. Finally, one of the other customers told me it was my responsibility to bag the groceries.

That was the only English I heard in this small town. No one wanted to speak English.

The bus arrived at the train station at 2:45 p.m. This was my transport to the ferry.

THE VISION

Everyone on the bus spoke English, and I made immediate friends.

I boarded the ferry and unloaded my gear in my cabin. Wow, nice cabin! I met Daniel from Montreal. He was my cabin mate. There were two sets of bunk beds against opposing walls—room for four. Daniel and I were the only ones in that cabin—or so I thought.

I contacted the crew and told them our door wouldn't lock. They said they would get someone to check it out.

All the workers on the boat spoke in an Irish accent. I love that sound.

Later that evening Daniel and I went to the bar and met Pat from Indianapolis and two other Americans, Brian and Joe.

We talked and drank until after midnight, then retired to our rooms.

Later that night the ferry was rocking and rolling. I was jarred awake. We were going through an intense storm.

I reached for my pack and found the Dramamine my friend Betty insisted I take with me. I downed one with my bottle of water and noticed Daniel was awake.

"Hey, man, take this."

"What is it?" he asked.

"It's Dramamine—a seasick pill."

"No, I'm feeling fine. I don't need it."

"You will," I said. "It won't work if you're already sick."

"No. I'm fine."

I crawled back in bed, hanging on to what I could to keep from falling on the floor.

The sun had just risen. Daniel was sitting on the edge of my bed, his hand on my shoulder, shaking me.

"Hey, can I have one of those seasick pills? I'm really sick."

Looking up at him with tired eyes I said, "If you're already sick, it won't work."

"I don't care. Can I please have one?"

"Sure." I sat up on the edge of the bed, retrieved some Dramamine, and gave him one.

Grabbing my clothes, I dressed and thought, "Boy, am I hungry!"

When I walked into the hall, there were lines of people trying to get into the bathroom. The maids and crew were mopping up vomit.

I walked to the restaurant for breakfast; the place was empty. There were people serving food, so I ate and walked up on deck. The waves were much smaller. The sun was shining, and I felt pretty good. Thank you, Betty!

When I returned to my cabin, there was an elderly man sleeping on the top bunk.

"Damn!" I thought. "They still haven't fixed the lock."

I put my hand on his shoulder and gave him a gentle push.

"Excuse me. This is my cabin. I think you're in the wrong place."

He groaned and turned his face to the wall.

THE VISION

"Excuse me," I repeated. "You're in the wrong cabin."

He mumbled something about it being his cabin and went back to sleep.

I walked into the hall and eventually found a member of the crew.

"Excuse me, miss, I have been trying to get the lock fixed on my door, and now there's a man sleeping on one of the bunks. I don't know who he is. I can't wake him."

"What's your cabin number?"

"Cabin 213, on the second deck."

She walked in that direction. I followed.

She walked into the room and shook the guy's shoulder.

"Hello, sir. Do you have your ticket?"

No response.

"Excuse me, sir. I need to see your ticket."

He reached into his pants pocket while still lying prone, eyes shut. He pulled out his ticket and handed it to the woman.

"Oh. Cabin 213, second deck." She looked at me and said, "I guess it's his cabin, too."

"Oh, he just showed up. He didn't sleep here last night."

As the crewmember left, the guy sat up on his bed. He was an older gentleman, about seventy years old.

"I'm awfully sorry, sir," I said with some embarrassment.

"That's OK. I would have done the same thing. My car is downstairs. I always reserve a cabin but usually sleep in my car. It was a rough night last night."

We introduced ourselves. His name was HG Dawe.

HG stretched out on his bunk and was, again, snoozing away.

Grabbing my book, I read until my eyelids drooped and went to sleep as well.

Waking to calm seas, I sat by the window and placed my bottle of wine, cheese, and bread on a small table. As I was opening the wine, HG leaned over and addressed me.

"Did you buy more than one bottle?" he asked.

"No, just the one. Would you like a glass?"

"No," he said. "It's just that you should have bought more. The wine isn't nearly as good in Ireland."

We arrived in Ireland. It was raining outside.

Daniel invited me to join him on his journey up the coast to Dublin. His friends were going with him; they were a fun group of guys.

The thing was that I had a more enticing invitation. HG lived in southwest Ireland in County Kerry, and he had asked me to join him.

THE VISION

We went to the car deck, found his car, and headed west.

HG was by far the most interesting person I had met on my trip. Maybe the most interesting person I had ever met.

His wife had recently had a stroke, and he had taken her to a rehab facility in Germany. He didn't trust the Irish medical system—or the English, for that matter. He had taken several trips back and forth to check on her.

HG had moved to Ireland from Germany. Even though he loved Ireland, he wasn't that crazy about the Irish people. He was convinced that the Irish were primitive and didn't have any interest in learning anything. They just wanted to frequent pubs and drink their lives away.

It was pouring rain during the drive to his home. He was an architect and had built his house when he and his wife moved there two years ago.

Raising sheep was his main focus, and he was anxious to see the twin lambs that were born the day he took his wife to Germany. He was concerned about them, hoping they were OK. His Irish neighbors were not all that excited about his moving there, so they often harassed him and his wife, thus his concern for the lambs.

When we arrived, I was blown away by the beautiful countryside and how well his house fit with the landscape. His home was amazing, with windows taking in his 360-degree view. Sheep roamed his land, but I didn't see any lambs.

He lived on a finger of land that protruded into the Atlantic Ocean.

"It is the most beautiful place in Ireland," he said.

HG showed me around his house and where my bedroom was located. I placed my bag next to the bed and joined him in the living room.

"I want to show you this," he said. "I had this book published seven years ago."

I took the book and sat down. It was filled with fantastic photography and was titled *TAIWAN: The Republic of China*, published in 1981.

This was a professional publication. I really didn't know what to say. "Wow" didn't do it justice. I just gazed at the book, page by page, scanning the descriptions of a trip he had taken to Asia.

"You did the photography, too?" I asked.

"Yes, I did, and I also had the opportunity to work for the United Nations. They sent me all over the world. My camera was always with me."

He then led me into his study. He was in the process of finishing a new book on Ireland. I had the privilege of seeing his layout and the photos he planned to use.

He had a few errands to run, so he told me he would be back soon.

"Please make yourself at home."

I went to my bedroom and unpacked the necessities. A nap sounded good, so I flopped on the bed and was out like a light.

That evening HG poured us both a glass of scotch. We sat in his living room and talked more about Ireland and the Irish people.

The talk about the Irish people faded away and was replaced by his fascination for the island. I think he expressed his view clearly.

THE VISION

I changed the subject to his lambs; I hadn't seen any since I arrived.

"Where are your twin lambs?" I asked.

He smiled and said, "They're at a neighbor's farm. I was going to get them this evening, but I thought I would wait until tomorrow. Maybe the weather will cooperate."

HG poured another round of scotch.

"Can I help you?"

"I don't need help, but if the weather is good, I want you to come. I'll give you a tour. If you think this place is nice, you should see the coast."

When I woke the next morning, HG had breakfast waiting. It was really good, but the interesting thing was how it was presented. A hardboiled egg was served in a tall ornate silver eggcup. He had the finest silverware and napkins, rolled and bound with a silver band. The rest of the meal would have been typical if not for its presentation—potatoes, toast, and bacon. They were in small portions on expensive China.

"It's better to not stuff yourself; it's healthier," said HG.

The weather did not cooperate that morning; in fact, it was worse. Rain was pouring down in sheets.

HG was clad in a raincoat and a water-resistant large-brimmed hat.

"Will you help me move my sheep to another pasture?"

"Sure!" I said. I put on a hooded poncho, and we walked out into the rain. He opened a gate, and we herded the sheep through the opening. He secured the gate, and we returned to the house to dry off—I did anyway. HG left his coat and hat on.

"I'm going to meet my neighbor. I'll be back with my lambs in a few hours."

"I can help!" I said.

"I would prefer you stay. If you come down with anything, it'll ruin your trip. You won't be able to see the sights in this weather anyway."

"Keep an eye out for those pesky Irish," he said. "They don't know you, so they won't bother you."

Raining or not, I pulled out my watercolor block, brushes, and paints. I found a dry place under a tree and started a painting of his property with sheep scattered over the landscape, munching on the lush grass.

When I was ready to head back to the house, I saw a figure walking toward me.

I've never seen a happier person than HG Dawe as he walked toward the house holding his two tiny baby lambs. He let me hold one.

I'm no stranger to sheep, being from Wyoming farm country. I had a ewe and a lamb in the 4-H Club; that was a long time ago. Lambs are beautiful and playful creatures.

I finished my painting that afternoon and early evening in the shelter of my room.

When I walked out, HG was setting the table for dinner. That man could do anything, including cook. We had pork chops, potatoes, and peas. After the meal, we retired to the living room and continued our talk, sipping on an excellent brandy. We stayed up well past midnight as I continued to learn about this amazing person.

We began by talking about world affairs as they were then. He was more knowledgeable about the States than I'll ever be. He didn't just talk about what was going on in the States but about our relationship with other countries.

The Arab countries were a major issue for him. He couldn't understand why we ever bothered with them. He felt that if the rest of the world had left them alone, the Arab factions would have continually fought each other. We had given them the means and know-how to amass modern arsenals and to develop a hatred toward us.

HG had been in the military during World War II on the German side. He had a totally different view than we Americans did. He blamed Churchill for the war.

"The British are a sneaky lot," he said.

According to him, Germany's beef was with the Soviet Union. And if we had allowed them to take over Russia, we would never have had problems with them.

The German attack on Poland was a defensive action. Just before this happened, Britain had signed an agreement with Poland that pledged to come to their aid if attacked by Germany.

Germany first annexed Austria and Czechoslovakia without hostilities. They thought they could do the same with Poland. When France and Britain declared war on Germany, Germany was forced to protect its rear by taking France and attempting to keep Britain at bay.

If the United States had stayed out of it, Germany's original plan to conquer Russia would have worked.

According to HG, if the British had stayed out of it, it also would have worked.

I failed to bring up the German atrocities and death camps. I should have. It was on my mind as we talked.

He said, "There are three countries in the world that are unique and different from the rest—Germany, the United States, and Japan. Their innovations have led the world in most of the strides and progress of the human race."

The last point that I recall from our conversations was when we were talking about the history of the world. I mentioned the Dark Ages.

HG looked at me and said, "What Dark Ages?"

This surprised me since I thought it was common knowledge.

I felt naïve spouting out things I knew something about but should know more about if I wanted to talk with authority.

"It's a period of time when past civilizations have perished, and all knowledge was lost. Things fell into disrepair; the populace was unable to maintain them. They resorted back to a more primitive existence. Prior knowledge was destroyed or lost."

"You know, like the period after the Roman Empire," I said

"I have never heard of the Dark Ages," he said. "The fall of Rome did not affect Germany, and we retained the knowledge we learned during that period—including what we have learned from Rome and other civilizations. Would you send me a book about that period when you get back to the States?"

"Sure," I said.

It was still raining the following morning. I had come to the conclusion that I needed to move on and see the rest of Ireland. HG would have been happier if I had stayed. We enjoyed each other's company. I think he was lonely without his wife, and the threat from his Irish neighbors was tempered by my presence.

I packed my bag. Leaving it on my bed, I walked outside my room. HG had placed a table with a red tablecloth under a window.

Displayed and perfectly organized was an astonishing gun collection. Not like one in the States where our gun people were proud of their AK-47 assault rifles, automatic pistols, and multi-ammo clips that showed their awesome mass-killing ability.

This collection was like one you would see in a museum—single-shot miniature pistols with redwood handles. They had ornately carved barrels and grips. Some must have been dated in the seventeenth century or earlier. They were in perfect condition.

Again, he had made a beautifully prepared breakfast. I sat down and complimented him on his gun collection. He beamed with pride. After we ate, he went over to the display and described the guns' origins and ages.

This made it more difficult to drop the news that I was leaving. There was still the coastline he raved about.

When I told him I had to move on, he looked disappointed but immediately took his raincoat and hat off the hook. He understood.

I felt bad—like I was deserting him. I would have enjoyed staying here.

The trains didn't run in this isolated part of the country. I needed to hitchhike to Tralee. HG took me to a spot where he said I would get a quick ride. Before he left, he handed me his phone number and said to call if I needed help. I thanked him for the wonderful hospitality and conversation.

Immediately an elderly local couple picked me up. Unfortunately, they dropped me off at an intersection a couple of miles away. I didn't see a car for two hours. It was raining hard, and I was getting a bit chilly.

Finally, off in the distance, I saw a cloud of smoke and heard the rattling of an old, out-of-tune vehicle with an occasional backfire. I think it was a '59 Chevy—yellow.

The car stopped next to me, and the driver said to hop in.

I felt like I stepped into a cartoon.

The driver looked like the perfect caricature of an Irishman. He had such a heavy Cork accent that I continually had to say, "What?"

He had orange-red hair with freckled skin, but his most obvious feature was his bright red nose. The car was filled with the stench of tobacco.

When he asked where I was coming from, I mentioned that I had been staying with a person I met on the ferry.

He asked if I was staying with that old German on the hill. I said "yes." (I bet this was one of the Irishmen that was bugging HG. I really hoped that HG would be OK.)

He took me to another spot where again I was picked up immediately. This time by a middle-aged English couple on vacation. They were really religious. You could tell by their constant referral to the Catholic Church and the iconic symbols placed around the car.

"Would you like to join us on a trip around the Ring of Kerry?"

"Sure!" I said. I might as well see the sights and get out of my point A to point B mode.

It was a pleasant tour. When we finished, they looked back at me and said, "We're planning to stop at Tralee for the night, but we can take you to Killarney first so you can catch the train."

"That won't be necessary," I said. "The train route starts at Tralee. I can leave from there."

They had a referral to a particular bed and breakfast. I found a room there as well, and the train station was only a ten-minute walk away.

That evening, I decided to do what the Irish do and hit the pubs. I would just do a smaller portion of that "drinking your life away" thing.

I visited three pubs, and the people were friendly and easy to talk to.

I have to say the Irish people rolled out the red carpet. They treated me better than I had ever been treated; the smiles were endless. This was especially true with a pub that was packed to the gills. There was an Irish band playing. They were fantastic, and the crowd was 100 percent involved.

My comprehension of their accent struggled at the start, but by the end of the evening, I understood them perfectly.

I caught the train early, so I could be in Dublin well before nightfall. It was an old rickety train to Mallow. At that point, I transferred to a modern smooth one for the remainder of the trip to Dublin.

When I arrived in Dublin, I wasn't sure where I was going, so I checked my duffel bag at the station and took my small backpack that housed my essentials.

On the ferry to Ireland, I had met several people. We had all grouped together drinking and talking. We had decided to meet in a few days at the oldest pub in Dublin, The Brazen Head. Arriving much earlier than I thought, I searched for the place and easily found it.

I hadn't eaten since early that morning, so I went to a different pub and had a meal. Digging into my bag, I found a map of Dublin that showed the bed and breakfasts in the area. The Sinclair House was highly recommended, so I found my way there and obtained a room. It was a decent room for very little money.

I called Anellina and filled her in on my travels. She was upset and convinced I was ignoring her. I was just tired of checking in.

That evening, I went to The Brazen Head at the prearranged time. Only one person showed—Joanne from Philadelphia. We wandered around Dublin talking and drinking beer. It turned out that her bed and breakfast was right next to mine. We walked there together and said our goodbyes.

THE VISION

There was a fun group of people at breakfast the following morning. Everyone was animated and happy. It was a great way to start my day.

Today was museum day. There were two that I wanted to see: the Irish Museum of Modern Art and the National Gallery of Ireland.

I had made the decision to go home on my originally reserved flight to San Diego. That would be in two days. I was running low on money. I thought about looking for a job. If I went back to France and visited Jean-Paul, he might help me with that. Or there was Linda in Spain.

I could do anything. Maybe I could move to a small island in Greece—live a simple life, paint, and find a menial job to get food and a studio.

I quickly vetoed those ideas. I wanted to get my van out of Anellina's garage. Seattle was beckoning me, and—truth be told—I was getting a bit tired of traveling. When I returned to San Diego, I could cash in my 401(k) plan from BTL and have enough money to move to Seattle.

Anyway, back to the museums. This would be the end of my museum visits. Seeing all the art around Europe had been fantastic. I had grown as a person, and my art knowledge had soared. This trip had inspired me; there was a fire blazing in my heart, and I had to do something with it.

The Irish Museum of Modern Art was a little disappointing. It was not artwork I was familiar with. There was a Russian exhibit upstairs, and I was curious about that. I had a little difficulty understanding their work. It seemed dark and a bit morbid, but it had its story to tell. In the long run and as I think back on it, the diversity was refreshing. It made me think. I guess I liked it after all.

The odd thing about this visit was that I was the only one viewing the work. The museum was empty.

There was one guard, and he followed me from gallery to gallery. As I moved to a new room, he walked in and stood by the door with his arms folded and his headset on. When I moved to the next room, he moved with me and assumed the same position.

When I reached the end of my viewing and started toward the exit, the guard stepped in front of me.

"So, what do you think about that Ronald Reagan?" he asked, as his serious demeanor dissolved into a smile.

And so, the conversation started. We talked about politics, art, and recent events for forty-five minutes.

He finally said, "Well, I'll leave you alone. I've taken enough of your time. Enjoy your stay."

I actually really enjoyed that conversation, especially since it was accompanied by his Irish accent. His interest in what was happening in the States and knowledge of world events impressed me.

The first thing I did after leaving the museum was check the ferry departure times to England. As often happens, the ferry workers were striking.

So, I bought an airline ticket to England.

Suddenly, I realized I was hungry. There was a pub just down the street. I had soup and a sandwich and then headed for the National Gallery of Ireland.

The National Gallery had a great collection—a lot of paintings by Jean-Baptiste-Camille Corot. These were beautiful paintings! Wow, another artist I was getting to know better.

I hopped on a green double-decker bus to go back to the train station and retrieve my duffel bag, then headed back to the bed and breakfast. I went out for dinner and hit the sack early. The next day, I would be flying to England.

CHAPTER THIRTEEN

It was a quick flight to London Luton Airport. From there, I caught a bus to the train station, and it connected with the Underground. The Underground took me to Heathrow Airport where I deposited my duffel bag and backpack in a storage locker.

A friend of Doug's, Karen Koppelman, had given me the phone number of her cousin in London and wanted me to contact her if I had time.

"Might as well," I thought.

I called the number, and Karen's cousin Gale Churney answered the phone. She was happy to hear from me, saying that Karen had contacted her and said I might call. Her couch was available if I wanted to spend the night.

Hopping back on the Underground, it took over an hour to get to her house on the other side of London.

Gale met me at the door. She was going to a concert, and her roommate Anita had invited a friend over for dinner. That fell through, so I took Anita out for dinner. We had a pleasant chat, and it made for a nice evening.

THE VISION

The next morning, Anita woke me up and offered to make me tea before she left for work.

"No, thanks. How about an aspirin?" I had a headache from whatever I had drunk the night before.

After leaving a thank you note for Gale, I took the lengthy trip back to Heathrow, grabbed my bags, and headed to my gate. I've never been searched so much in my life—three times.

It was a long flight to LAX. I had a three-hour layover, then flew to San Diego.

Anellina picked me up from the San Diego Airport. We talked a bit about my travels and my flight as we drove to her house in La Mesa. It felt good to be back home. She said I was welcome to stay with her until I decided what to do.

The first thing I did was rescue my van from her garage. I think Anellina felt relieved to have her unwanted guest out of there. She didn't say that, but I would have felt that way if I had been her. Three months can be a long time.

I backed the van out on my mostly flat tires and used a hand pump to partially inflate them—enough to make it to a local gas station. Then I drove back to Anellina's house.

"I'm dead tired, Anellina. Is it OK if I take a nap?"

"Of course, you can," she said smiling. "Want to go out for dinner this evening?"

"Oh, yeah! Sushi?"

Doug met Anellina and me at Yakitori II. I had been eating there for fifteen years. I had introduced my friends to this fantastic restaurant, and it had been a hangout for all of us since. This was the place where it all started.

The chefs and half the clientele knew me. They gave me a great welcome back. Even the owner came out and talked.

They were excited that I had visited Linda in Granada, and I filled them in on some of the high points. Linda had worked there for at least three years. We all had great times and great sushi, and the chefs were hilarious.

Even though I knew what my plans were, I felt unsettled—not grounded. Doug was living in my studio, and that was good. I had a lease, and he was willing to take it over.

Anellina was particularly gracious for letting me stay there. I think she still had hopes of a potential relationship. She was ready to settle down with somebody.

I had bad insomnia—probably due to jet lag. In the middle of the night, I asked Anellina if I could go to her living room and watch TV—something I had been deprived of, not just in the last three months, but also because I had been living in studios with no TV for fifteen years. I was amazed by the technological advancement of the information and entertainment that came from this box.

That probably sounds weird to all of us now. The television medium has grown by leaps and bounds since my days in San Diego.

I visited BTL. I needed to cash in my 401(k) plan, but that turned out to be a sideshow compared to the delight I felt when I walked around to the different departments to see all the people I used to work with. I was greeted with warm smiles and hugs.

THE VISION

The only negative part was when I poked my nose in Marks's office to say "hi."

"I'm not hiring you back," he said.

You just can't be nice to some people.

My biggest problem was how to take my belongings to Seattle. My personal items were few, but I had a ton of paintings—way too many to fit in my van.

But as fate would have it (probably due to that guardian angel that had been paving the way for me my whole life), there was a couple in the process of moving to San Diego from Seattle; they were friends of Doug. They had already moved some of their belongings down and planned to take an empty truck back to Seattle to pick up the rest of their stuff.

They not only offered to take the rest of my paintings to Seattle, but they also had family who would store them until I arrived. In addition, the girl's mother was on the Seattle Arts Commission. Since I would be a new artist in Seattle, she was interested in seeing my work.

After a week, Anellina decided that I should move out. I kind of wanted to also.

Doug's friends brought their truck over, and we loaded it with paintings. They planned to leave for Seattle the next morning.

I actually left a lot behind—mostly sculpture. I had sculpted a life-size nude sitting on a barstool that had really turned out nice. I also had castings of huge faces I couldn't take.

Oh, yeah, and I left my softball trophies.

I wonder what happened to that stuff?

Well, there was nothing holding me in Sand Diego now.

I spent the next week meeting with friends and saying goodbye over a meal or in a bar, discussing Seattle and the good times we had in San Diego.

I woke up early on the first of June and headed north. Seattle, here I come!

It was slow and easy. I followed Highway One and camped where I could. This was the fifth time I had traveled to Seattle on my own, so I had my favorite spots.

My friend Mark Zingarelli was expecting me. He allowed me to stay until I found a place to live. I told him that it wouldn't be long.

Mark introduced me to northwest brews. There were many local breweries, and they each had a unique taste. He also introduced me to Kristie. She was too good for me—not her determination but mine. We spent fun times together until she knew I had my feet planted firmly on the ground. (Since I was new to the Seattle area).

My first act was to find a figure-drawing workshop. I really missed that. There was an art school just east of downtown at the south end of Seattle by Pioneer Square. The workshops were three hours long as was usual. I find it easy to meet people at figure-drawing workshops; I'm in my element.

There was one thing I wanted to do before I dove back into my art.

At BTL, I had designed a bald eagle for a client. I was anxious to see it as an inflatable. Before it went to production, some salesmen and the owners had nixed it. They said my design could never be done, and it would cost too much.

It was true that the client had limited funds.

A year earlier, we had made an inflatable pigeon for someone. It was the massive creative brainpower of BTL that decided to use the pigeon patterns and paint it to look like an eagle.

To me, it looked like a pigeon wearing an eagle costume. I was embarrassed to say I worked there.

When I arrived in Seattle, I wanted to make a twenty-five-foot-tall bald eagle. To do this, I called around Seattle to find shops that dealt with fabrics I was familiar with and that used heavy-duty industrial sewing machines. This meant fabricators of awnings or banners or maybe even backpacks. I settled on the ideal place—a shop that made parachutes. They also repaired and folded them. Their hangar was at Boeing Field.

The owners, Bill and Alice, were excited about my idea. I told them I would teach them how to make inflatables step by step if I could make myself a huge inflatable bald eagle. They agreed. It was a fun experience.

Bill and Alice were amazing people; they were open to new and exciting things. They were also probably the most eccentric people I have ever known.

It was at this parachute shop where I met a great friend. That friendship is alive to this day.

Rip did professional technical drawings, and this was before computer-aided design was common.

He also loved playing bass guitar. I had brought my drum set from San Diego. We set up in an empty hangar and jammed practically every night.

Fabricating the eagle was time-consuming but it went well. It was nice to be in total control and not have idiots sabotage its potential. The eagle that could not be done was a huge success. In the next eight years, I had numerous front-page photos and articles about it in the major local newspapers and publications.

During the production of the eagle, I found a small place to live on Alki Point in West Seattle. This was temporary until I could find a studio. It was a beautiful place with beaches to the south and to the north. The area had a great view of Puget Sound, the ships, the ferries, and the Olympic Mountains.

I also picked up my paintings that Doug's friend had moved here. I met her mother who worked for the Seattle Arts Commission. She really liked my work and had the paintings spread out for viewing in her living room. She told me to organize some slides and send them to her. She would set up a show for me at the Smith Tower.

The Commission did a show once a month and invited all the major gallery owners; I was sure to be connected to galleries who would show my work.

How lucky can I get, having these coincidences that offer me these opportunities? There was something bothering me about this, however. Moving to the Northwest, I wanted to do all new work and go in another direction with my painting. I put the presentation of my old work on the back burner. When I completed my next series, I would send in slides.

It was time to get serious about a job. I always go for what I want. There were two custom picture frame shops that were more professional than the others in Seattle. One was Artech. I stopped by and applied. They seemed a little aloof as if to say, "Yeah, everyone wants to be a picture framer." I filled out an application.

The other one was Artform. It was in Pioneer Square and in the back of the best quality gallery in the city—Davidson Gallery.

Artform looked as if there were only two people working there. One was the owner, Penny Auge. The other was Kat, fitter and mat cutter extraordinaire. It didn't look like they needed anyone.

Artech was much larger with more employees. They were the ones that should have been hiring.

I talked to the owner of Artform. Penny was really an open person and knew her stuff. I filled her in on my experiences. She hired me on the spot. She wanted me to come in the next day.

When I arrived for work, I entered through a door in the alley; Pioneer Square has fantastic alleys, kind of like a movie set.

Kat was there; Penny usually came in later. We went through their system. There were three copies to each order sheet, which had the client, the size of the frame, and the mat-opening size. It showed the type and color of the mat and the details of the frame. It had the due date and a description of the artwork. Basically, all the information needed to do the job.

Looking at the artwork made me realize that this was the place I wanted to work. We were framing fantastic artwork and preparing them for shows. It was not "decorator" framing. It was museum framing—acid-free—with mostly white or off-white rag and acid free mats. Every aspect was museum quality, down to the tape and foam backing.

Kat was fast and did quality work. She cut the mats and fit the pieces at lightning speed. She did give me "a go" on cutting a few mats to see how I did. I had my own mat cutter and was proud of my corners—no overcuts. I also learned their techniques: the backing and ratio of the placement of the screw eyes and the proportion of the mats, making the bottom a quarter or a half-inch wider. Visually, it looked the same as the other sides.

Kat also did the sanding and cutting of the frames. She joined the frames and developed her own acrylic, pearlescent finishes. My main responsibility in the operation would be to sand the molding, miter the corners, and join the frames. Kat would do the finishing.

Penny wanted a line of frames that involved wood stains or oils to bring out the grain and character of the wood; that was my job. I had learned this type of framing when I worked for David at the Reuter Gallery in San Diego and at The Fine Art Store. I was a perfect fit.

I had to prove myself though. Penny was a tough cookie. The tiniest mistake sent her ranting and raging for hours.

Even though I had my forte, I was also depended upon to do fitting and mat cutting along with Kat when it was needed, which it often was. Kat could also take a vacation now and then. Penny hated to let her go. I wasn't as good, but I could handle it, and Penny felt a little better that her duties were covered when Kat was gone.

Another "blow my mind" moment was when I went downstairs to see the woodworking and finishing rooms. It was the Seattle underground. There were brick hallways and rooms that looked like jail cells. I spent much of my time down in this dungeon and loved every minute of it, chopping and staining frames.

When I went upstairs, I was surrounded by the great artwork that we were framing. We were also working in the backroom of a top-notch gallery; they always showed excellent work.

Artform was the chosen framer for all the top photographers in the area. To top that off, they also framed the original sketches of Dale Chihuly, done when he designed his glass pieces. He sometimes exchanged his glass art for framing.

Another plus was getting to know the artists, collectors, and gallery owners. When these people showed up, the environment brought out the best in people. Penny was very good at conversation; even Kat and I were involved.

One day, as Kat and I were working together, she asked me if I wanted to go to a party the following Saturday.

"Sure!" I said. (Oh, boy. A party!)

"Here's the address. It starts at seven. You don't have to be on time."

That Saturday, I attended the party—not on time.

It was packed with people. They were all friendly.

Kat saw me and took me over to meet the hostess. She was a beautiful woman, and our short conversation seemed to indicate she was a very smart woman as well. After a brief chat, we parted, and I continued to meet and talk to other partiers. I touched bases with Kat every now and then. She seemed to disappear often. That wasn't too hard to figure out. She's less than five feet in height.

The following Monday, we chatted about the party and the interesting people.

"So, your friend who hosted the party, she's a beautiful and smart woman."

"Don't even think about it," Kat said, as she wired and backed a frame job at record speed.

"No, I understand. She's beyond me," I said in defense.

"She has her own agenda."

"And what might that be?"

"She plans to find a really rich man; marry him; get pregnant; divorce him; acquire a new house; collect thousands of dollars a month for eighteen years. She has always wanted to raise a child, but not with a man."

And this is how it unfolded, narration by Kat:

Three months after the party: guess who is dating a filthy rich man?

Six months after the party: guess who just married her filthy rich boyfriend?

One year after the party: guess who's pregnant?

One year six months after the party: guess who just got a divorce?

Two years after the party: guess who has a brand-new house? Oh, she's also getting an undisclosed amount of money, per month, for the next eighteen years.

Wow! That actually happened!

The final required element fell firmly into place. I found the ideal studio.

Less than half a block away and kitty-corner to Occidental Square was an old shoe factory. Artist studios were being rented out on the fifth floor. I rented one in the northwest corner. It looked out over Occidental Square, Puget Sound, and the Seattle skyline. It was less than fifty yards from where I worked.

The floor also had a common kitchen, shower, and toilet.

Building stretcher bars and stretching canvases were first on my list. I started by preparing twelve large canvases. I dove in immediately.

There was also a corner common room with the same view I had—actually better. It had a stage in it. Within two weeks, I had organized a weekly figure-drawing workshop. I had access to the same models used at the art schools and universities in the area. The models liked the three-hour sessions and the environment. They loved coming back.

Oh, yes. Rip and I started a co-ed softball team. We also played music in his basement a couple of nights a week.

The *I Ching* has always interested me since I read Carl Jung's volume set. It is one of the world's oldest books. This book of changes is full of symbolism. Modern books transcribe these symbols so that western civilization can understand them—even though the symbols are universal. It works on the premise that the world and our lives constantly change. The randomness of throwing sticks or coins creates a hexagram. From this, you refer to the book to decipher what it is telling you about the changes yet to come. It is almost impossible to throw the same hexagram twice in a row due to the many possible combinations.

During my last year in San Diego, I threw the coins three different times. I got the same hexagram three times in a row. It said, "Advantage will be found in the northwest." Couple that with my trips to the Seattle area over the last several years. Every time I made that trip, I felt like I was going home. I fit in perfectly. It was meant to be.

The way things had unfolded for me since my arrival in Seattle confirmed all of this for me. This was my home.

One final thing had to happen: find my special sushi bar. And I did find it!

Maneki was four blocks to the east of my studio. Kozo Nakayama was the chef. That was the beginning of many wonderful sushi experiences. I also introduced this place to many people, as I had done with Yakitori II in San Diego. It was the final piece to my happy life.

As I had in San Diego, I painted like a maniac. The artists on the floor became involved in the monthly art walks. The middle of the floor had been transformed into a gallery before I arrived. We changed shows every month. Pioneer Square was ripe with art lovers during the art walks. Crowds of people climbed the five flights to see what was there. It helped that we put a sign with an arrow.

Michael Andeel and I hung out a lot. He was an excellent photographer, and he had built a darkroom in his studio. Michael was the only other person on the floor who lived in his studio and who was devoted to his art as much as I was. He produced unique black and white photos.

One of his things was to follow the Seattle music scene. His shots were from the most unexpected angles you could imagine. He depicted the musicians and the crowds in a most professional way. I saw some of his work in local publications. He deserved much more attention than he was getting.

We found a bar that was just a walk down the alley. It was a Mexican restaurant and bar. Taco Tuesday provided us with a warm gathering of other artists. It also fit our starving-artist income—two bucks for a beer and all the tacos you could eat. I was doing better than most because of my job at Artform. The artists and photographers we hung out with there were the real deal.

I entered juried shows and was accepted to many of them. The quantity of work I expected to produce was still in process. I just loved to paint. It was nice having the stretched and sized canvases ready to go. I never have painter's block. There are more ideas bouncing around in my brain than I can keep up with.

After over twenty years of drawing from a model, I realized that it had become an addiction—a good addiction. Sketching things from a trained eye is rewarding. It's an eye-to-brain and out-the-hand expression. You can train the artist's eye to be like another limb of your body.

Unfortunately, the artists on our floor were mostly "wannabes." They thought it was neat to have a studio and live in their homes in the suburbs.

Until recently, it had not been that way. From what I heard, there had been a group of artists in the studios with different skills; these had been people with performance art skills as well as a love for the visual arts.

They had a good thing going for years. Unfortunately, the person holding the lease had some medical issues and had to hand the lease down. No one wanted it. The group that was there seemed to be dissipating and wanting to move to their next stage in life.

A "wannabe" artist who had just moved in said, "I'll take it!"

That turned out to be a big mistake. It had been a great co-op, splitting all costs among the artists who were living on the floor until it fell into the hands of Melanie, a latent capitalist. She was thinking more about the profits that could be made than providing spaces for artists.

This was a space that had great energy, inundating the floor with creativity and production.

Melanie's art leaned heavily toward the satanic side. The one-piece I remembered was a creepy devil doll she placed on her windowsill.

Artists in the area, as well as in other cities or communities, were always looking for venues to show their work. If not at galleries, artists discovered different establishments to display their creations.

That was a good thing. They became places where artists could show their work in public and the owners were more than happy to have their walls decorated. They were great supporters of the arts. It helped build the character of the crowd and the establishment.

I found my space in the Pioneer Square Saloon. They had high walls—the perfect place to display my strata series. These oil paintings were just under seven feet tall.

Evenings brought a creative crowd. The bartenders were ideal for maintaining the mood and carefree attitudes. It was a good place for artists to convene and have profound conversations.

There were two different directions I was focused on with my paintings.

One was my pipe series—somewhat surrealistic—that involved figurative work and landscape. Working on a figure, I would replace an arm with a pipe, for example. Or I would paint a forest—instead of tree trunks, I used pipes.

My purpose in doing this was purely symbolic. The rest of the work had more recognizable images, except for the loose brushstroke I was using.

To start a painting, I prepared a washy base and applied it to the surface. I textured it with splatters, towels, and brushstrokes—all in washes. This was an extension of how I painted in San Diego by allowing unintended shapes to come through and be part of the dynamics of the painting.

The purpose was to show conflicting energies: one was life itself, and the other was the inferior human influence on life.

The other direction was my strata paintings. I used to love looking at cross-sections of the Earth in science books. It occurred to me that instead of being geographically accurate, I could make symbolic images depicting the vast unknown mysteries of the depth of the Earth. There was no limit to what I could do.

I could also relate that to the awareness of the human and the depths of his mind—the mysteries and symbolic nature of human existence. I stretched canvases that were tall and thin. The first ones I painted were seventy-six inches tall and thirty-six inches wide. I later reduced the size to fifty-three inches high and twenty-five inches wide—the same proportions. I even did a series of smaller ones fifteen inches high with water base paints.

All in all, I did about sixty strata paintings—probably more.

I also had fun combining the strata paintings with the pipes.

The techniques I described were dependent on continual studies in landscapes and figure drawing. The more strength I had in these two areas, the better my "out of my head" paintings were.

One day in the early afternoon, I was focused on some work when the phone rang. We only had one phone located in the common kitchen.

Mike answered it. "Paul, it's for you!" he yelled.

A lady was on the phone from a software company. She wanted to see my work. They needed to have a mural painted. Another artist had recommended me.

THE VISION

The next day, a couple of sharp women in business suits came to visit me. They looked around with smiles on their faces. They were sold right away.

The bummer was that I couldn't paint what I wanted to paint. They wanted a large, three-panel mural, a total of twelve feet by six feet.

They wanted it to look like a Rousseau—a jungle scene with animals. Other than that, I could paint what I wanted. It didn't need to be a copy—just a jungle.

They flew me down to New Orleans. Megan, the woman I was working with, sat next to me on the plane. She was pleasant to talk with and was also drop-dead gorgeous. She explained how things would work. We would be in New Orleans for four nights. I would paint the panels during a trade show. They thought it would attract people.

At the end of the trade show, they would give the painting to whoever drew the lucky number.

When we arrived at the hotel, Megan handed me the key to my room. It turned out that she had a room next to mine.

"How strange," she said. "The rest of the company is on the third floor. I wonder why they put us on the sixth floor?"

That evening, the company reserved a cruise boat for a private party and a trip up the Mississippi. We were served fantastic food and had an open bar.

During the trip, Megan explained that she was married.

"You know, after this trade show, we won't need your services anymore, so this is the last we will see each other."

I actually presumed that, but the message was not lost on me. When we returned to the hotel, she said, "Well, I guess I'll take a bottle of wine up to my room and watch TV."

One of the men in the company invited me to join him and another guy. They were going to Bourbon Street. I accepted his offer, and we had a great time, returning to the hotel at two in the morning.

It was fun hanging out on Bourbon Street, listening to great music, and eating good food.

The trade show went as planned, and I enjoyed painting on stage.

I feel bad about Megan. I just couldn't flip the switch. Every evening, she told me she was planning on staying in her room alone, and every evening, I went to Bourbon Street. If I could imagine the best possible scenario for a tryst with a beautiful woman—a four-day fling—this would be it.

Sometimes, I hate myself. As I proclaimed earlier, it's hard for me to get involved this way. Why didn't she just say, "I'm taking a bottle of wine to my room. Come join me."?

Ideally, it would have been perfect to have Megan join us on Bourbon Street. We could have easily ended up in the same room afterward. Everyone knew her. She couldn't let on that she was luring me to her room. They knew she was married.

On the flight home, Megan again sat next to me. She was pissed and wouldn't talk to me.

Working at Artform became routine but not lacking in the flow of good art. That translated into sparking my creative juices.

THE VISION

Penny and her lady friend met some of us at Maneki once. That evolved into more sushi get-togethers. We reserved a private room with pillows and a rectangular well under the foot high table—in case you were uncomfortable sitting cross-legged.

We left our shoes at the door—which was a sliding screen covered in ornate Japanese art. We had many righteous feasts in that place. The food was fantastic. Our private waitress made sure that our sake was full, the empty trays were removed, and more tasty delights were placed before us. We were sated to the point of being not just satisfied, but uncomfortably bloated.

Back at the frame shop, the routine was broken by an international event. The wall in Berlin was taken down.

Shortly after that, we receive about fifteen large paintings from the fading Soviet Union. They were oil paintings that were not stretched but were rolled and put in tubes. When I unrolled them, I saw that my work was cut out for me. None of them were square and not by just a little. Some stuck out six inches beyond a square border. The sizes ranged from eight feet by five feet down to three feet by four feet.

I had to stretch them square and fit them into a floater frame. This type of frame has an inset thin frame that is below the surface of the painting. It is usually black. Another frame is placed around that one. The result is the appearance of a painting floating inside the frame. You can see the edge of the painting.

Before placing the work inside the frame, the extra canvas was carefully folded around the stretcher bars. I could not cut it off; that was a no-no. I also slightly rounded the stretchers so that no sharp corners would crack the gesso or whatever the artists had used as a primer. The idea was that the artist could take them off the stretcher bars and return them to their original condition.

The paintings themselves were loosely painted. The brush strokes were apparent.

The colors were very dark and the subject matter depressing—actually morbid.

Rip contacted me and invited me to a party at the Ballard Locks. He lived with Dennis, a good friend of his. Dennis knew some women from the Denver area who had found an amazing house built on stilts overhanging the canal that leads to the locks.

Their house had lots of windows and a nice deck. We drank, munched on hors d'oeuvres, and watched the boats cruise in and out of the locks. You could hear the waves lapping underneath, especially when a wake from a passing boat hit the pylons and the shore.

There was one animated woman I ended up talking to for most of the evening. She said they had to move but were enjoying the house while they could.

Her name was Martha, and she was from Pueblo, Colorado. We had a fantastic conversation covering politics, the arts, and just general bullshit. She was very intelligent and a good speaker—very entertaining.

She worked at the Seattle Trade Center and loved her job. The Seattle Trade Center was eventually renamed the World Trade Center Seattle.

I told her that I was in the arts and worked at a frame shop in Pioneer Square. My living situation was exactly what I was looking for—a work studio where I could live in Pioneer Square.

THE VISION

Speaking of Pioneer Square, a new nightclub had opened underneath the viaduct, across the street from the docks—the OK Hotel.

I was already familiar with this place. It had been an actual old hotel that artists used for installations. The hotel itself was not fit for occupancy. It didn't meet the city's building codes.

Each artist was assigned to a room. They had free rein to use it for an art installation. It became an art show where one could wander down the halls and enter each room. The artist had his or her little cubicle of self-expression. One room had mouse traps spaced a couple of inches from each other, covering the walls and ceiling—all of them cocked and ready to snap. There was amazing diversity in each room.

The building had now been turned into one of the most unusual nightclubs in the city. It had a huge bar with a greasy spoon, but the highlight was the two separate stages in two different rooms. The best and the most avant-garde musicians and bands played here, including Nirvana, Flop, and Soundgarden.

There was one fantastic and truly unique band that I had heard before. They had played at several art openings. I knew some of the members. It basically was a neo-Jewish band that had that modern touch—a little jazz, a little rock. There were string instruments, a horn section, drums, bass guitar, keyboards—I can't remember all the instruments, but I do remember their sound. When you started listening, you couldn't stop.

David Byrne, founder and lead singer/songwriter for the band Talking Heads, lived in the area and used to jog around the streets. He dropped into the OK and walked into the room where this band was playing.

They played music on his next CD.

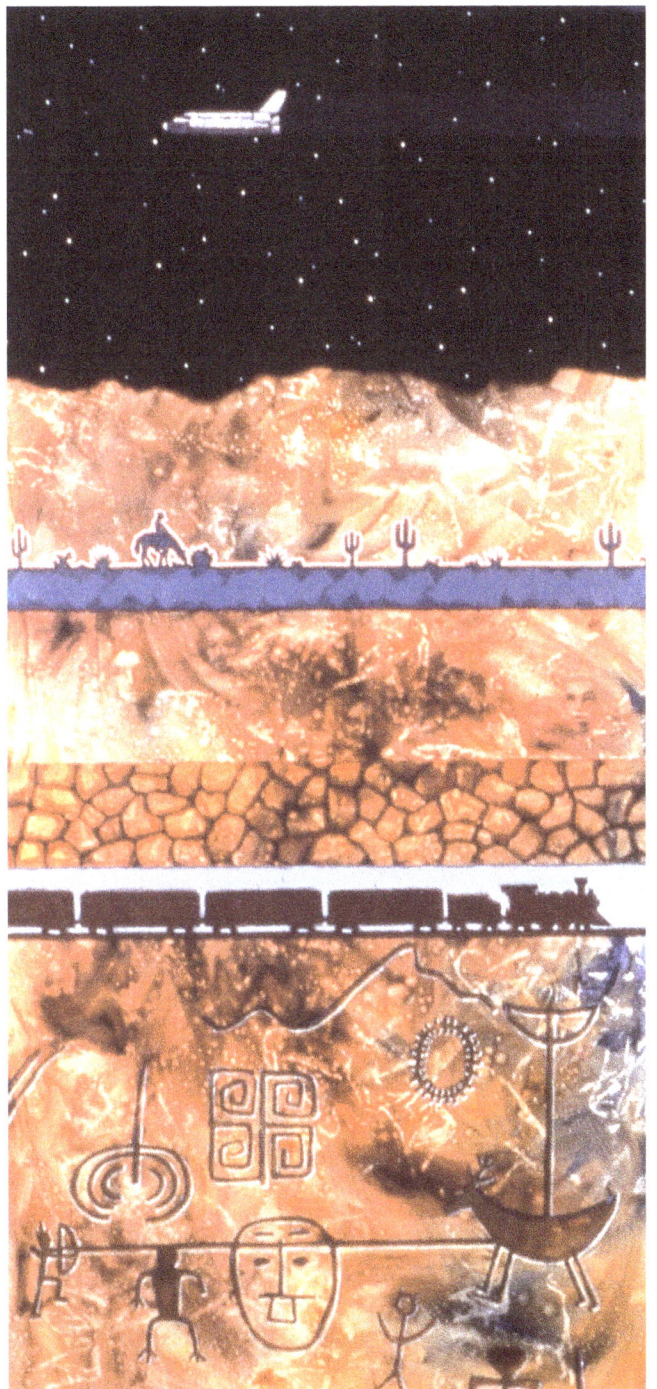

CHAPTER FOURTEEN

When I returned to my studio, there were five flights of stairs to reach our floor and each floor had approximately twelve-foot ceilings—maybe they were fourteen feet. I ran up the stairs—all the way—every time. That's one of the ways I stayed in shape besides softball.

Panting heavily, I unlocked the door at the top stairs and immediately ran into Melanie—the infamous holder of the lease—as she was leaving to go to her house in the suburbs.

"I found a renter for the studio next to yours," she said.

That was one of the signs of the emerging dictatorship. No one on the floor had a choice of who they would be living with.

Thinking, "I probably should introduce myself to the new tenant or artist," I walked to the door and knocked.

This was a particularly nice studio. It was large, and all the windows faced north. The room had a full view of the Seattle skyline. It was one of two studios that had an actual door. The rest of the studios were open to anyone roaming around the space.

The door opened.

There stood Martha, the woman I met at the party in Ballard a week ago.

"Oh!" She smiled. "Fancy meeting you here. Want to go out for a drink?"

"Uh, okay?"

"Do you know a good place? I'm a bit hungry, too."

"Sure," I said, as I recovered from my surprise.

"I saw your studio, you do nice work," she said, shutting the door behind her.

We both walked down the stairs and went to FX McRory's—just around the corner.

We each ordered a beer; it was beer heaven. Local brews on tap ran the length of the bar—over forty feet long.

"Do you like clams or oysters?" I asked.

"I love both."

We ordered Oysters Rockefeller and a large bowl of clams to share.

"I'm sorry to surprise you like that. I was thinking about what you said about your studio, and I thought I would see if there were any more available."

Our conversation continued from where it left off at the Ballard party. I enjoy intelligent conversation. I take life seriously but feel it is important to deal with the humor in it; even sarcasm adds the ingredients to take a serious thing lightly, to me anyway. I understand that it annoys some people. Martha was good at dealing with it and throwing it back.

Martha took out a card and paid the bill.

"Tomorrow is Friday. Want to go out for coffee before work?"

"Sounds good," I said. "I know just the place."

We returned to FX McRory's on occasion, but instead of going into the main restaurant, we preferred the small oyster bar just outside the door. It was more intimate, and it was fun chatting with the chef as we sampled the menu.

It was Friday morning. Martha and I strolled through the beauty of Occidental Square and stopped in at the Grand Central Bakery. I had my everyday breakfast consisting of drip coffee and one of the best cinnamon rolls I have ever had. Martha had a latte and a cinnamon roll.

"Oh, man, these are good," she said.

The interior of the Grand Central was huge and old in its construction, fitting well with the Pioneer Square motif. There were a few businesses on the outer edges of the open space. One of them was the bakery.

After our morning treat, Martha followed the waterfront to the Seattle Trade Center, and I walked a block to Artform.

Having the key, I entered the back door, filled a bucket with water, and washed the filth from the steps, left by whatever bum had used it the night before.

No one had arrived yet; I was there early as usual. My chop list to cut the frame molding was already organized from the day before and waiting downstairs. I replaced the blade on the circular chop saw and began my workday.

Martha was to become an everyday item, even on my walks to Maneki for sushi. I'm not sure if she was into sushi when I first met her, but she was now.

That evening, I was in my studio working when Martha walked in. She sat down and watched while I finished the detail on a canvas.

During our conversation the day before, I had told her about the OK Hotel. Since it was Friday night, she wanted to check it out.

As we walked the two blocks to the OK, we almost passed Elliot Bay Books. Martha was already familiar with the place; I guess most people in the area were.

Not being in a hurry, we independently caroused the aisles of books; the atmosphere was great. As I soon found out, Martha was an avid reader. We met downstairs and had a light meal and another coffee.

When we walked into the OK, it was still early in the evening. A woman in leather—decked out with tattoos, a nose ring, and net leggings—played her guitar and sang. It was a solo act. Oh, yeah, you couldn't miss the turquoise hair either. She was good.

Arnis Sarma was sitting at the bar drinking whiskey. He was one of the creative photographers who lived in the area. Originally, he came from some Slavic country. I introduced him to Martha, and they hit it off pretty well.

Martha's claims to fame were her photography and writing skills. It was nice to know that Melanie had picked someone with talent to rent the studio to. You couldn't say that about a few of the others she had allowed in.

We walked into the back room where the larger bands played and watched as a band carried in their amps, guitars, and the usual performance items used to enhance their wild presentation.

It was way too early for them to play so we returned to the bar, sat with Arnie, and ordered a drink—then another one, followed by more.

I knew a lot of the artists who frequented the place, and we bounced our conversation and jokes off each other as the night wore on.

The band in the back room began playing, and most of the crowd filed in to watch.

At about one in the morning, Martha and I staggered back to our studios. We ended up spending the night together.

Things were coming together on the art scene. The paintings I worked on quickly grew in numbers. It was time I set a date for a one-man show in the studio gallery. I talked to Melanie and the rest of the renters; everyone was OK with it.

Eagle Eye Gallery on Capitol Hill wanted to show my work. They also set up a one-man show for me for the following year. It was great having something to work toward.

It was a plus that I had venues in which to show my work; however, my drive to paint was not affected by whether I showed or not. Being in the studio working was what I really enjoyed. Showing my work was like undressing in front of the world. The paintings I did spewed out of my thoughts and emotions without orderly intent. Personally, I feel that there is no need to have a consistent show of work that sells. My work is a visual diary of my life and my experiences. The world inside my head wants an outlet. I create this work with symbolism and spontaneity.

I did have my show in the studio gallery. The opening night was during the monthly Pioneer Square art walk. We had lots of people willing to take that five-story hike to our floor; it added to the excitement of the art scene.

I had a great response, but no sales. I only showed large works, and the viewers were mostly artists themselves.

There was also a lot of interest in renting my inflatable eagle. The extra income was nice. It was rented mostly for events and promotions.

Sometimes, I inflated it in ideal locations—mostly for exposure. Once people saw it, they were amazed at its realism.

A good example of this was the Fourth of July.

The Seattle Trade Center—Martha's workplace—was located on the waterfront.

One day, when meeting Martha for lunch, we walked down to Elliot Bay.

I looked back at the trade center and pointed at the roof.

"See that platform on top of the trade center?" The platform itself must have been thirty feet high. It was once used to support a huge water tank that was no longer needed.

"Yes," she said.

"I want to put the eagle on it for the Fourth of July."

"Let's do it!" Martha exclaimed. "I'll just contact the powers that be and let them know. I'm sure it will be OK."

It was more than OK. Early on July 4, we hauled the eagle to the top of the platform and inflated it. You could see it from miles away. It looked beautiful. Everyone we talked to was excited about it. The trade center people thanked Martha for the publicity.

There was one problem. There was a seagull nest on the roof, and mommy seagull kept dive-bombing the eagle, trying to scare it away. It took a while to wash the bird poop off after we took it down.

Martha liked to get out of town. She enjoyed camping and hiking, so I took her to my favorite spot—Shi Shi Beach.

To get there, we drove across the top of the Olympic Peninsula, passed the beautiful Lake Crescent, and continued on to Lake Ozette.

We set up camp on the north edge of the lake for the night.

We spent the weekend taking the trails to Cape Alava and Sand Point and then the highlight—Shi Shi Beach. We planned on staying there for the night. Martha was amazed. Even though I had been there twice before, I continued to be awed—so peaceful!

Martha and I trekked around the Northwest a lot.

Once we went to the tiny town of Gold Bar in the Cascade Mountains northeast of Seattle. Some friends drove us there for dinner. When we were done, we told our friends to leave us. We could get back to Seattle on foot. The following morning, after spending a night at the inn, we followed an old logging road and walked for most of the day.

We finally came across a paved road and a bus stop. We rode the bus from there.

We went to Snoqualmie Falls, the Hoh Rainforest, the hills around Mount Rainier, and we frequented the Ocean Crest Resort in Moclips several times. The first time we went to Moclips was because of a first-place prize at a Halloween contest.

Speaking of Halloween, I had been tiring of the same costume and thought I would do something different that year. There was something I wanted to try that was sure to be a hit.

The next time I saw Martha, I asked her if she wanted to be involved. When I laid out the details, she was excited. Michael Andeel was up for it too. We needed at least six people for this to work. Martha, Mike, and I could do the fabrication.

I bought a roll of chicken wire and formed the shapes of six tropical fish. They had to be somewhat consistent, so I made the basic shapes. Each fish was about thirty-six inches long with a high, exaggerated back fin and tail—you know, like real tropical fish. We covered each with paper mache and painted them in beautiful iridescent colors. We painted tiger stripes, polka dots, etc.—you know, like real tropical fish.

Each fish was structured to act as a helmet. You pulled it over your head, and it rested on your shoulders. The open mouth was for viewing. There were fins on the side behind each gill that were attached to a stiff metal wire. Moving it up and down made the fins flap.

Come Halloween night, we needed to find a venue that was large and packed with people. The perfect place was right across the street from our studio. I wasn't going to participate, since there was another Halloween competition two blocks away. I would do the outhouse costume at that venue.

It was easy to find friends who wanted to be involved with our "school of fish." Each person wore black. The idea was to walk through the crowd and—on cue—change direction—then change again and again, as the "school of fish" made its way through the crowd.

I was late arriving at the costume party I attended, but it didn't matter. They put me in with the finalists. As usual, I got first place—a two-night stay at the Ocean Crest Resort in Moclips.

Back at the studio, Martha and the crew were hanging out in the kitchen talking and laughing as I walked in.

"How did it go?" I asked.

"Great!" Martha said. "First place. It worked out just as you said."

"What was the prize?"

There was a big box on the table. It was an inflatable hot tub.

It was kind of lame. We never did use it, so we gave it away. Getting first place was award enough.

"How did you do?" Martha asked.

"First place," I said. "A trip to Moclips at some resort."

Since meeting Martha, I noticed that I never saw her working on anything. She said she did photography and writing, then showed me some photos she had taken. They were excellent.

She finally put that skill into action.

Pioneer Square decided to do a monthly publication. In the first issue—Volume One—Martha took a fantastic photo of my inflatable eagle and wrote an equally fantastic article. They not only accepted the article but they also paid her for it. The story was on the front page.

They were excited to have her on board and asked her if she would do another article for the next publication.

"Sure!" she said. "Can I pick the topic?"

They agreed.

Martha wrote a scathing article about the Seattle police. The Pioneer Square Star refused to publish it and asked her if she would write another article or at least tone this one down.

"No way. If I can't write what I want, I'm not interested in writing for your paper."

At least Martha had that rebellious, artistic attitude. She was amazingly talented. The only thing she lacked was the drive and passion to produce.

The shit finally hit the fan. Melanie was tired of delaying her capitalist plans for the studio. Each tenant on the fifth floor had a sublease, but there was a stipulation that if she sold her lease or passed it on to another person, the leases were void.

There were rumors of a ruthless asshole, with mafia ties, on a floor below us. Melanie said she sold the lease to him.

This all began with Melanie gathering us together for a studio meeting. She said that there were issues with the legality of our living in the studios. She had asked a lawyer to come over to protect "all of our rights" and discuss our options.

This was a setup. She just wanted to evict us and have her lawyer there when she did. The rest of us didn't really like Melanie, and she knew it. There were many reasons why she wasn't liked; you can add ruthless coward to that list.

We were given a month to leave.

We had to have a party before we left. It was a potluck, and all our friends were invited. We drank and partied through the night.

We had a long table in the kitchen area and decided to do a photo of a staged *Last Supper*. Using a copy of Da Vinci's painting, we arranged the proper number of people at the table in the correct poses and placed food and drinks in front of each person. We tried to make it look as correct as possible.

Mike Andeel took the center "Christ" spot, and everyone else studied the painting so they would know their poses.

I put my camera on a tripod and shot a few exposures. The photos turned out great!

This inspired me to do a painting: *The Last Last Supper*.

THE VISION

It sold immediately at Eagle Eye Gallery.

The person who bought it liked the image so much, he felt like others should enjoy it. He paid to have 500 posters and 500 photolithographs made from the image, then gave them to me.

"Be sure to sign and number the lithos," he said.

Shortly after getting our eviction notice, the jerk from downstairs came up to our floor and began berating us, telling us to get the hell out. He even placed a butcher knife on the gallery walls and sprayed its silhouette on the wall with red spray paint.

Michael—our hero—said that if there was anything we wanted to throw away, even trash with old food, put it in his room.

It just so happened that the elevator mechanisms were in Michael's studio. After the rest of us left the building, he piled all the trash on top of the gears, pulleys, and wheels used to make the old elevator work and tamped it all down. I swear, the pile was at least six feet high. From the inside, he nailed the studio door shut and piled more trash against the door. He then climbed out his window and up the fire escape to the roof. He went down the stairwell to make his escape. I heard they had to break the door down to get in.

We never really knew what transpired with the transaction Melanie made, but years later, you could still see her "devil doll" in the window of her studio.

Martha and I found a studio, not far away on Western Avenue. It had been renovated for the purpose of providing studios for artists. The waterfront was a block away, and our studio was next to the greatest restaurant ever—Wild Ginger.

There was a loft for a bed and a small, enclosed space that we turned into a dark room. Martha's brother sent her some developing supplies. I was hoping it would get Martha excited about her photography.

I set up my easel, stretched some canvases, and started painting. The environment felt good. My work seemed like it came together more easily than it had in the last studio.

I did some good work in that studio. I stretched some large canvases: seventy-six inches high by thirty-six inches wide. I worked on my continuing strata series. Two of these paintings were sold at Eagle Eye Gallery.

The New Year was coming soon. Martha and I decided to take a trip to San Diego. It was fun showing Martha around. I introduced her to my friends, favorite places, and old haunts. I even took her to Bigger Than Life.

Again, the employees were excited to see me. I had sent them a photo of my eagle, and they had pinned it to a bulletin board in the break room.

Sunset Cliffs had been a magical place for me when I lived in San Diego. I had my own special spot where someone had carved a profile of an Indian's face. This area of the coast was all cliffs, caves, and large rocks protruding from the surf. The waves were great for surfing, and I used to take my board there on many occasions. The sound of the waves crashing against the rocks and the swells rising and dropping reminded me of happy days. I used to sit there for hours watching the sunset. I also did several paintings there.

That is where I took Martha on New Year's Eve.

THE VISION

I proposed to her. The date was set for September of that coming year.

After returning to Seattle, the Gulf War was winding down. There were multiple successes, and by early February 1991, the United States claimed victory. The Iraqi army was driven from Kuwait, leaving their leadership and military beaten but intact.

I heard a lot of talks—some of it reflecting my thoughts—that we should have driven into Baghdad to finish the job.

As it turned out, Daddy Bush made the right move. It left the Middle East a functional area regardless of their problems.

We found out the results of what "finishing the job" meant when President Bush's son became president and decided that, if his dad wouldn't do it, he would. He blew up Iraq, killed Saddam, and disbanded the military. The aftermath blew up the whole Middle East, leading the world on a path that caused the extreme instability and horror that we have today.

Winning the Gulf War developed pride in Americans, and we wanted to celebrate it.

The City of Seattle made plans to have a military parade downtown. This was aggressively curtailed. It was not something the citizens of Seattle would accept.

Somehow, the planners heard about my inflatable eagle, and they wanted to put it behind the reviewing stand during the parade.

Even though I was a bit disappointed that the parade did not happen—only because of the opportunity to show off my eagle—I agreed with the decision to not flaunt our military power.

Thinking that this was over, I found out that the "powers that be" still wanted to honor the troops. They were pursuing different plans.

I was contacted by the Seattle Seahawks to be part of a tribute to our military for halftime at a Seahawk game. They wanted to see the eagle, so they invited me—and my eagle—to their training facility in Renton.

Part of boasting about the eagle was my claim that it could be inflated in sixty seconds. They wanted to see if that was true.

I took Martha with me. We laid out the inflatable and connected it to the blower. After we were directed to a power source, a couple of their decision-makers came out to where we were set up.

"Sixty seconds, huh? We're going to walk back into the building. When we disappear inside the door, start the inflation. We will come back out in exactly sixty seconds."

They disappeared. Exactly one minute later, they came back out to the full glory of the eagle. Not only were they impressed; they were in awe of the detail and realism of my creation.

"Great! You've got the job."

On game day, we went to the Kingdome stadium early to practice with the rest of the participants.

During halftime, they unfurled a flag, almost as big as the field itself. The eagle popped up—as expected—on the fifty-yard line.

THE VISION

Part of our responsibility was to deflate it and remove it as quickly as possible.

We did the inflation on a huge tarp. To deflate it, I had a large deflation panel on the eagle's back. I yanked the ripcord, and the eagle dropped immediately into a heap. Martha disconnected the blower, so the air could vent out the fan tunnel.

The next step was to grab the two front corners of the tarp and pull the whole thing off the field.

I ran to one side and grabbed one corner. As I was rushing to the other corner, there stood an Army captain. He already had the corner in hand and gave it to me. I gave him a quick "Thank you, sir" and pulled it off the field.

Wow, our military is really on the ball! They do things as needed—even if not asked. That small act made me appreciate our armed forces even more than I already did. It's no wonder we won the war.

Martha and I jumped up in the air and high-fived. Success!

They sent me a videotape of the halftime show. It was very impressive.

Even though the eagle was twenty-four feet tall, it looked pretty small compared to the vastness of the field.

On September 23, 1991, I woke to the rays of the rising sun lighting up a corner of my tent. There was a chill in the air, and I could hear the sound of birds.

I opened the flap and crawled out into the crisp fresh air.

We were camped on the north shore of Lake Ozette. This was the day Martha and I were to be married.

There weren't many attending—Martha's parents and a few friends from her work; other than that, just the minister who would marry us.

The minister, John Wingfield, was from the Unity Church. Martha had found him. He had the reputation of hitching people in unusual places, like the top of Mount Rainier. He would go pretty much anywhere. He would probably marry someone under the waters of Puget Sound in scuba gear.

For us, it was Shi Shi Beach. Martha and I were the only ones who had been there. The rest were in for a pleasant surprise.

We lucked out. We found an old logging road that went within a half-mile of the beach. Normally, it is a pretty long hike.

A smaller road took us even closer. It was so overgrown that the minister complained about its scratching the side of his van.

All was forgiven when we walked the rest of the way to the beach.

John, the minister, jogged the length of the beach, took his flute out of his bag, and played it at the water's edge for an hour. He had the biggest smile on his face—to hell with the scratches on his van.

John asked Martha and me to pick the spot where we wanted the ceremony to take place. Behind the driftwood and just inside the woods, there were cozy little dens that people used as campsites. After checking a few out, we found the perfect one. I could feel the calming energy in this little nook. The forest around it seemed to make a cozy room.

He asked us for our rings.

I had carved the rings out of wax and had them cast in twenty-four-karat gold.

John wanted to be alone in our chosen spot.

The ceremony began inside our little den with friends and family forming a circle. The words were all prearranged and confirmed. When it came time for the rings, John held them out in the palm of his hand. A beam of light passed through the canopy of trees and struck his palm. The rings lit up as if they had an internal light. He handed hers to me and mine to her. We placed them on each other's ring fingers after finishing our vows.

The deed was done.

The minister and Martha's parents left to find more civilized accommodations. Martha and I set up our campsite inside our chosen room of trees. Martha's friends camped in their chosen site a half-mile up the beach.

In the middle of the night, Martha crawled outside the tent and threw up among the ferns.

She was pregnant with our soon-to-be daughter, Shawn Claire.

There was an item I had put on the back burner. I had several rolls of black and white film from Europe and really wanted to develop them myself. We were all set up in our dark room. I asked Martha if she would mind if I used it. I didn't want to be an obstacle if she wanted to keep it available, just in case the bug hit her. I would have loved to see her shooting black and whites and developing them. It would be nice to see her driven by her creativity.

I had developed film before, but not much; it had been a while. Martha filled me in on the process until I became comfortable with it. We had everything we needed. The darkroom was just sitting there waiting to be used.

I became obsessed with wanting to see my Europe photos. I would hang out developing film for hours—listening to music or not—sometimes drinking wine as I worked. The process threw me back into the past to relive those three months. I was also learning more film-developing techniques and understanding the exposure time more as I went along.

During this time, Martha was working at the trade center, and, when she arrived home, she was usually tired and not feeling too well.

We purchased a TV and would lie on the bed together, checking out what was happening in the world, as well as movies and sitcoms.

I had lived in studios painting for such a long time that I had lost touch with this little box.

We ended up watching reruns of *Star Trek*. It was our favorite. I knew about the popularity of it but had never partaken.

I did see the *Star Trek* movies as they came out.

I could say that we became Trekkies during that period except for the fact that I still to this day cannot recall all the characters or episodes. It was a diversion that Martha and I enjoyed.

Martha's pregnancy was beginning to show. She came home from work one evening a little distraught. Things weren't going well with her supervisor.

The people at the trade center seemed to like Martha. They were friendly to me and accepted me at the parties they had. It came as a surprise when she was laid off. As I got to know Martha, her personality revealed its feistiness. She was also confrontational. I learned much more about this as our relationship continued.

While living at the Western Avenue studio, I had a very pleasant surprise—one of the most wonderful surprises I have ever had.

My brother Don called. He was an instructor in structural engineering at UW.

I don't know how he had done it, but he had arranged to have my son Kevin and my daughter Kim visit me. The next day, I bought their airline tickets. I hadn't seen them since I was "allowed" to see them for twenty minutes in 1975 after traveling 1,200 miles. I still held the bitterness from how I was treated by Barbara. For her, it was a punishment. She enjoyed standing in the living room of her parents' house with her arms folded, smiling and glaring at me.

"Sorry, your twenty minutes are up. Good-bye."

Kevin was attending UW, and my brother Don was his advisor. His major was in structural engineering. My brother and Kevin had developed a good relationship during his years in school.

Kim had finished high school the previous year.

Don was familiar with our situation. He knew that Kevin and Kim wanted to see me and that I wanted to see them.

Kevin told me years later that Barbara was angrily against it, but her husband had made the case for the kids.

"Let them go visit him. They need to see their biological father."

She relented.

At first, it was just Kevin. He was old enough to make his own decisions. When Kim found out, she insisted on going as well.

When I picked them up at the airport, I was thrilled and so were they. It had been a long time. Barbara had sent photos of them growing up to my parents. My parents had forwarded the photos to me.

I brought Kevin and Kim back to the studio. I had so much to say and show them. They were excited to tell me about their lives and experiences.

We were so wound up that we walked to Wild Ginger for dessert at one in the morning. They were really happy and animated—playing off each other and confirming each other's stories.

That night, Kevin asked if he could have the key to the studio. He wanted to walk around the waterfront and downtown Seattle by himself. I gladly gave him the key.

The next morning, I took them on a tour of some of Seattle's highlights. We went to the top of the Space Needle and wandered around Seattle.

They were there for a whole week.

During that time, we took the ferry to Bainbridge Island—it was like a tour of Puget Sound with Mount Rainier standing majestically on the horizon. The Olympics and Cascades—one range to the west, one to the east—were snow-capped and beautiful. To top that off was the Seattle skyline. I was blown away when I first saw it and so were they.

THE VISION

There was one thing I wanted them to experience and they wanted to as well—the Seattle music scene. We looked through local papers to see who was playing and where. Unfortunately, Kim was too young to be admitted to nightclubs.

There was a band that was just hitting it big. They were playing at the OK Hotel. Since I knew the owner, I walked in and talked to him. I asked if we could bring my daughter through the back door, but he was hesitant and didn't want to take the risk. We decided we didn't want to leave her out. It turned out the band was Nirvana.

We opted for a comedy show instead. It was kind of lame, but we had a great time. Just the fact that we were spending time together was enough.

Little did Kevin and I know that about six years from that point in time, we would be playing in our own original band in Seattle and Kitsap County.

It was sad to see them go, but the door had finally been opened. There was the possibility of getting to know each other—to actually build the relationship we had been denied.

As the months of Martha's pregnancy continued, we decided that once our daughter was born, it would be nice if we could live in a more rural environment. Bainbridge Island was our first choice. It was also just a ferry ride to work. When I disembarked from the ferry, I would be three blocks from Artform. The ferry arrived in Seattle early. That would give me time to stop at the Grand Central Bakery for my coffee and cinnamon roll and time to work on the daily crossword.

We found a large A-frame on the north end of the Island. It had two stories and a large basement. One-half of the A-frame had the kitchen, living room, bedroom, and bathroom. The other half was completely open. The second floor was like a balcony looking out over this huge space. It also had a large deck looking out over trees.

This large open space became my studio.

I didn't waste any time. I set up my easel and started painting immediately.

CHAPTER FIFTEEN

Working at Artform continued. It was a big part of my life. I loved this place and the people I worked with.

Penny was amazing. With everything going on in my life, she allowed me to take time off as needed.

She was the instigator of an episode that she knew would be important to me.

One day when I arrived at work, Penny said that her sister, Andrea, worked at a prop and costume shop owned by an interesting character, Jerry Chin. Andrea wanted me to come to their shop and talk to her boss about a project he was making a proposal for.

When I arrived, I found myself in a most interesting place. Jerry was an intelligent, high-energy person. His warehouse was huge. It was filled with everything a movie producer could imagine. This was a place that provided the props and costumes for movies depicting any time and place. If a movie was being made in the 1920s, he would provide furniture, styles of dress, and knick-knacks depicting that era.

In this case, the proposal didn't really have anything to do with this particular business. Jerry had unbelievable connections in Los Angeles. He was asked to do a fourteen-foot by forty-eight-foot billboard on Sunset Strip in Hollywood. The Alaska Tourist Bureau wanted a giant three-dimensional moose head with two life-size (fake) people—one hanging from an antler and the other filming it.

The purpose of this was to encourage the movie industry to film in Alaska. Jerry heard about me from Andrea and had seen my eagle. He proposed doing the moose head as an inflatable.

Jerry landed the job. After doing detailed drawings, I sculpted the moose head and antlers, then patterned it. I was ready to move ahead.

I still needed to buy a sewing machine.

At the same time and perhaps because I was preparing to be a father, I decided to attend church. Martha wasn't interested. I went for a few months, but the same thing happened as times before when I tried to be a good Mormon. The church demanded most of my time. I still hadn't advanced far enough in the priesthood, and I was put in a class with younger boys and learned things I had learned before.

All in all, as an artist, I needed my freedom to do my work and learn about the world. To be a good Mormon, you had to tuck yourself inside its wing. Each night of the week, I had duties that I could miss, but I was strongly encouraged to participate. I decided again that it was not for me; I had God's work to do from the gifts he gave me. I truly believe that.

It was not that I didn't believe in the church; it was just that it was perfect for some people and families, but not for me or mine. Mormons are good people.

THE VISION

The reason I bring this up is that I ran into a man at church who owned an awning shop in Seattle. He said I could use his sewing machine. Better yet, they would do the sewing for the moose head for a small price.

Before sewing on the antlers, I needed to paint them. I used a large spray booth at the awning shop and painted each one separately.

The fabrication of the moose went flawlessly. When the inflatable was finished, Jerry found a warehouse where I could do the final airbrush and hand painting.

One problem was how to add support to an antler that stuck out twenty feet from the billboard. This was mostly accomplished with the air pressure provided by the blower, but I needed to hang one of the human figures from the tip of the antler. I used PVC pipe and installed it internally for extra support.

To make the figures, I used chicken wire wrapped around PVC pipe and used duct tape to cover the surface. I dressed them in real clothes. The faces were sculpted from clay and then cast in rubber that was mixed with a powdered flesh pigment. I painted the face inside the mold and strengthened it with burlap. When I peeled it out, it had a nice matte finish. I then painted the eyes, lips, and teeth on the outside. They came out glossy. The burlap extended beyond the edge of the face so it could be sewn into the figure's head.

Jerry and I flew to Los Angeles to install it. The finished product turned out perfect. Everyone I talked to thought the figures were real.

The move from Pioneer Square to Bainbridge Island offered a nice contrast—city to country—linked by a thirty-five-minute ferry ride.

I didn't see the extra time going to work as a hardship; I saw it as a beautiful enhancement of my life.

Let's not forget softball. I contacted the Bainbridge Island Recreation Department.

"Hello. I just moved to Bainbridge Island, and I'm interested in playing on a softball team."

"OK, great. What's your name?"

I gave them my name and number.

"I can put you on the list. Women are more in demand, but you can probably get on a team eventually."

"Oh, OK."

"There is another option," the person on the other end of the line offered. "You can start your own team. I have a list of people who want to play."

"That sounds great. I'll drive by and talk with you. I would like the information on the interested people."

Perfect, I can start my own team again like I had done in San Diego and in Seattle.

The co-ed team I assembled was filled with beautiful, fun people.

"So, what shall we name the team?"

THE VISION

After bandying around options, the perfect name presented itself: The Extras.

All of these players were there because they really wanted to play softball. In my experience, most teams are formed from employees of businesses or some group that wants to play softball.

Been there, done that.

They have excellent players who want to play, but to form a team, you need to convince others that it is fun, great exercise, and a bonding experience with each other—all striving for the same goal.

Great! I applaud them. That is what softball leagues are for—especially co-ed. All men's teams have a little more of that macho stuff. That's OK, too. I've played in both.

The point I am making is that *all* the players on The Extras *really* wanted to play and have fun! The women not only held their own but they also outplayed the men on many occasions.

The result was that we were always a competitive team, always finishing in the top three.

Sportsmanship was a dominant aspect of this team. We had fun amongst ourselves, and we had fun with the other teams.

We respected the players on other teams. We respected their abilities and their feelings. We rooted for and encouraged players that weren't as good, even though it might be another team's players. We all wanted to play and have fun.

The team expanded their yearly presence on the Bainbridge Island league to the North Kitsap league.

It worked perfectly. When the season was over at Bainbridge, the North Kitsap league was just starting. That worked out well for some of The Extras. Half the team lived in North Kitsap.

The Extras debuted in 1992, and they are still playing today. The players changed as the team traveled through time, but it has always had the same aura.

Unfortunately, I dropped out in 2008. Even though I stretched and did sprints before each game, I continued to pull calf muscles and hamstrings. I had played sports my whole life and had never had an injury.

At first, my thought was that I needed to face the fact that I was getting old. What I needed to do when I hit the ball was jog to first base. After all, it was just a game. Or if I was on a base and someone else hit the ball, I needed to jog to the next base.

That didn't work out. When the ball was hit, my conditioned self had to move at a sprint to the next base. Damn, pulled another muscle!

Commuting to Seattle involved getting up early and driving the van to a park and ride. It was still dark at that hour. From there, the bus took us to the ferry terminal. By that time, the sun began to show itself.

The early morning ferry ride was beautiful. Instead of sitting comfortably inside the ferry, I chose to climb to the top deck where I could feel the cool breeze.

Seattle glittered as we approached, and the mountains either showed themselves or not. Sometimes, I would walk aft and gaze at the wake, watching the receding islands topped by the Olympics on clear days.

When we arrived in the bustling city, I walked to the Grand Central Bakery and did my usual coffee and roll and absorbed myself in my crossword.

As usual, it was a delight working at Artform.

I enjoyed the trip to Bainbridge Island at the end of the workday, too. At certain times of the year, you could watch the sunset over the Olympics. I had to take a step back and realize where I was. I had experienced the ice-cold, windy weather of Wyoming and the heat and constant sun of the Southwest. Here, I was truly in heaven. I couldn't believe it was real.

Things became a little harder after the money from the moose billboard faded away. Martha was no longer working and was awaiting the baby. We relied on my income.

I was proud of Martha. She was an avid smoker—drum tobacco, roll your own cigarettes. When she found out she was pregnant, she quit—cold turkey.

Halloween rolled around again. We were having difficulty making ends meet. Caught up in my routine, I didn't think of Halloween contests until the day was upon us.

The lack of money was a bit depressing.

Martha was lying in bed.

"Why don't you find a Halloween party and make us some money?"

On one hand, I wanted to stay there with Martha; on the other hand, she was giving me the OK to go out and party.

I threw the outhouse in the back of the van and headed to Seattle.

I returned home at one in the morning. When I walked into the bedroom, the light was still on.

"How did you do?" she asked.

I smiled and threw 500 dollars' worth of five-dollar bills up in the air. They showered down, as we both grinned and relaxed. We could at least catch up on our bills and go out for dinner.

Even though financial woes continued to plague us, things kept happening that seemed to give us an infusion of cash when it was most needed.

We talked my friend Rip into renting the basement bedroom. I had been going to his place in Seattle to play music on occasion. The sound of his bass rising from the basement was a common occurrence while he was there. Even though Martha restrained herself, I got the impression that it bothered her.

I would have really enjoyed playing music with Rip, but I didn't join him as much as I wanted to. I thought it would be worse for Martha if I spent my free time downstairs.

The eagle was still being rented often. I needed to install it and pack it up at the end of each event.

I also donated it to schools. They usually provided us with a lot of press—even front-page photos in many publications.

For ten years, I installed the eagle on Winslow Way at the Bainbridge Fourth of July celebration and parade.

Martha also started working at Eagle Eye Gallery. The job was casual. She tended the gallery, allowing people to browse, and offering her assistance if she was needed.

Finally, the day came for Martha to take the trip to the hospital. We drove to the ferry dock, and they moved us to the front of the line for boarding.

Shawn Claire was knocking at the door. She was born on May 7, 1992, at Virginia Mason Hospital in Seattle.

The hospital encouraged fathers to be involved—unlike when Kevin and Kim were born. In those days, I had had to stay in the waiting room until I was told to come in.

Watching Claire emerge into this world was a precious experience, as was cutting her umbilical cord and giving her a bath (as the nurse instructed me).

I am so glad I had the opportunity to experience Claire's birth and to be a part of it. Of course, the part Martha played was much greater than I could have offered. It was her first child.

Martha and I went through the nights being awakened by Claire's cry to be fed, to change an uncomfortable diaper, or because of a bad dream.

I loved to hop out of bed and lift her out of her crib, hold her against my shoulder, and comfort her. I loved that little face tucked into my neck. I would check to see what the problem was. If it was a diaper, I could fix that. If she had a bad dream, I loved that part: I would hug her and pat her back, walk her, and talk to her. If it was feeding time, I would take her to Martha and lay Claire down next to her mother.

Then came the call from Jerry Chinn. He had landed another inflatable billboard job—actually two—for the FIFA World Cup soccer match. It was being held in Los Angeles that year.

The sponsor was Mars Chocolate company. They wanted a giant inflatable SNICKERS candy bar next to a huge inflatable soccer ball with three-dimensional peanuts scattered over the whole billboard.

This job was a dream. I really liked starting a job from scratch. Stretching a large sheet of grid vellum on my drawing table was the most enjoyable part of my job. I loved to figure out the math and develop the patterns.

Actually, I enjoyed every aspect of making inflatables—even making a supply list and ordering the materials was fun.

The pay gave me the opportunity to focus on the project at hand and not fret about our finances.

The only part that stressed me was when the deadline approached. That made me shift into a higher gear. Completing a project was the ultimate highlight.

This job came off without a hitch. The sewing was done at the same awning shop as the moose head had been, but I needed to get my own facility.

I began to check out possible spaces in the area and found an ideal spot. The building was in a rural area just outside of Poulsbo—a fifteen-minute drive from our home. It had 2,500 square feet and high ceilings—high enough, anyway.

I showed the space to Martha.

"This will work great! You won't have to drive to Seattle and use someone else's business space."

I bought two sewing machines and built a long sewing table. The machines fit into two notches that I added to the table during construction. It was large enough to roll out lengths of fabric and do the cutting.

This facility was also big enough to set up a sculpture and woodworking area.

"I have something else I want to show you." I smiled at Martha in anticipation of her response.

We drove down a two-mile-long road that ended in a tiny town on the shore of Puget Sound. It had a long pier and a south-facing beach.

The town was called Indianola. It consisted of a general store and a clubhouse with a dance floor and stage. It also had a post office. There was a small population of houses that spread both directions along the shoreline and into the woods.

Martha was as surprised by the town as I was.

Martha checked an information board by the post office: "Lost cat, please call," "Will do house cleaning., "Band playing at the clubhouse this Saturday," and "House available for rent."

We called the phone number for the house.

"I am in the area. Can you meet me now?" said the voice.

We drove about three short blocks into the woods, and there stood a beautiful cabin amongst the trees. There was land around it and privacy.

The owner only lived in it while on vacation. She was from Washington, D.C. She had fallen in love with the house when she saw it—and with the community. She asked what I did for a living, and I gave her the short version.

"You're perfect!" she said. "This is an artists' community. It would be nice to keep it that way."

As it turned out, she was senior art editor for *Smithsonian Magazine*.

"If you want it, it's yours."

The answer was, "Oh, yeah!"

We signed a one-year lease.

We had lived in the Bainbridge Island A-frame for two years. It was nice, but the landlady was a tyrant. She was only there in the summers; there was a small locked apartment downstairs where she lived when she was there. The lease was a typical lease with typical responsibilities.

The landlady sent a letter stating that when she arrived, she expected us to have things in good shape, according to the lease. However, the letter ended with: oh, by the way, paint the fence and the kitchen walls, clean the roof, and do several other things that should be the owner's responsibilities. Then she ended with a statement equivalent to "Or else!"

THE VISION

We packed up and moved to our quaint little home in Indianola with our delightful daughter Shawn Claire. We called her Claire. She was a little over one year old.

Claire delighted me. I loved to see her change and grow, and she loved me.

She knew I loved her.

Every child is unique, and Claire carved out her niche early.

She never crawled. She never scurried around on hands and knees scooping up everything in her path that interested her.

Her interest was in standing up.

Claire would pull herself across the floor on her stomach, to anything vertical. Then she would climb it and walk around the room.

I know that is a stage that most children go through, but Claire skipped the crawling part.

Shortly after moving in, Martha said, "Guess what?"

"What?"

"I'm pregnant."

I had my one-man show at Eagle Eye Gallery. The opening didn't draw a lot of people like the art walks in Pioneer Square had, but during the following month, there was a lot of traffic. I sold two more large paintings.

Jerry called again with yet another inflatable job for AirTouch Cellular. This time, it was four billboards. The design was simple. I needed to make a forty-foot-long blimp for each ad. The hard part was to outline the letters on each blimp with rope light. I placed grommets outlining each letter and attached the lights with pull ties.

To start this project, I made a list of supplies. Seattle was so close that I decided to go to my suppliers and pick out what I needed.

The fabric for the job was different. There was a specific fabric that couldn't be substituted. It was vinyl-coated nylon. There were three vendors that I knew of. My favorite was in Los Angeles. You could call in an order and give them a Pantone color, and they would match it exactly. It usually took two weeks, but you could order a minimum of 100 yards. Most fabric companies demand a minimum of 1,000 yards to custom coat a fabric.

The other two fabric vendors had stock colors. They could overnight the fabric if you needed it for a project with a quick turnaround.

I finally had the facility I needed to do a whole inflatable by myself. Everything was set up and ready to go.

One of the first things I did was build an actual billboard in the shop. To attach an inflatable to it, I made brackets with hook Velcro under a three-inch lip. When I finished a blimp, I would sew loop Velcro around the edges. I attached the blimp to the brackets and inflated it in my shop to make sure I had patterned it right. I then painted it while it was inflated.

The work was long and tedious. When we finished the first one, Jerry and I took it to Los Angeles to install it. I had packed it so tight that it damaged some of the rope light. I had taken extra lights so I could replace the ones that didn't work. Having learned my lesson, I didn't have that problem packing the other three.

Because of the billboards, *Outdoor Magazine* contacted us. At first, they wanted us to buy an ad. We weren't prepared for extra costs at the time.

They were still intrigued by our inflatables. They asked if we wanted to do an article on the work we do. Martha did most of the talking and said she could write the article.

When she finished, she sent it in with photographs.

They loved it so much, they put a photo of the moose billboard on the cover. It was their feature article—about eight pages with the photos. These photos included the World Cup Soccer and AirTouch blimp billboards.

The article also described my history with Inflatables in San Diego, the process I used, and the benefits of using inflatables for outdoor advertising. Big Air Productions, Inc. became a well-known name in the inflatable industry.

I wanted to work on some ideas for inflatables—things that might be rentable. Having a family, I needed to create an income.

I decided on a "Kilroy Was Here" character. We could put it on top of a building with Kilroy's nose and fingers hanging over the side.

This was a fun inflatable and was rented out regularly.

A huge grocery store, Central Market, had just finished constructing their store at the same time I had finished Kilroy. I asked them if I could put it on top of their store for a photoshoot. They hadn't opened yet.

Once they saw it, they rented it on a regular basis for at least four years. Whenever I installed it, they said their sales doubled.

Kilroy dates back to the early 1940s. It was a popular graffiti drawn by soldiers in World War II.

James J. Kilroy started the phrase. He was an inspector at the shipyards during the construction of military vehicles. Workers were paid for what they accomplished. Sometimes, the workers would run an item through twice to get extra credit. Kilroy noticed this, so he would label the manufactured items with the phrase "Kilroy was here."

As the war progressed, the need for more arms and ships forced these war machines to be rushed to the war theater before Kilroy's label could be painted over or cleaned off.

Thus "Kilroy was here" kept showing up. It became an icon used by the troops as they advanced into enemy territory.

Rumor has it that an astronaut scrawled it in the dust on the moon. It has been found on the underside of the Arc de Triomphe, on the Statue of Liberty, and atop Mt. Everest.

During the Potsdam Conference at the end of World War II, Truman, Stalin, and Churchill were in attendance. There was an outhouse on the premises. Stalin was the first to use it. When he came out, his first remark was "Who is Kilroy?"

I also made a twenty-five-foot dinosaur. I regularly used this at schools. It looked like it was coming to life as I inflated it. Some kids ran away screaming in fright.

I gave tours of my business to groups—mostly grade school classes. The dinosaur was a great hit. As I ended the tour, I would stand under the inflatable as I finished my "Thank you for coming" and "Goodbye." I had an employee turn off the fan, and the dinosaur mouth would lower and wrap around me as it had just found lunch. I had to repeat this several times, so all the children would have the chance to be eaten by the dinosaur while parents and teachers snapped photos.

Martha's trip to Swedish Hospital to give birth began at one o'clock in the morning. After the ferries closed down for the evening, an emergency helicopter was used to take patients to a hospital in Seattle. We called 911, and we were told to drive to the football field at Bainbridge High School and wait for the chopper.

On the way to this meeting, we dropped Claire off at a friend's house.

The helicopter arrived shortly after we did. It was too small for me to go with Martha, and it was more important to make room for the EMTs. The local fire department invited me to stay at their station to wait for the morning ferry. They had a TV room, but I spent more time watching the clock.

Finally, at five in the morning, I drove to the ferry and boarded.

As I was trying to decide which of the hundreds of empty seats I would use to rest my tired butt, I saw a familiar face. It was Liz.

Liz played on our softball team, and she was a nurse at Swedish Hospital. She did this commute every workday. When she arrived in Seattle, she walked to the hospital—uphill and in the dark. Liz was really excited to hear that Martha had arrived at emergency and was being prepped for delivery.

I drove her to the hospital.

"I'll check-in and see you shortly," she said.

Within minutes of my arrival in Martha's room, Liz arrived with breakfast.

Jessie Paige was born on September 11, 1994.

As with Claire, I was invited to participate. I did what I could to comfort Martha. Watching Jessie's birth and cutting the cord was special to me. Liz immediately picked Jessie up and held her tenderly—giving Jessie a huge smile and loving words—then handed her to me. Another beautiful girl. I placed Jessie next to her mom, and she fumbled a little before latching on to Martha's breast to begin her first meal. Another nurse took Jessie and me to a different room, and I was instructed on how to bathe her.

Throughout my daughters' early years, we found another preschool for the girls in Indianola—owned by Mary Katherine Kolb. The school was well run and an excellent place to leave our daughters. Mary Katherine was a great teacher and understood children more than anyone I ever knew. Claire and Jessie met most of their dearest friends at this place, friends they continued to have through their later school years.

THE VISION

After living in our Indianola house for a year, I decided that we needed to prepare for future slow times. I had not been spending much time at Artform, and the commute was beginning to wear on me. Since I seemed to be on my way to providing an income from inflatables, I thanked Penny, gave her my resignation, and told her if she ever needed my help to let me know.

I built a loft apartment inside the shop. If we move out of the Indianola house and into the shop, we could drastically reduce our living costs.

I am pretty detail-oriented, so I bought some books and made stairs that rose to a split-level bedroom area. There were two rooms—one for the girls and one for Martha and me.

Next to the existing bathroom downstairs, I put in a double sink and a claw foot bathtub with a shower. We added a refrigerator, a microwave, and a hotplate. A plug-in skillet also proved useful.

I loved living like this. It reminded me of studios I had lived in previously. Martha was into it as well—at least she said she was. She was with me as we bought the building supplies. She found the sink and the bathtub.

There was a new addition to the office area. Martha's mother sent her a computer.

My business—Big Air Productions, Inc.—suddenly had jobs flooding in. There were no sales call; it was all word of mouth.

This required hiring people. I was unable to do it all myself.

Finding a good accountant was first on my agenda.

In 1995, The Becker Group took an interest in our inflatables. They made Christmas decorations for malls around the world.

They asked us if we could make an inflatable jingle bell out of gold fabric. One of the main designers from Becker came out from Baltimore to view it.

This resulted in Big Air fabricating Christmas ornaments, snowmen, and toys for malls around the world. We fabricated inflatables for malls in Dubai, London, Paris, Rio de Janeiro, and countless places in the United States. Within fifteen years, we fabricated at least 2,000 inflatables for Becker. The quality of these inflatables was beyond anything else found on the market.

As jobs began coming in, I hired friends on occasion, but they had their own jobs.

Finally, I advertised for a cutter and sewing machine operator. I ended up getting the two best employees I have ever had. They stayed with me for at least fifteen years.

One was a Japanese woman, Kukiko. She was a great cutter—fast and precise. If I needed help in other areas of the business, she was happy to help.

The other was Karen. Karen was a whiz at the sewing machine—also very fast, producing quality work.

The best thing about these talented women was that, if we were between jobs, they both were agreeable to taking time off.

Kukiko had a family—two sons and her Navy husband. She had financial security and had her own projects going on at home.

Karen had her own business and a husband, son, and daughter.

THE VISION

When a new job came in, I called those two immediately after I designed it. They enjoyed making inflatables.

When I moved to the Northwest, I continued hearing the name Dillon Works. When I did hear it, it was said with respect in relation to quality fabrication. Mike Dillon had started his business in his garage. As it developed, his company moved to an old closed motel. I still try to recall the memories of when I first saw his work and met him. It was shortly after my arrival in Seattle.

He asked me to do an inflatable of the body of a rocket that needed to fit perfectly with the fins he had fabricated. It fit perfectly. This job was for Sony Interactive Entertainment's PlayStation, and it led to future jobs for Big Air. The following year, Sony wanted Big Air to make five twenty-foot-high PlayStation characters for an interactive games convention in Los Angeles. They liked them so much they ordered five more.

Since I last saw my son Kevin, he had been more than busy.

After our initial visit, Kevin went on a Mormon mission. He was placed in an area encompassing part of Georgia and northern Florida.

When he returned, he enrolled at UW to finish his degree in structural engineering. My brother Don continued as his advisor.

Kevin struggled, but Don coached him through the difficult classes.

UW was well funded and had highly ranked colleges in most areas. A degree from UW is respected around the country. Wyoming has a lot of resources and few people. They made it a point to fund a quality faculty with the buildings and tools they needed. This was especially true in structural engineering.

I had some reservations about majoring in art when I attended UW, but I realized—especially after the fact—that I was well prepared when I went into the world.

Kevin could get a job anywhere with anybody.

He chose Seattle. He fell in love with the city when he visited, and—most valuable to me—it was important for him to develop a relationship with his biological father.

Kevin landed a job in Seattle at a structural engineering firm and quickly transferred to an even larger firm, Seattle Structural.

When he arrived in the Northwest on the first of February 1997, he moved in with us for three months. That gave him time to look for an apartment in Seattle and settle in.

It was fun having Kevin there. The girls loved him. He also helped me finish the painting on an inflatable I was making.

He was anxious to start playing music, so we regularly visited Rip and played in his basement. We played some oldies, but Kevin had written some original songs that he taught us.

By May, the softball league was starting, and Kevin joined the team.

Kim and I kept in contact, and I visited Laramie several times. Kim was always excited to see me.

She remarried. With her new husband, Dave, she came to the Seattle area to visit. I took them out for sushi. On our way to the restaurant, Kim told me that her husband liked steak. She didn't think Dave would like sushi. When I brought it up, Dave said it was fine.

THE VISION

After that, when I visited them in Laramie, we went out for sushi. They both loved one particular restaurant. It was unbelievably good for being in Wyoming.

Kim worked at the university and was also working on a degree.

When I arrived in Laramie, she introduced me to her boss and co-workers. She seemed proud to call me her dad. She had a beautiful smile on her face.

CHAPTER SIXTEEN

Martha thought it was important to enroll Claire and Jessie in preschool.

We started with the Island Cooperative Preschool on Bainbridge Island.

This was a co-op because the parents participated. When a child was one year old, he or she attended one day a week. (It wasn't a full day.) A parent of each child had to be there the whole time. Parents were given duties like snack mom, playroom supervisor, etc. When a child was two, he or she came twice a week, and parents alternated helping. This worked its way up to five-year-olds going five times a week. There was also a parent meeting at the first of each month to discuss what was going on with each child and to get lessons on raising children.

When the actual classes started, I usually took our girls to daycare and picked them up. I loved it.

We installed the computer that Martha's mother had given her, along with a printer, in the office. The screen was in black and white. The concept of using a computer was new to me. Martha immediately became obsessed. I think she used one when she worked at the trade center.

Martha started by doing invoices, bids, and correspondence with interested buyers. She would also answer the phone and make calls. The fax machine became a necessary and commonly used asset.

I walked into the office one day as Martha was focused on the computer and stood over her shoulder. She was smiling—sometimes laughing.

I couldn't understand anything on the screen. It looked like some alien language.

"What is that?" I asked.

"It's a programming language. I learned how it works!"

"So, what are you doing?"

"You can talk to people around the world. The first thing you do is program your own living area. I chose a studio. We play this game; it's like a scavenger hunt. You visit people at their homes and they can choose to invite you in. Or someone will visit you. Each person has a list of items to be found, and they are scattered throughout all the participants' abodes. You win if you find everything on your list."

"Wow! It sounds like fun, but complicated," I said.

"It's not that complicated," Martha said. "I figured it out, and, yes, it is fun. You don't just look for things; you sit in their living room and chat about life, politics—whatever comes to mind."

That sounded like something Martha would get into. She was really smart. She could read a book in one day. Her fingers were a blur on the keyboard, and she could make a living as a writer if she wanted to.

The girls and I rose early. I made breakfast and made sure they were fed and dressed. I took Claire to school and Jessie to preschool. Then I worked in the shop on the latest project as my employees filed in and continued their duties.

I loved getting up with the girls and seeing their smiley faces. Claire enjoyed school. Sometimes, I took her to the bus stop; sometimes, I drove her. Jessie stayed in the shop when she didn't have preschool. She liked to sit on the worktables and entertain the sewing machine operators, cutters, and other employees.

Jessie would do drawings on the tabletops with a sharpie. She was amazingly talented. At three years old, she sat on the lawn and braided three blades of grass together without being taught. It was a tight, perfect braid.

I could not stand being without a pen or pencil while at work, and I didn't want to run around trying to find one. Therefore, I bought hundreds of them and spread them throughout the shop.

One day, they all disappeared.

I asked my employees if they had a pencil I could use to figure out a particular problem I was working on. They looked around, scratched their heads, and were confused along with me.

We heard Jessie walking down the stairs. When we focused our gaze on her smiley face as she descended, we noticed she was holding high a huge mobile she had made out of pens, pencils, and string. It was all perfectly balanced.

As time went on, I began to realize that Martha seemed unhappy with our marriage. We seemed to be on a path of distancing ourselves—

THE VISION

falling into an abyss of discontent and resentment. Martha only wanted to be at the computer.

This was the usual slow time of the year for the business. It was the perfect time to get out of our normal routine. The family could be together, and Martha would be away from her computer. We could talk.

We packed up our Ford Windstar and headed for the coast. It was a nice feeling—like a family again. We had been to the Ocean Crest Resort three times; the first was because of my outhouse costume.

The Ocean Crest Resort was poised over a cliff above a beautiful wide beach. Long zigzag stairs connected the rooms to the sand.

It had a fabulous restaurant with huge windows allowing the beautiful ocean view to pour in. Dinner during sunset was the best.

The resort had a gym, a masseuse, and a swimming pool across the street.

It was a pleasant stay, and the girls enjoyed it. Martha and I spent a lot of time with them at the pool. We would get up early and walk on the beach while Claire and Jessie scoured the beach for shells and artifacts.

Martha and I had productive and fun conversations like before. Everything felt like it was back to normal.

It was late summer 1997, and the girls were excited about the school starting. On top of that, Big Air was hit with a massive order from Becker. We made 224 Christmas inflatables—very high quality, not like what you normally see on the market.

After ordering the supplies for the ornaments, I generated the patterns. I called Kukiko to come help. She showed up the next day ready to go. I called Karen, and she was there the next day as well. As the workload began to build, I hired more help—sewing machine operators, painters, and workers who had wood and metal experience. Most had worked at Big Air before and were excited to get the call. The season had begun.

Martha fell into the rhythm. During working hours, she did office work, answered the phones, and handled correspondence with Becker.

We actually put the girls to bed together. Most importantly, *we* went to bed together.

Late one night, the phone rang. It was on Martha's side of the bed, and she answered it.

"Paul, it's for you. It's your mom."

"Hello." It was strange that my mom was calling this late.

"Paul, Kay disappeared. She's been gone for three days."

Kay was my sister—one year older than me. Being so close in age, we didn't get along. I really tried.

Kay had been dealt the wrong cards in this life. In the late fifties, she developed a bad acne problem. Boys weren't attracted to her and didn't notice her.

I was just the opposite. I had good, olive-colored skin and tanned easily. It's not that I didn't have small eruptions; it's that they were few and not so noticeable. Even though girls were attracted to me, I really didn't know how to handle it. I stayed pretty much aloof.

THE VISION

Kay was overwhelmed with girls from her class showing an interest in me. They had, on occasion, asked if she could introduce us. She hated me for that.

After we graduated and moved apart, our relationship greatly improved. Kay moved to Las Vegas, married, and had three children.

It seemed like a wonderful marriage, but after several years, something happened, and they divorced.

Kay had graduated from college as a registered nurse and had a job at a correctional facility. She loved her job.

My brother Don had helped her buy a condo.

The devil soon descended on my sister. Kay developed a gambling problem. She had a good salary, plenty to pay the mortgage and raise her children. Instead, she used her money to take that risk of doubling or tripling it. Cashing in on occasion must have encouraged her. More often than not, she lost and couldn't pay her mortgage. She lost her condo.

It was early February 1998. Kay's daughter and two sons were in their early teens when my mom called me.

"What do you mean she's been gone for three days?"

"The last we saw her was when she drove to our house and asked Dad for five dollars for gas."

Kay's children and co-workers had raised the alarm. She was on all the news channels—disappeared without a trace. Was it foul play? The nurse who worked at the prison had disappeared and could not be found.

A week later, I received another call from Mom.

"Paul, they found Kay's car. It's on a road near the top of Mount Charleston."

Two days later, there was another call.

"They found Kay's body."

She was found at a bottom of a ravine. The police found two bottles of wine and an empty medicine bottle. She had done the deed at the top. When she lost consciousness, she apparently toppled over the edge.

I flew to Las Vegas for her funeral. What a waste. The pain her children felt must have been enormous.

My sister's taking of her own life caused a domino effect.

My dad passed away from a stroke three months after Kay died. He blamed himself for giving her the five dollars for gas. Her death affected him very deeply.

My mom and dad had always been together. As a result, Mom was lost and alone without him.

Mom died three months after my dad from heart failure.

Before Mom passed, I decided to take a trip to Laramie with my girls to visit my brother. Mom knew that I would be there. She hadn't had much of a chance to get to know my daughters, so she traveled to Laramie so we could all be together.

When I arrived at Don's house, I asked if Claire and Jessie could take a bath.

"Of course," said Don.

My mom lit up and asked if she could bathe them.

"Sure," I said.

That meant a lot to her. I overheard her talking to them through the bathroom door. She was telling them stories about me when I was young and telling them how lucky they were to have me as a father. All three came out of the bathroom with smiles on their faces.

We only stayed a few days.

The morning the girls and I left to make the drive back home, I noticed Mom in the kitchen preparing dinner for that evening. I gave her a big hug and told her I loved her. The girls and I loaded the car, climbed in, and headed home.

Mom died in her sleep that night. My brother had a message waiting for me when we arrived home.

CHAPTER SEVENTEEN

The inevitable finally occurred between Martha and me. Our marriage was over. The good news was that during the two years it took to resolve our divorce, my business grew by leaps and bounds.

I made two important additions to my life and business. One was a person to run the office, and the other was a nanny to make sure my girls were well taken care of when I was busy. The nanny was only needed until both girls were old enough to go to elementary school, and the office manager was only needed during busy times. Both were essential when it came to being able to function in a busy environment.

One of my softball team members had a job as an architect. He was working on designing the new flagship store for Nordstrom in downtown Seattle. They were looking for a spectacular event to kick off the opening celebration when it was finished.

At one of our softball games, I brought the inflatable eagle I had made when I first arrived in Seattle. The team was blown away. Ed asked me if I had a brochure or photos that he could take to work.

I received a call from Nordstrom eight months before the store opened. They were looking for an idea to promote the opening. They wanted to highlight their shoes.

I suggested a pair of legs hanging over the side of their roof as if someone was sitting on the building dangling their legs over the edge.

They loved the idea; in fact, they wanted three pairs of legs—a man's, a woman's, and a child's. They figured fifty-five feet in length would attract everyone's attention.

"Can you do that?"

"You bet I can!"

The opening was a grand success. We inflated the legs on cue with the national press waiting to film it. We flopped the legs over the side and inflated them all at once. It hit the front pages across the country.

They kept the legs up on the roof for the whole summer—June 1 to August 31. There was only one problem. After a rainstorm, the man's legs filled with water and tore.

We repaired them and had them back up in a couple of hours.

A year later, Nordstrom went public. We inflated the legs on the roof of the New York Stock Exchange.

The Bon Marché is two blocks from Nordstrom. Having seen the legs, they asked me if I would meet with them.

They had two items on their agenda.

The Bon wanted twenty-one Christmas elves to put on the side of their building. They needed them to look like they were climbing up the side.

They also asked if I could make inflatable floats on golf carts for the holiday parade.

I said I could—to both; they were asking the right man.

After seeing the legs fly from the Nordstrom building, they needed little convincing. I got both jobs.

The twenty-one elves were not inflatable. They were built with chicken wire on a flexible base. I ordered six five-gallon containers of "Plasti Dip", each a different color (This is a rubbery compound used to coat the handles of tools).

We mixed a flesh color (with different ethnic complexions), wrapped the bodies like mummies using a loosely woven material, and painted each body with "Plasti Dip". I then sculpted elf faces and cast them using the same material. We made red and green clothes and hats and then gave each elf a backpack with a wrapped gift sticking out the top.

Because the elves' substructure was flexible, the installers could change the body position to whatever they liked. Some simply hung from window sills; others were in the act of swinging a leg up, so they could stand on a sill; others were standing in windows. They were all scattered across the building like an army assaulting a castle.

This turned out to be yet another front-page news story in the Seattle paper. Some office workers freaked out when they walked into their offices and saw strange elfin characters staring back at them from outside their windows.

The inflatable holiday floats, each powered by an internal golf cart, became the beginning of a fifteen-year stint of fabricating floats

THE VISION

and being in charge of maintaining them. Finding drivers for the Seattle Holiday Parade was a yearly ordeal that took place on the day after Thanksgiving. Most of them were harvested from friends and the staff of my favorite haunt, Whiskey Creek. Big Air also sent maintenance people to Portland to train the workers of another company, SCI 3.2. They were in charge of the Macy's parade in their area.

I made approximately twenty-five floats for each city over those fifteen years. I also had an awesome maintenance crew that could solve any problem on the parade route, usually within a minute.

Before Big Air arrived on the scene, the floats had been made by a Texas company using tens of thousands of balloons tied across a chicken-wire frame. They were on golf carts.

The Bon had not been getting along with the company that made these floats. That was when they asked me if Big Air could make them. I told them we would give it a try. We took over without a problem.

As the years went by, all of these balloon floats were replaced by our inflatables.

Being involved in the parade was quite the occasion for my forty-five workers and volunteer drivers. I provided them with hotel rooms while they labored to prepare the floats at the Washington State Convention Center. At the end of each twelve-hour workday, they transformed themselves into party animals, but they always showed up the next day, raring to go and amazingly proficient with their duties.

Each person had his or her stories to tell. It was quite the adventure.

Oh! And I can't forget. Since we worked through Thanksgiving, the Bon—which later became Macy's—provided us with an excellent turkey dinner with all the fixings.

Back on the home front, a lot was happening. The year 2000 was upon us, and the worst of the divorce was behind me—almost anyway. Martha and I still did not get along well. For the girl's sake, I wish we had.

Claire was in third grade, and Jessie was in kindergarten at Suquamish Elementary School.

They were both into soccer and loving it.

I volunteered as an art docent at the school and continued to do so for many years—in my daughters' classes, as well as others. I love teaching art, and I had no qualms about teaching first graders how to mix colors, learn perspective, and other basics that children should learn along with the ABCs.

The rules for a docent required twenty minutes of teaching art history. The school had a small library of large art posters depicting work from the great artists—a good sampling anyway. That was a good thing. I had plenty to talk about with each artist I chose to present.

The school also sent each class on a field trip to my studio. I inflated my twenty-five-foot-long dinosaur at the end of the tour. The students loved it.

Word got around, and I gave tours to many of the elementary schools in Kitsap County, as well as to art schools and the Boy Scouts.

THE VISION

My landlord asked if I would rent more shops if he built them.

I said I would definitely rent them. I ended up with four shops on four acres; each was 2,500 square feet with a high ceiling.

One shop contained the office and the sewing department, as well as my upstairs apartment that I was still living in with the girls. Another shop was for woodworking and welding. The third shop was the painting shop where we painted the inflatables while they were inflated. I stored the Macy's parade floats in the fourth building. They paid me rent for housing them.

Big Air was doing well enough at the time that I was able to buy the best quality machines and tools I could find.

I saw a lot of Kevin. We played softball together, and he was part of the crew for the Macy's parade. The most exciting aspect of our relationship was that we started a band together. We did original work written and composed by Kevin. We played in Kitsap County and Seattle. After seven years, we cut two CDs. Kevin developed a relationship with Annie, our lead singer. They married and gave me four wonderful grandsons—Peter, Steven, Samuel, and James.

Kim was busy with school and her family. We didn't communicate much. I traveled to Laramie on occasion and always contacted her. She and her husband had become fans of a new sushi bar—in Wyoming no less—and it was fresh. I've eaten at many sushi bars, and this one was easily in the top five percent. My brother, his wife Leslie, and I would meet Kim and Dave at the restaurant. The sushi was amazing, and the conversation was light and fun.

Since the first day I saw the beautiful city of Seattle and Puget Sound, since breathing the fresh air with the salt and evergreen aromas, since experiencing the islands and gazing at two snow-capped mountain ranges, the thought entered my mind: "If I ever buy a house, I want to live in the forest. I want a lot of land and a view of the Olympic Mountains."

My company was doing well enough that I could finally look for a house. Immediately, an ideal opportunity opened up.

It wasn't the house so much as the property. The house was OK. It was built in 1952 and large enough that my daughters could each have their own room. There was work that initially needed to be done. The deck was not there. The previous owner tore it down because it was rotten. For safety's sake, the sliding door was screwed shut so people couldn't walk out and fall five feet to the ground. I had a new deck built.

The front porch was actually sagging and rotten. I had the porch rebuilt.

The repairs were capped off with a new roof.

That was the major work that needed to be done to make the place livable.

The barn was worse. It had no roof at all. It was a small barn and was filled with the remnants of chickens (hay, feathers, and poop) and a small stall for one or two cows.

Jessie was so excited about the barn that she ran into the old building and immediately fell through the floor. She was OK—whew!

I couldn't bear to tear the barn down—hence a new roof, new floor, and a huge deck with a protective overhang. I cleaned out the hay and unnecessary structures. Then I put up the wallboard and painted everything white.

Voilà! I had a magnificent painting studio.

One obvious requirement was to put track lights on the ceiling above the painting area. There couldn't be enough lighting. I also put two rows of track lights on the sidewalls. They were attached vertically on each side with independent switches and a dimmer.

Then I built two small studios as private painting areas for my daughters, and installing a wood stove was a necessity.

So, back to the property. The house was on five and a half acres with a gorgeous view of the Olympic Mountains—not a partial view—the whole blessed range with the Hood Canal in the foreground. The house was on a rise overlooking a horse ranch; I would never lose that view.

There was also a pond on the property with an island. It had an incoming stream and an outgoing stream that eventually emptied into the Hood Canal.

Over half of the property was a dense forest. I attached a wildlife easement that not only saved on property taxes but also provided an abundance of wildlife. Deer, bear, and many unusual species appeared on occasion. I saw a couple of lynx and a tiny fox popped into view once. They all emerged from the forest on occasion. The deer loved to dine on the apple trees. There was also a plum tree and a cherry tree, not to mention the blackberry bushes.

Oh, yeah. There were plenty of coyotes, and I saw a wolf once.

A snow owl made its presence known, too, looking for mice and filling the night with its hoots. During the day, woodpeckers knocked out their rhythm. I could go on.

The pond had its own visitors. There were plenty of ducks and a blue heron that made its usual yearly visit to her nest. Two river otters slept lazily on the island on two occasions.

Finally, I can't forget the domestic inhabitants—my dogs. I have had three Vizslas at different points in time. When the first one passed, she was replaced with a new pup. The dogs could run around the property without a leash but never lost sight of me. They wouldn't go outside without me, even though the door was often left open. They ran circles around me or would wait next to the open door with their heads tilted to one side.

"Come on, Dad. Let's go run around!"

I have never thought of myself as a businessman.

Painting and working in my studio have always been my loves, and I have made a lot of sacrifices to do that. We live in a society where the amount of money and the material items you amass in your life determine your success.

I have never thought of it that way. I would have been happy experiencing life and producing art, not as a tool to make money. Success to me is the internal growth and awareness you amass as you journey through life. That is what you carry with you after your death. Painting is meditation as well as expression. My work became a visual diary of my mind with the acknowledgment that I really didn't understand what I was expressing; however, it was real, and it did emerge as a baby born to this world. I will leave it to others to figure it out.

That's not true for many artists. It is common for artists to paint from photographs, maybe enhancing their work to be more interesting and attractive. These artists stay on the realistic plane of life and determine their success by how much they sell. After all, we all need to make a living, preferably doing something we love.

As far as fabricating inflatable sculpture, the one thing that dawned on me is that I have never made a sales call. Making inflatables was a path that life put me on—probably for a reason. I did love the challenge. It would not have been possible to make inflatables without the knowledge and growth I acquired during my manic obsession with my art for the previous thirty-five years.

Making an inflatable began by creating concept art, making a clay sculpture, forming it in fabric and compressed air, and then painting it—all on a massive scale. I was still honing my art. The fact that it became an external process and not an internal one was the only difference; however, one did create the other. Inflatables emerged from my ability and obsession with my personal internal art. I just took the path where it led me.

One morning while working on an inflatable project, I was interrupted by the telephone—a common occurrence that happened endlessly as I blundered through my shop. This was different. This was a phone call that became the beginning of a project I will always be proud of.

I ran into the office and answered the phone. I needed to run to get there in time.

"Big Air Productions," I said, slightly out of breath.

"Hello. Is this Paul?"

"Yes, it is. Can I help you?" I took a seat at the desk.

"I think you can. My name is Randy Buck. I'm a producer for Troika Entertainment. Are you familiar with the Broadway production of *Cats*?"

"Yes," I said. "I saw it live in London."

"Great. Do you think you can make the set as an inflatable?"

"Sure, I can!" My usual response to all inquiries.

"What is your best guess on how much it would cost?"

"I would need to see some photos or drawings of the set. It will be at least $20,000."

"I'll tell you what. I'm going to expedite our program and some photos for you. Call me when they arrive."

"I'll do that. Thanks."

Two days later, a large envelope was delivered. Opening it revealed an eight-and-a-half-by-eleven glossy brochure that is handed out to the audience at the beginning of performances. There were detailed photos but it mostly showed the performers. You could see sections of the set but not enough to show the scope of the project.

I picked up the phone and called Randy. He answered immediately.

"Hello. This is Randy."

THE VISION

"Hi, Randy. This is Paul from Big Air. I received the brochure."

"I know it doesn't show much of the set, but maybe it will give you a better idea. I don't have much more than that at the moment."

"It looks pretty detailed and complicated," I said, as I flipped back and forth through the program.

"It is. There are also a lot of lighting and strobes built into the wall. There must be at least forty cats' eyes that light up. What do you think? Price-wise, I mean."

I stalled a few seconds—long seconds.

"Well, I feel that the price I originally gave you was really low. We could be talking $50,000."

Randy paused with his response, then said, "So what are you doing this coming Friday?"

"Nothing important."

"I'll tell you what. I'll have a ticket to Boston waiting for you at the Seattle airport. It's an early flight. I'll book you a room in a hotel next to the theater and send you the details. When you arrive, check into your room and relax or see the sites. I'll meet you at the back door of the theater at eight o'clock."

"Great. I'll be there."

I hung up the phone in shock. Could this really be happening?

The flight to Boston was pleasant but long. It was early February 2002, and I was departing from the usual drizzle and temperate weather of Seattle. I had always wanted to visit Boston. There were so many interesting things I had heard about. It almost had the same lure as Seattle had.

Boston has a history—old architecture and monuments. To name all its virtues would take a while, with its support of the arts and the part it played in our rise as an independent nation. There are sure to be more attributes I had yet to discover.

During the flight, I continued to read my book of the moment, *Passage to Juneau* by Jonathan Raban. The thought of the possibilities from this job distracted me from reading. On occasion, I would fade off into my thoughts only to realize I had read two pages and hadn't absorbed any of it. Instead, I was wondering how I would make this inflatable set—how would it work? Then I returned to the last part of the book I remembered and began reading again. Usually, I napped on flights, but not this time.

I arrived in Boston to an "all-out" snowstorm. There were huge snowflakes and no wind. A cab driver was waiting for me with my name on a rectangle of white cardboard. He drove me directly to the Shubert Theatre. Next to the theatre was an old hotel.

I tipped the cabby; my ride was paid for. Retrieving my bag, I entered the hotel and was directed to my room.

Throwing my bag on my bed, I opened it and removed my winter coat, hat, and gloves. Walking around Boston intrigued me, and the weather reminded me of Wyoming—without the wind. I walked through parks and across huge bridges. There weren't many people out in this weather. I was probably the only crazy one.

At eight o'clock that evening, I knocked on the backstage door. When it opened, I asked to see Randy Buck. He was expecting me. In less than a minute, he was shaking my hand and inviting me in. The place was hectic with all the performers running around half-dressed, trying to prepare for their moment on stage. It was opening night. He introduced me to several people—mostly stagehands and managers and a few "cats" as well.

We meandered around backstage. Randy led me to the set and quickly showed me its construction and characteristics. He then opened the side curtain. The place was sold out; only one seat was empty, middle front. We walked down some steps, and he led me to my seat.

"When the musical is over, meet me back on stage. We can talk."

Anybody who has seen *Cats*—especially for the first time—is usually blown away. It is a very dynamic performance. The tour is so physically taxing that Troika has to recast most parts every year. The leaping and dancing are hard on the body after a year of continual performances, which are only broken up by travel from city to city.

I met Randy on stage after the show. As it turned out, not all parts could be inflatable. There was a huge tire that rose to heaven with cast members on it. There were doorways through large sewer pipes and an oven that the "cats" could crawl through to make a grand entrance.

The inflatable set needed to fit perfectly around the solid obstacles. Cats' eyes would be scattered throughout the set. An access panel would need to be made in the back of the wall so that each set of eyes could be easily installed. The lights would be attached with Velcro inside little chambers with its electrical wiring passing through the back. A framework had to be built to keep the walls firm and to support the wiring.

Randy shook my hand, thanked me for coming, and told me to go home and think about it. We could discuss the details later.

"By the way, on opening night, we have a party. You're invited. It is immediately after the show in the lounge inside your hotel."

My flight didn't leave for a couple of days.

"Relax, and see Boston," he said. 'Your room is taken care of."

The next day, the snow had stopped, and the chill that followed the snowstorm required that I bundle up. I was glad I had come prepared. I walked around Boston, had a couple of beers at the Cheers bar, and used the subway to explore. On my last night there, I had sushi then retired to my hotel room. It was an early flight home the next day.

The back-and-forth negotiations, discussions, and a trip to yet another opening night in a different city—Baltimore—followed.

"Can you do a prototype?" Randy asked.

"Yes, I can."

I took a section of the set and made an eight-foot-high and six-foot-wide inflatable wall in the technique I planned to use. I sent him photos as it progressed to see if he had any input.

Randy liked it.

"So, what are you doing this Friday?"

So, it was off to Baltimore. When the wall was deflated, it was amazingly small and fit easily into a carry bag the size of a suitcase. This time, I took my girls with me. Martha offered to watch the girls if she could accompany us. I agreed. Otherwise, I would need to leave them in the hotel while we tested the prototype.

When I arrived at the venue, I was told to go to the Lyric Theatre at the Modell Performing Arts Center. This was an immaculate theater. The solid set had already been installed.

I walked out to mid-stage, took the inflatable out of the bag, inflated it, and compared it to the real set. It was a very good likeness. They tried different lighting and were impressed. The sound of the fan wasn't that noticeable. We would use bigger fans, but the production was so loud that the audience wouldn't notice.

We watched the Baltimore opening performance that night and went to their party. Claire and Jessie were able to go backstage, see the performance, and attend the party. They both were given *Cats* brochures, and they ran around getting signatures from all the performers.

Randy wanted to make sure that I had the financing to finish the job. We finally agreed on $170,000.

"Oh, and by the way. If you complete the job on time, I will add another $10,000 as a bonus."

One final trip had to be made—to the Queen Elizabeth Theatre in Vancouver, British Columbia.

When the production reached Vancouver, a couple of hours north of Seattle, I drove up to watch them unload their five—or was it seven?—semi-trucks with fifty-four-foot trailers.

As the trucks were unloaded, the crew held each piece of the set in front of me to be photographed. Randy had also sent me immaculate technical drawings.

The solid set took a crew of fifty installers over a week to install. When I finished the inflatables set, it took a crew of four one day to install, and it fit in a mid-sized U-Haul truck.

When the inflatables were finished six months later, four of us from Big Air traveled to Biloxi, Mississippi, to help install them for their opening night. It was the beginning of that year's tour with a new cast and a new set. They also wanted us available to make any changes that were necessary. It was a great success!

Throughout the first year, Troika sent us to a few cities—including Ottawa, Canada—to go over the inflatables and make minor changes and check for damage.

After ten years of production, Randy called and said that *Cats*—the longest-running show in theater history at that time—had come to an end. The inflatable set had worked great and was still in excellent condition. It had made them millions. They could do one-night stands and fit it in theaters where the solid set couldn't go.

"Just to let you know," said Randy, "when I proposed the inflatable idea to Troika over ten years ago, they didn't like the idea. I searched the Internet for inflatable companies. When I found your site, I knew you could do it. I was so confident that it could be done that I used my own money. By the way, I'm now president of Troika Entertainment."

What a fabulous man!

I glow with pride when friends tell me I'm a good father. They are familiar with me and know what I went through while raising my daughters. They know nothing of my first marriage when I was forced to choose between being with my son and daughter and pursuing the life I was meant to live. I believe my marriage could have included both. I still defend my actions due to the situation. I definitely believe that we have been placed on this planet to find meaning and grow, to have goals, and to make use of our gifts. After all, that's what gifts are for. It's also important that children experience the dreams and accomplishments of their parents. Sadly, it was not to be in the case of my first marriage.

Wanting to be a good father is not the same as being a good father. I believe I have always *wanted* to be a good father; I just hope that it resulted in my *being* a good father.

Having grown up in Wyoming in a poor yet loving family was a good thing.

During my second marriage, I made the classic mistake of wanting my daughters to have everything that I never could.

It was not just a coincidence that my direction in art led to an inflatable business and a dramatic increase in my financial stability. It was meant to be. Things happen for a reason. It's human destiny.

Some things were basically the same whether we had money or not. At least once a week, we had dinner at the kitchen table. We took turns saying grace. Sometimes, on winter evenings when the sunset early and it was dark at dinnertime, I would light a candle and place it at the center of the table. The girls loved typical low-cost meals such as spaghetti or macaroni. Sometimes, it was meat with a baked potato and salad. They loved it when I made hamburgers.

Regardless of the food, the romantic soft candlelight at dinner made our conversations fun and intimate. Sometimes, we would order pizza and sit in front of the TV. Breakfasts were usually a bowl of cereal or French toast, and lunches were in the genre of grilled cheese or tuna-fish sandwiches. All meals were accompanied by juice or milk.

Red Robin was the restaurant they preferred, although we sometimes experimented when we went out.

Bedtime was special for both the girls and me. They were excited when I read to them. We would always go to Jessie's room, mainly because Jessie fell asleep in the middle of our reading sessions. I read the whole *Harry Potter* series to them. I tried to change my voice to match the characters, but they didn't like that so I just read. I was as enthralled with these stories as the girls were. When the movies came out, we made them a priority to attend.

I enjoyed rousing them from bed to prepare for school. They were both smiley-faced and animated, and they took care of things themselves—dressing and brushing their teeth. I would help with their hair.

Other than these normal things, I overextended when we went shopping for clothes. It was common to let them spend up to $300 each. They loved picking out shoes.

I took them on trips when I had time between jobs. Once we took a cruise up the inside passage to Juno, Alaska. We also visited Hawaii.

We had a scary incident in Kauai.

Having rented snorkeling gear, we found a common tourist spot with a small reef protecting an area of safe calm water. As we swam around, I noticed the water was quickly getting deeper. We were being swept into the ocean outside the reef. It was no use trying to swim back. The current was too strong. The girls were happily swimming around enjoying themselves. I immediately got their attention.

I pointed to some rocks that were perpendicular to the direction of the riptide and expressed the urgency. We swam to the rocks; it was our only option. It wasn't that deep when we arrived, and the bottom was sandy, but with the force of the waves hitting the rocks, I thought it best that we climb out and crawl across the rocks to safety. Jessie and I both had cuts from the coral. Claire came out intact but lost her mask. I looked around and couldn't find it.

It was a lucky thing that my girls were both excellent swimmers—thanks to their mom. She had insisted they take swimming lessons. I took them to their classes for several years. They were both naturals.

When cell phones appeared, it wasn't long before I bought Claire and Jessie one. If our family had acted as a whole unit that worked together, I would have probably waited. As it was, when they were with their mom, I worried. I wanted to be able to connect with them and to be there for them if they needed me. It came in handy on many an occasion.

Since I was an art docent for eight years, I became well acquainted with the teachers at Suquamish Elementary. I was assigned to my daughters' classes. I really wanted to be involved with their education.

There was homework every day, and I loved to help them when they would let me. Later on, they were learning the new math. I was lost. I'm good at math and can figure out the problems, but I have to do it my way. I'm still confused about why they changed it. It seems there are more people confused about math than before. That really showed with my employees. They were good workers and knew how to do their jobs, but they ran into a wall when it came to math. Kukiko was an exception. She went to school in Japan, and I could trust her to figure things out.

I always encouraged my daughters to participate in sports. I realized that I could not force this, but I could encourage it.

Before children are offered sports in junior high and high school, there are city leagues or organizations that offer a variety of team sports. They do not have the pressure of school sports and can be introduced as something that is just plain old fun. By the time the kids are in junior high, they should have an idea of whether they want to pursue sports or not. Sports really shouldn't be required, but it definitely builds character along with the ability to work as a team.

Music is another important thing for children to understand and experience. I loved taking the girls to their lessons. I purchased a piano, a flute, and guitars for the girls. I even bought a cello at one point—anything to help them experience music. Claire wanted voice lessons, and it turned out she was a natural.

So, yes, I tried my hardest to be a good father. I have to admit that sometimes, I tried a little too hard.

BILLBOARDS

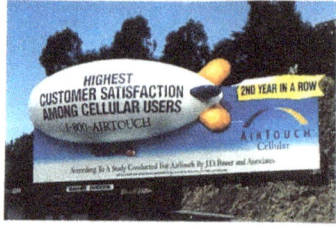

CHAPTER EIGHTEEN

Claire was an interesting child. I have delighted in this opportunity to grow close to this person who came into my life.

There was no question as to the direction Claire was going. She loved music, and she loved to sing. She was anxious to take her first piano lesson. Not knowing where to find a teacher, I finally found a notice of one posted on the wall of a music store. The teacher was in East Bremerton, about a half-hour drive.

This was an odd experience. Claire must have been around nine years old at the time. I stayed in my van during her first lesson and worked on a crossword puzzle.

At the end of her lesson, the teacher walked Claire out to meet me. She had a list of books that we needed to buy for her next lesson. She looked at me with an accusatory expression.

"I thought you said she has never had piano lessons."

"She hasn't," I said.

"She must have. I introduced her to the basics, and she played through it with no hesitation. She's done it before."

"No. This is her first time. We don't have a piano."

"Here is a list of books for her to get started. I'll see her next week." Walking away, she hesitated, looked back, and said, "She's played before." Then she disappeared back into her house.

"What's that all about?" I asked Claire.

"I don't know. She's weird."

At her next lesson, Claire took her new lesson books in with her. Ten minutes later, the teacher stomped out with Claire at her heels. She gave back the books and all the cash I had given her.

"I can't teach her," she said as if she were scolding me. "Look. Her first lesson is on page six." She flipped through the pages and pointed out several other sixes. "It's a sign of evil, and she plays like she's done it before. I can't teach her. This is a bad sign!"

She frantically ran back inside. Claire climbed into the passenger seat.

"What the heck? Is she for real?" I asked Claire.

"I don't know, Dad. She is really weird."

Fortunately, we were referred to a teacher that lived five minutes away from our house. Her name was Sherri Danielson. She was fabulous! Not only did she give Claire piano lessons but she also gave her vocal lessons.

"Claire is amazingly talented," Sherri said. "I will enjoy having her as a student."

She taught Claire until she graduated from high school.

THE VISION

The first piano teacher called me six months after Claire's lessons with her. She apologized, saying that she hadn't been taking her medications.

Claire took band lessons in sixth grade. Mr. Haag, the junior high school music teacher, taught a music class at the elementary level to give the students experience. He wanted the students to be more prepared when they were in junior high.

Claire chose the flute.

Mr. Haag had his students compete across the state. He had a quality, well-disciplined band and was asked to march in several parades, including one in Victoria, Canada. Every year, he took the band to Disneyland to march in parades and take classes.

Claire loved music and received a scholarship award presented by the Bremerton Youth Symphony. She could go to any summer music camp she wanted; she chose Jazz Camp West just south of San Francisco. It lasted eight days, and the teachers were the best you could find in the Bay Area. The camp was in the redwood trees of La Honda.

Claire enjoyed it so much that she went there every summer for three years. It was a vacation for me. I flew down with Claire and rented a car. We found a hotel in Half Moon Bay, and I drove her to the camp early the next morning. She had to be there at nine o'clock and was assigned to a cabin with other girls her age.

I returned to work at Big Air, only to hop on a plane again a week later to pick her up.

Sherri, Claire's private lessons teacher, had a recital twice a year for her students. She would find a decent-sized room—generally with a stage—and she packed the place with students, friends, and family.

Claire was a little shy and was a nervous wreck when it was her time to perform. Sherri saved her for last, and she blew everyone away with her voice.

Funny thing, I never heard Claire sing at home, so I was in awe every time I attended an event where she did sing. She was also the vocalist for the Kingston High Jazz Band.

Claire didn't stop there. She was chosen to be the drum major for the marching band. She was a natural leader.

In her junior year, the school put on a musical. Claire wanted to play in the pit, and she thoroughly enjoyed it. It also sparked her interest in trying out for a musical the following year, *Anything Goes* by Cole Porter.

"I really want to try out, Dad," she told me when she heard about it. "I don't care if it's a minor part. It will just be fun to be on stage."

She got one of the lead roles—Reno Sweeney—and she nailed it. The whole school was in shock when they watched her perform and sing. I was amazed, too. I had no idea she was that good. Sherri attended a performance and was delighted. Musical theater turned out to be Claire's major when she later attended UW.

As I stated before, I encouraged activities outside regular school time. Martha discouraged it, especially in sports.

"I don't want Claire to take any outside activities until she gets better grades!"

"Are you kidding me? She is getting good grades. She has to get good grades, or the school won't let her participate. If she has a problem with any class, they have time before and after school to get special help so they can continue their activities."

Claire lettered in three sports: soccer, basketball, and track. She was really good. Like me, she liked sports but her heart wasn't into it like music. She didn't have that aggressive "win at all costs" attitude.

I didn't expect her to excel in sports. Just being involved made her a well-rounded person, and she was in great shape.

Midway through Claire's junior year, Martha and I made arrangements for Claire to stay with me until she graduated from high school. It really helped her to be in a more stable and consistent environment. Continually going back and forth from her mom's house to mine seemed to frustrate her.

Claire's senior year was the year she was drum major for the band and had a lead role in *Anything Goes*. She was also the vocalist for the school's jazz band.

She was in love, too. She had a boyfriend. They were happy together.

Jessie began her experiment with out-of-school activities as Claire did. She was an amazingly talented person and excited about the world around her. By the time she reached junior high, Jessie took a starkly different path.

I signed Jessie up for music classes with Sherri when she was seven or eight years old. She started with the piano and performed—her first time on stage—at the recital halfway through the year. Jessie was over two years younger than Claire. She didn't really want to follow in her sister's footsteps, so she didn't.

After that first performance, Jessie wanted to learn bass guitar; she wasn't drawn to the piano.

I mentioned this to Sherri, and she brightened up.

"I teach bass guitar, too. That's great!"

Jessie and I took a trip to the music store and bought her a bass guitar. In the following recital six months later, Jessie went up on stage—solo—and played the theme song to *Pirates of the Caribbean*. She didn't miss a note.

Since Kevin and I were playing in a band together, we thought it would be fun to get together with the girls and make music.

We sounded awesome. Unfortunately, Claire had to be prodded to play with us, and Jessie lay on her back on my bed—bored—and played bass.

Kevin and I tried that twice before we gave up. The girls just weren't into it.

The biggest interest for Jessie was soccer. Her coaches loved her. Better yet, so did her teammates.

Jessie probably scored three-quarters of the goals. In one game, she scored four goals. Jessie's team won 4 to 0.

It wasn't that she was a ball hog; she was definitely a team player. She would pass to a teammate running towards the net. Her teammate would attempt to kick it into the goal. Jessie followed up on her pass, and when the girl's kick bounced off the goalie, Jessie was there to slam it into the net.

Once I saw her sprint to the net with two defenders blocking her. Jessie would kick it between them and—at a full sprint—pass them and kick the ball in the net before the defenders had a chance to turn around. She was a natural.

I also saw her kick a line drive into the net from midfield. She was a strong girl then and a fast runner.

I will never forget Jessie's huge, beautiful, mischievous smile. She was a delight. When she started seventh grade, everything changed. She tried out for the volleyball team with her friend Brooke. Halfway through the selection process, they put their heads together and decided that they didn't want to make the team, so they purposely sabotaged their chances. I told her not to do that, but she wouldn't listen. They both disliked the coach.

According to Jessie, the coach said the team members could not go to any other school events. They had to focus on volleyball and not be distracted.

That seemed pretty strict for seventh graders. I couldn't believe that would be true, but maybe it was.

Nevertheless, I lost Jessie at that point. She discovered pot and became rebellious at school. She skipped classes, and her grades showed it.

I don't know what influenced her, but she became involved in the Goth movement. Jessie wore black clothing and painted her face as if she wore a mask. Her sweet smile turned into an emotionless frown, and she would continually sneak off to attend all-night raves in Seattle.

It became impossible for her mom and me to work together. Martha was in complete denial about Jessie's drug use and behavior. She took Jessie's side, saying that I was accusing her of doing things that she wasn't doing.

I knew Jessie. I knew what was going on. Dropping her off and picking her up from school every day, I became acquainted with her friends and her teachers. Martha was at work in Seattle twelve hours a day. She didn't seem concerned about what Jessie did. That was part of her latchkey philosophy.

I felt helpless.

Late one evening, a night when Jessie was supposed to be with her mother, I received a phone call from an ambulance that was taking Jessie to Harrison Medical Center. She was out cold and unresponsive.

Jessie had been at a friend's house when she passed out. Her two friends called the ambulance. When the EMTs arrived, the girls said they had been drinking Four Loko. I called one of Jessie's friends who had been with her. She gave me the same story. There had been news accounts that described college parties where everyone passed out. There was speculation that they were poisoned or the punch bowl was laced with "something."

When I arrived at the emergency room, Jessie was awake. She had been on IVs to clear her system.

The doctor handed me a sheet of paper with recommendations that called for a drug abuse program.

"Your daughter needs to change her lifestyle."

"Did you test her for drugs?"

"No," the doctor responded. "We are normally urged to call the police in a situation like this. We are just telling you that she needs intervention."

The next day, I dropped Jessie off at her mom's house. I told her what had happened.

THE VISION

Months before Jessie took her ambulance trip, I had been concerned about her drug use and sneaking off to raves.

I made a point of not giving her the opportunity to go to a particular rave that she was looking forward to. She stopped complaining and relented. She asked if she could visit a friend instead. I agreed.

That turned out to be a mistake. Jessie talked her friend into sneaking off to the rave. Her friend's mother called me and told me they had taken off for Seattle. I continually called Jessie's cell phone but didn't see or hear from her for three days.

Her girlfriend returned home after one day. I found out from her mother that Jessie had left her cell phone at her girlfriend's house on purpose. I drove over and picked it up.

I called Martha to see if she had heard from Jessie. She hadn't. It is a horrible feeling having your daughter disappear. I couldn't sleep. I called the police and called her friends.

When Jessie finally showed up, she immediately apologized. She said she would never do that to me again. She realized how much it scared me and how concerned I was.

I didn't give her cell phone back. Not right away. After she pleaded with me for two weeks, I finally agreed to give it back *if* she would see a counselor for six months. She agreed.

Jessie was true to her word. She regularly saw her counselor once a week. This was supposed to be an honest interaction between the therapist and the patient. Parents did not have a right to know what was going on. I suppose there is a reason for that. Kids could be abused if the parent found out certain information. If the child understands this confidentiality principle, they just might be honest—not having any fear.

So, I needed to trust that the sessions would be constructive.

Back to Jessie's ride to the hospital in an ambulance. After I brought her home and delivered her to her mom, I called her counselor and told her what just happened. Her counselor was royally pissed.

"Jessie has been lying to me the whole time!" she angrily retorted. "I refuse to see her any more. She needs to go to Cascade Recovery."

This was an outpatient facility for teens that had behavior problems or were hooked on drugs.

I was surprised that Jessie's counselor responded the way she did. She just discarded Jessie. Why wouldn't she have Jessie come in once more and confront her? She could then recommend that she go to a drug treatment facility if she couldn't help her.

Armed with the letter from the emergency room and a referral from her therapist, I walked into the Cascade Recovery Center and talked to them.

"You do realize that Jessie needs to be arrested or willing to volunteer to be admitted to the program," the Cascade supervisor told me.

"I do know," I said. "How can I work this? Her therapist and Harrison Medical Center referred her here."

"Does she know that she is supposed to get help?"

"Yes."

"We'll just be honest. Bring her in, and we'll tell her that she was referred here. We'll ask her to sign the papers, and she will come in twice a week. One day, she will see a therapist, and the other day, she will be in a group. We will routinely test her for drugs."

This continued for about six months. All her drug tests were positive.

It was around this time that Jessie stopped going to school. As a result, she flunked all her classes.

I finally stepped in and enrolled Jessie in Spectrum Community School—a special school for students that could not deal with the routines and expectations of the school system.

That meant I was back to picking Jessie up to take her to school and dropping her off at her mother's house on days that she was supposed to be with her.

That didn't last long either. When I dropped Jessie off at Spectrum, she walked in the front door and out the back.

It was a futile battle. She officially dropped out of school. Her mom and I signed the papers that allowed this to happen.

Martha eventually got a job at a satellite phone company. This job consisted of her being sent to different parts of the country to test the reception for satellite phones. For instance, she was flown to Phoenix for two weeks. They rented her a car and booked a hotel, and she traveled around to see what the phone reception was like in surrounding areas.

She then had two weeks off. Martha loved doing this. She finally was able to travel around the country and get paid well, all expenses covered. She liked it so much that she volunteered to do it on her two weeks off. That meant that Jessie was back living with me full time.

Throughout the ordeals and expenses of Martha and my girls, I was inundated with fantastic inflatable jobs that I had never expected. I had many clients who proclaimed that I was the best inflatable fabricator they knew. I received many "one of a kind" quality jobs from excellent clients. These included Cirque du Soleil, Radio City Music Hall, and Sony Interactive Entertainment. There was one specific designer in San Francisco who saw me as a person who could pull off the impossible. That was Mitchell Mauk from Mauk Design, Inc.

I was doing well enough financially that I was able to buy my business property—four buildings on four acres. I remortgaged my house and paid off my shops in full.

Along with these jobs, I continued my seasonal work for Becker, averaging 100 inflatable ornaments and toys a year for malls around the world.

I also continued to fabricate floats for the Seattle and Portland MACY'S Parades. That included being in charge of finding the maintenance people and the drivers for the Seattle parade. We loaded trucks from my facility and delivered them to the Washington State Convention Center. Thanksgiving week was spent assembling the floats. We organized and drove them during the parade, then loaded them back in the trucks and delivered them to my shops for storage.

I first met Mitchell Mauk when I did a job for Sony Interactive Entertainment's PlayStation. I made inflatables of the main characters of the video games that were hitting the scene at the time. I did five characters, and Sony ordered two of each. This included Lara Croft, Spyro, and Crash Bandicoot.

THE VISION

That was a fun project, and they turned out great.

Over a year later, I received a call from Mitchell.

"I need your help," said Mitchell. "Can you make a sixty-foot-long Teflon molecule? It's due in two weeks."

"Do you have a photo?"

"Yes. I will send it to you now."

Seconds later, a digital photo was on my screen of a model of the molecule. It was all spheres and tubes.

"I can make that. It's a pretty short lead time."

"I need to figure something out," said Mitchell. "The design I did for a trade show in Las Vegas fell through. My client needs something."

"OK. I'm pretty sure I can do that. Can you send me the model?"

"Yes, I can. What do you think it will cost?"

"$20,000."

"OK. Go ahead and invoice me. I'll overnight the model."

When the model arrived overnight, I opened the box. The model had been made with Christmas ornaments. There were hundreds of tiny pieces in the box. The model had disintegrated.

I hopped in my truck and drove to a Michaels arts and crafts store. Amazingly, I found wooden spheres and dowels that were in the exact proportion as the sample.

I drilled holes in the spheres to fit the dowels and recreated the model. After painting it, I sent a photo to Mitchell.

"Looks great. Go for it."

This was an unusual job in that I didn't use a fabric-based material; I used clear vinyl. The tubes were navy blue, and the spheres were a light, more transparent blue. The inflatable was coming together beautifully.

I was put in contact with the installation company based in New York City. I sent them a technical drawing of how the molecule would be hung. It would hang from a truss that was sixty feet long. Each sphere had a D-ring at the top, and the length of the support cable varied depending on the place it occupied in space.

The installation crew was freaked out.

"We know this isn't going to work. If it doesn't, we're the ones who will look bad."

"It's going to work," I said.

They countered with, "You need to ship this to us so we can do a test inflation."

"Can't do," I said. "I have two weeks to make this. It will arrive in Las Vegas just in time for the installation."

When I arrived at the convention center, the truss was in place with the cables hanging from their assigned spots. I spread the inflatable out to make sure it wasn't twisted and attached all the cables.

THE VISION

The New York crew was standing around—arms folded—glaring at me. They thought I was going to single-handedly embarrass them and ruin their reputation.

Mitchell showed up, ready for the show.

"OK," I said. "When I yell go, raise the truss and turn the three blowers on at the same time."

I gave the "go" sign. The truss began to rise, and the air blew into each tube and then into each sphere. When it reached the designated height, the truss stopped, and there hung the most beautiful, awe-inspiring sight I have ever seen.

The jaws of everybody in the area dropped, followed by huge smiles. It was perfect. It looked better than I could have imagined.

The crew responded with handshakes and pats on the back. The most rewarding were the smiles—especially on Mitchell, who was running around taking photos.

After this show, the inflatable was moved to the Jacob K. Javits Convention Center in New York City. The same crew was there when I arrived to install it—my newfound friends. I was treated with handshakes and smiles.

This exhibit received a silver award from *Exhibitor Magazine* as the second-best exhibit in the nation that year.

Each job was an adventure. I was dealing with high-level clients and also dealing with the reality of being an employer.

For someone who never planned to be a businessman, I was flung into the middle of its complexities. When I first started making inflatables, I welcomed the challenges and viewed them as an adventure.

The good thing was that clients called me. I didn't have to make sales calls; they were already sold by the time I was contacted. This was because of my website and just plain old word of mouth.

My employees were excited about having a job that was creative and fun. Being able to see a project progress from a sketch to a finished product was rewarding. Everyone always gathered together to see the first inflation of each project.

As time moved on, I began realizing the weakness in my business. That was the fact that my capacity to produce was not able to match the amount of business I was getting.

I needed employees who could take over certain aspects of fabrication, as well as people who could work with my clients.

At the time, it all fell on my shoulders.

I usually tried not to inundate myself with too much business. Jobs seemed to space themselves out enough to make them manageable. But the more business I had, the harder it was to control the ensuing situations.

There was one job that was the epitome of what I am talking about.

The producers of *Mystère*—a Cirque du Soleil production in Vegas—called me and asked if I could make a forty-foot snail and replace an old one they were using. The one they had was literally falling apart.

THE VISION

The time and cost to maintain it made them realize that they might as well get a new one.

I sent them a formal proposal.

It was going on three weeks, and I hadn't heard back from Cirque.

I did get a call for that year's Sony PlayStation exhibit. These were intense shows. This would be my fourth year, and the exhibit would be designed and coordinated by Pinnacle Exhibits.

Many businesses were involved. There was a company that handled the lighting, another company handled the solid work, and Dillon fabricated the more specialty items. There were also the shippers and installers. Pinnacle Exhibits designed the exhibit, and Mauk Design designed the project I would be working on—a 1,500-pound afterburner.

Because of this, we had many conference calls with all of the vendors who were putting in their two bits and vying for importance. Everyone seemed to feel that their role in the exhibit was the most important and their concerns were to come first.

When the topic was on the giant inflatable afterburner, there were so many people making demands that I just sat back, feeling helpless.

I knew exactly how to fabricate this—what materials needed to be used and how it would work.

The lighting people were the first to insist that their part in the project was to be the most important.

"We need to install the lighting before the afterburner is inflated. It would take too much time to install it after inflation."

"How much weight are we talking about?" I asked.

"About 1,000 pounds."

"Can you figure out a way to make it lighter?"

"No. These are the lights we need to use."

Mitchell's input was, "We need to use clear vinyl fabric for the base."

"That will be risky. If there is no fabric base, it will be too weak to support the inflatable."

"We need to do it anyway. We need to figure out a way."

"OK, then. We need to lift the inflatable from the top. Attach it to a truss."

"No," responded the installers and the designers. "We don't want the appearance that it is being hung."

And so it went. There were a lot of assertions that weakened the chance of this working.

There were so many conference calls that nothing was finalized until three weeks before the due date.

I had already received the one-half down payment for the afterburner when my infamous telephone rang.

It was Cirque du Soleil.

"We have decided to go ahead with the snail project. Send us an invoice. You'll have the check in two days."

THE VISION

The snail—named Alice—was the job I favored. Sony was a great account and offered future work possibilities, and I also had a history with them, but I had to wrestle with their egos. They wanted to tell me how I should make an inflatable.

Cirque du Soleil, on the other hand, respected my experience and allowed me to take the bull by the horns and accomplish the mission.

Alice wasn't due until two weeks after the Sony project, so I took both jobs. I was cornered. I had already received payment to start working on the afterburner and Cirque du Soleil was depending on me to remake Alice.

If I could design and pattern the afterburner, I could put it in production and then do the clay sculpture for Alice.

We were on track to finish the afterburner when there was a prearranged visit from "The Team." There were two weeks to go until we were to install it in Los Angeles. The lighting people were not happy with the route we had taken to present their lights, even though it had been preapproved. They changed their minds.

We spent the whole next week ripping out the old areas that would accommodate the lights and remaking them to the lighting company's satisfaction.

That left us one week to finish the inflatable.

After a whole week of working long hours—with overtime and no sleep—we rolled up and crated the afterburner as the truck waited at our door. There was no time to do a test inflation

I arrived in Los Angeles late in the afternoon. The inflatable afterburner was spread out on the floor. It actually looked beautiful.

Everyone was ready to leave. The company had a suite reserved at a Dodgers baseball game with vast quantities of food and drink.

I was zoned out from lack of sleep, but it had progressed to the point that I was totally wired and couldn't sleep.

Chris from Pinnacle Exhibits asked if I was alright. He was also wondering how I thought the inflation would go.

All I could do was shrug my shoulders. I had no idea if it would work, but my gut instinct was that we had pushed it too far.

The next morning, I began mounting blowers and attaching the inflatable to the wide stairway, the grand entrance to the exhibit.

There were about twenty lighting people who were scurrying around.

"Wait a minute. We need to install all the lighting before you inflate it."

They were all frantically assembling lights and wires.

"Relax!" I told them. "I need to make sure it works. If it does, I will drop it back down."

When I turned the blowers on, my worst fears came true. When it started to rise, there was a loud pop, and it collapsed. The clear vinyl couldn't hold the weight.

I was distraught.

"OK, plan B. What can we do?" asked Chris.

"Well, I can go home and work on another big job deadline before it's too late."

He said that would be OK.

Actually, I did have a plan B: sew up the rip, sew in sleeves on top, and lift the inflatable in place using a truss. I would cut off the airflow to the base. By doing this, the air would seep into the base, and the pressure would be workable.

At the time, I didn't mention that. I was angry that I hadn't been stronger when I first dealt with the problems of the project. I let them talk me into doing something that I knew wouldn't work.

I was dead tired and flew back to Seattle. If I hadn't had the Cirque du Soleil job due in two weeks, I would have stayed. I still regret leaving it like that.

When I returned to my shops, the crew was waiting for me and ready to proceed. They were lost without me.

I had them do some prep work while I was gone. When the afterburner was in production, I finished the clay for Alice. We were ready to pattern the shape and proceed.

The timeline was extended, and two of my sewing machine operators and I flew to Las Vegas for a couple of days to go over details.

The project turned out beautifully. It was nice having control of the production.

As the years rolled on, I did many projects. I did several more projects for Radio City Music Hall and Cirque du Soleil, as well as rock tours in Europe.

In 2008, the economy went on the skids. It didn't affect me at first, but in the next few years, the Becker Group's owner retired and sold the business to Global Experience Specialists (GES). They decided not to pursue the Christmas side of the business.

Macy's also was having financial difficulties. They sent a person to Seattle to lay off all the events people. To continue the parade, they had to keep me, but they cut and slashed my compensation for doing the parade.

I put in my notice and stayed one more year to break in the Portland people I had trained. They could run the Seattle parade.

The number of companies making inflatables had grown rapidly since I began my venture into the field. By 2008, I had been doing it for twenty-six years. During that time, the design had become computerized, along with much of the production. The final straw was when these companies sold inflatables and had them fabricated in Taiwan, China, and India. People didn't care about quality anymore. They wanted them quick, cheap, and dirty.

I was getting fed up with employees who had at first respected my skill. As I became busier, I still made the clays and patterned the projects, but my employees began complaining and thought they knew more than I did. Egos ran rampant. I found myself in the office doing bids, developing concept art, invoicing, and dealing with clients over the phone. I missed the hands-on aspect of making inflatables.

I also became tired of dealing with difficult clients and just didn't need it anymore. I missed my old creative self. I wanted to work alone and make what I wanted to make.

I began designing and building inflatables in 1982. I helped two companies, who pioneered the industry, grow into thriving businesses before I started my own business in 1994. The work I was asked to do and the high-end clients I had went beyond what I had expected.

In 2014, after many challenges and adventures, I retired and sold my shops. Finally, I was able to get back to my painting. My barn made an excellent studio and I started showing my work again. I was *so* much happier.

CHAPTER NINETEEN

Panda is not a bear. Panda is a black and white Dutch rabbit.

When Jessie dropped out of school, she wanted to live with me. The first thing we did was sign her up for the General Education Development (GED) orientation.

The second thing we did was purchase a rabbit.

"Dad, can I get a rabbit?" she asked.

"Sure you can, if you take care of it."

I thought that would be a good idea. Maybe it would help her be more responsible. Maybe it would be a friend and a companion for her.

We drove to a feed store in Old Town Silverdale. It was rumored that they carried rabbits.

When we entered, we were directed to a back room. There were several cages and a good variety of rabbits. They were all different colors. One cage had three white rabbits huddled in the far corner; then there was a solid black one who looked at us and wiggled its nose; and on we went, down the line of cages. All of them just sat there and looked at us or ignored us.

THE VISION

Finally, we approached a cage with a young black and white bunny. It immediately hopped over to us and stuck its nose through the wire. Jessie held her finger up and touched the bunny's nose. It didn't recoil; it just sniffed. When Jessie moved her hand to a different area, it followed and again sniffed at her finger.

"I want this one!" Jessie said with a big smile on her face.

"Good pick!" I exclaimed.

I walked to the front and returned with an attendant.

"Oh, the Dutch rabbit," he said. "They make the best pets. She's a girl about six months old. She's had her shots."

He put her in a cardboard box and made air holes. We bought a large bag of straw and a bag of rabbit food. We also found a cage that was big enough for the rabbit to hop around in and a litter box.

As we drove away with the box on Jessie's lap, she looked at me.

"Her name is Panda."

Arriving home, Jessie searched through her cell phone to find instructions for taking care of her new pet. She loved Panda. She changed her straw and litter box regularly. She fed her and let her run around her room. She even took her outside on occasion. It looked like a good buy.

There were certain situations, such as when Jessie spent the night with a friend or visited her mom, which gave me the opportunity to take care of Panda. I actually loved it.

One thing I did was find a cardboard box and cut out a door. On the opposite side, I cut out a window, just big enough for her to get through.

Panda loved that box. When we took her out of her cage for any length of time, she would crawl in the box and stay a while. I think she needed the retreat and darkness. She felt safe.

Jessie took three orientation classes for her GED. Through testing, we found that her reading and writing were already at a high school graduate level. She needed to take math and a couple of other courses. I think it was science and history.

However, when it came time to take her GED classes, she decided she didn't want to take them.

I was really concerned. From the age of thirteen (when she sabotaged her chances to get on the volleyball team), she had quit everything she started.

I told her that many people make it a point to finish everything they start. It is also my belief that anyone can do what he or she wants in life if they have patience—especially if they continue to work toward their dream. I was hoping she would take the hint.

I realized that when I made a suggestion, she definitely wouldn't do it. It was frustrating for me. All I wanted to do was help her. It became clear that I had to back off and let her make her own decisions.

So, Jessie decided she was going to move to Houston, Texas with her boyfriend. They were going to live with his father until they got on their feet.

THE VISION

She was at least formulating a plan for her life.

She left Panda with me and moved to Houston.

Being a parent who had a child give up on taking care of her pet, you would think that my first thought would be, "Who wants a rabbit?"

Not me; I was enjoying Panda. I liked to spend time with her. It was like therapy.

Jessie didn't really give up on her pet; she just had other priorities. She asked if I would send Panda to Houston when she did eventually get settled. If I changed Panda's straw and litter box every day, she seemed much happier. I also let her out of her cage twice a day to run around.

Sometimes I lay on the floor and did my crossword. On several occasions, Panda hopped up to me, grabbed the corner of my crossword, took it to the other side of the room, and start flipping it around.

Panda was a hilarious rabbit. I couldn't help but laugh out loud when I saw her antics. She was amazingly entertaining.

It was common for her to run circles around me as fast as she could. She liked me to rub the top of her nose. I would slide my finger up to her head and scratch behind her ears. We would end our play periods with my picking her up; it was also a game to see if I could catch her. When I did, I cradled her in my arms—belly down with one front leg hanging over my forearm. When I put her down, she jumped out of my arms, or if she wanted more, she refused to jump down. Then I would hold her and pet her until she gets tired of it.

Jessie eventually came back home. I was excited to show her the things Panda and I did together. She almost seemed annoyed. I think it made Jessie feel bad that she hadn't been here for her.

The next day when I poked my head in her room, I noticed that Jessie hadn't changed Panda's straw and her litter box was piled high.

"Can I clean Panda's cage, Jessie?"

"Yes, go ahead."

I shut the door and let Panda run around while I cleaned her cage and litter box. After washing out her cage, I put her back in and fed her.

This happened often. I eventually just went into Jessie's room and took care of her on a regular basis.

Job hunting was a priority when Jessie returned. Unfortunately, she was discouraged after a week of letdowns. She didn't really try that hard. She would fill out an application and then not take it back to the establishment that had given it to her. When they told her she needed to apply online, she just blew them off. I couldn't say anything; I wanted to help but I didn't know what to do.

Jessie did accomplish one goal that took perseverance, a bit of stamina, and even rejection. I was really proud of her for that. She passed her written drivers' test after four tries. Then it was on to the actual driving test. She failed it twice but finally passed.

I pointed out to her that if she had that attitude toward everything she did in life, there would be nothing to stop her. She could do whatever she wants.

THE VISION

Finally, Jessie was ready to make another move. Her friend Skyler was moving to San Diego, and she wanted Jessie to go with her. I'm not sure how she got the money—maybe from her mom. Skyler had friends that they could stay with for a while.

A few days after arriving in San Diego, Jessie called me.

"Hey, Dad, I just got a hostess job at a Gaslamp steak house. It is really nice." She sent me photos from her iPhone. "It's on Fifth Avenue. Didn't you live here?"

She gave me the address.

"Yes! My ballroom studio was four blocks north of there, above San Diego Hardware."

I was really happy for her. She had actually landed her first job—by herself. She really liked her job. They had her come in often that first week. The second week, she didn't work a lot. I then received a text that she was laid off. When I asked why, she said that she didn't have a happy voice when she answered the phone.

That confused me. Why wouldn't they sit her down and talk to her? Maybe help her practice a happy voice? Maybe they did, and maybe Jessie couldn't do it. I really don't know. Her explanation didn't seem complete. I didn't press her.

After a couple of weeks at her friend's house, there was some trouble—enough to make it uncomfortable. I guess one of the girls they were with broke up with her boyfriend. I think he was renting the house.

"Hey, Dad," came the text. "Can I come home and live with you?"

"Yes, you can, hon."

I picked her up at the airport the next day. Jessie had her own money to buy a plane ticket.

When Jessie first left for San Diego, I felt sorry for Panda, but I was happy to have my time with her again.

I decided that I would turn Jessie's room into Panda's own little apartment. I put her cage on the floor and left the cage door open. She could run around and use her cage to go potty and munch on her straw. I put her food bowl just outside the cage door.

Panda had a regular routine of retiring to her cardboard box at the same time each day to take a nap. She would crawl in at noon and come out around two o'clock.

When I first let Panda run around the room, she ran under Jessie's chest of drawers. It was a task to get her out. I put a board along the long side and surrounded it with pillows. On the end, I stuffed pillows under the edge between the feet of the chest so that she couldn't have access.

After a while, I realized that it wasn't necessary to keep her from hiding. The room was her safe haven in the only secure home she had ever had.

One day, I was cleaning out her cage and spaced out. I left the door open. Looking around, I didn't see her anywhere.

"Oops," I thought.

I stood up and walked into the living room. There was Panda sitting smack dab in the middle of the living room.

"Oh, man. Now I have to catch you."

She looked at me for about five seconds and then darted between my legs and back into her room.

One touching moment I had with Panda had to do with blocking her access to the area under Jessie's chest of drawers.

It made me understand the importance of having an escape hole. It was definitely important to her.

When I walked into her room one afternoon, I was in for a little surprise. She was sitting next to the dresser. She glanced over at the dresser and back to me. One of the pillows had been removed. She had dragged it across the floor to the corner. There was a hole big enough to scamper through.

Panda made as if to run to her hole but stopped short. She then ran back to the spot where she was originally and looked at me. Then she did it again: ran to the hole and ran back. She looked at me as if to say, "Look what I did!"

"Looks like you've been busy," I said as if she were a human. "I think we should put the pillow back."

I walked over to the corner, picked up the pillow, and stuffed it back in the hole.

Panda looked frantic. She ran to the pillow and started tugging at it with her teeth, then started clawing at it as if she were digging a hole. She ran back to her spot and glared at me, then ran back to the pillow, and again tried to grab it with her teeth to pull it away.

"OK, Panda. You win," I said, as I reached down, pulled the pillow back out, and tossed it in the corner. And there it stayed.

She hopped over to the entrance and sniffed around the edges to make sure everything was OK.

She never went under the chest of drawers when I was with her. That was for emergencies.

Pet rabbit owners are more than likely familiar with the bunny flop. Rabbits only do it if they are comfortable being around you. It puts them in a vulnerable position.

Rabbits are bottom-heavy, and when they want to stretch out and relax, they flip over on their side. In that process, they look really uncoordinated and seem to be having a spaz attack. They flail about, kicking their feet and twisting their head. I really did think she was having a seizure when I first saw it. She ended up in the most beautiful sphinx-like position. Her back legs both to one side and her head had a bit of a "look how beautiful I am" essence to it. She looked completely relaxed.

I felt honored when I would lie on my side with my crossword or book and she would hop up, tickle my face with her whiskers, and bunny flop right next to me. Yes, I fell in love with this adorable creature. It wasn't easy to gain her trust.

Rabbits are completely different from dogs and cats; I've had both.

Now that Panda had her freedom, it became a wonderful feeling to join her in what I called "my therapy session."

I was delighted at feeding time when she saw me open her food bag. She came running over and did figure eights around my ankles. I totally spoiled her. When I put her bowl of food on the floor, she poked around until she found her favorite treats, then take them aside and relish their taste.

THE VISION

Panda only used her escape hole once.

When Jessie returned from San Diego, she opened her window to air her room out. The bottom of the window was only six inches from the floor.

Jessie left to do other things around the house, and when she returned, Panda was gone.

Jessie came to my room and frantically told me that she couldn't find Panda.

"I left the window open, and she jumped out while I was gone. Will you help me look for her?"

"Sure, I will."

We went outside and called her name, looking for places she might have gone. She was nowhere in sight.

"Just a minute, Jess. I'll be right back."

I went back into her room, pulled the pillows away from the dresser, slid the board back, and gently said, "Panda, are you in there?"

She hopped out.

When we made eye contact, I felt this message, "I'm OK, Dad," and she hopped back in. I replaced the board and pillows.

I yelled out the window, "She's OK, Jessie. Panda's in here."

Her room was her safe place. Having the window open was a threat.

Jessie stayed with me for a month or so after returning from San Diego.

After recovering from her San Diego trip, she began spending a lot more time in Seattle. She said she was seeing more of her mom as well.

She would spend time with me, but she didn't make attempts to find work.

After not hearing much from her for a few weeks, she called me with some exciting news. She got a job in Seattle and rented her first apartment in Belltown.

"And guess what, Dad? I got my own cell phone and service with AT&T. You don't have to pay my way anymore."

I was really excited for her.

"Can I come over and take you out for sushi?" I asked.

"I would love to. This Friday at six?"

"It's a date."

On Friday, I took the ferry to Seattle and walked up First Avenue. Jessie walked down First Avenue, and we met at a fantastic sushi bar that neither of us had been to.

We had to wait for twenty minutes for a place at the bar. It was *so* good, I would have waited an hour.

When we seated ourselves at the bar and placed our order, I asked the question, "You haven't told me about your job. What are you doing?"

THE VISION

"I'm camming."

"So, explain that to me. What is camming?"

"Well, Dad, I sit in front of the computer's camera and do things. I don't have to do anything I don't want to do. I work for a company that accepts credit cards, and my real name and location are kept private."

This really didn't surprise me since her job in Houston was at an exotic dancing club. This seemed safer, but I didn't agree with her following this line of work.

Jessie continued, "I can make as much money as I want. I have a beautiful studio apartment with a slight view of Puget Sound. The rent is $2,000 a month."

The subject changed, and we talked of other things. I was interested in seeing her apartment, but I wanted her to invite me. She didn't.

After dinner, we parted. I hugged her and told her I loved her.

I didn't hear much from Jessie in the next month. I thought about her often. I worried, but at least she was taking the world by the horns and tasting the realities of life. I still knew her as an intelligent, creative person. This could be a stepping-stone to a better life—a learning experience.

It was at this point that things went horribly wrong.

I received a phone call from Jessie.

"Dad? Are you OK? Is everything all right?"

"Things are great, honey. What's up?"

"I was just worried about you."

"Are you OK?" I asked. "You sound worried."

"Yeah, I'm OK. I love you."

"I love you, too, Jessie."

A week passed. Her mom received a similar phone call. I tried to text Jessie a couple of times that week. I called, and there was no answer.

Jessie finally called, and the first words out of her mouth were, "Dad, I made a big mistake."

"What's up, honey?"

"I'm afraid. I did something really stupid."

"Where are you?"

"I'm in Kennewick."

"Where is Kennewick?'

By this time, I had turned on the computer and typed in Kennewick. I put my shoes on and pulled out a Washington state atlas.

It was four in the afternoon, Thursday, January 8.

"It's in southeastern Washington by the Oregon border."

"Why are you in Kennewick, honey?"

THE VISION

"I don't know. I threw my phone away and bought a bus ticket to Denver. When I got here, I decided to get off the bus and go back home. I took a couple of buses, and they all ended up back here."

"I'm really confused," she said. "I got a room at the Red Lion."

"Dad, everyone is looking at me."

"Jessie, give me the address." She did.

"What's the phone number?" She gave me the number. "And your room number?"

By this time, I was in my Dodge Ram heading for the Bainbridge ferry.

"Are you there alone?"

"I don't know. I think so."

"Does anyone else know you're there?"

"I think so. I'm scared, Dad. I think someone is going to hurt me."

"Who's going to hurt you?"

"I don't know."

"Jessie, you need to call the police."

"Will you call them for me, Dad?"

"Yes, I will. Stay there and just relax. I'll call the police, and then I'll call you right back."

The first thing that crossed my mind was the large number of young women who disappear in the Seattle area and are never heard from again.

I called the Kennewick police and explained the situation to them. They dispatched a car to Jessie's location.

My phone rang. It was the officer who was checking on Jessie.

"Mr. Polson?"

"Yes."

"I'm with your daughter now. She seems safe. It's a really nice room. She seems disoriented and confused. I'm not sure what I can do at this point."

"I'm on my way there now," I said. "It will take few hours. Will you tell her to please stay there until I arrive?"

The police officer left, and I called Jessie.

"Jessie, I am on my way, but it will take a while."

"Dad, I'm going to die tonight."

"What do you mean you're going to die tonight?"

"I don't know. I just know I'm going to die tonight."

"Is someone else going to hurt you?"

"I think so."

"Jessie, I will be right there. Just wait for me."

THE VISION

I called the police back, and they connected me to the same officer. I explained to the officer what Jessie had just said.

He told me that he was sitting outside the hotel, keeping an eye on it.

"She didn't want me to leave. She is really scared and confused. She's not making much sense," he said.

"Is there any way you can take her back to the station until I arrive?"

"I can't do that. What I can do is take her to the crisis center. It's a brand-new facility and opens all night."

"That would be great. Please do that."

"OK. I'll call you when she's admitted."

I called Jessie and told her what was going to happen.

"OK, Dad."

I received the call that she was safely admitted to the crisis center. You wouldn't believe how relieved I was. I relaxed and drove the speed limit. Driving over the Cascade mountain range was a bit difficult. It was mid-January, and there was a snowstorm with high winds.

I kept referring to the Washington atlas to make sure I was prepared for exits that I had to take. It seemed to take forever. It took six hours.

At least, Jessie was safe.

When I arrived at the crisis center, they showed me her room. It had a large window where she could be observed. The door was locked. Jessie was lying in a bed with a cover over her. She opened her eyes and had a relieved look on her face.

"Please follow me," the nurse said, as she led me to a room across the hall.

Before I followed her, I raised a finger and smiled at Jessie. She understood that I would be right back. She lay back down and pulled the blanket over herself.

The nurse said that Jessie had signed a paper saying that the hospital had permission to talk to me about her condition.

"Your daughter is extremely disoriented and paranoid. She says she keeps seeing a blue light that is telling her what to do. I think she needs to be hospitalized, but we can't do that. There was no crime committed, and no one has been hurt. All we can do is recommend that she see someone when she returns to Seattle."

When Jessie and I left the hospital, she looked at me and said, "Dad, I realized how important family is. You can always trust your family."

"Shall we find a hotel for tonight, or do you want to go home now?" I asked.

"Can we please go home?"

"Yes, we can." I was wired and still in a shocked state. I wouldn't be able to sleep anyway. Jessie was in the same condition.

As we drove home, we had conversations that were unusual, only because we had never really talked much since she was a young teenager. She always stuck her earphones in her ears and listened to music. She didn't want to talk. Jessie explained what had happened.

Jessie felt really good about starting her own business—finding a fabulous apartment and being self-sufficient.

THE VISION

She had spent years going to raves and wandering around Seattle. She saw the business people, the workers in restaurants, and the delivery people. She also saw the bums, the drunks, and the down-and-outers who just hung out on the streets.

Jessie appreciated what she had. She thought it would be a caring move to talk and hang out with people on the lower rungs of life. She was making the statement that she had not been corrupted by success.

Anyway, this one particular group of young men who regularly hung out downtown shared drinks and smoked pot with Jessie, and who knows what else they shared or if the alcohol or pot was laced.

At one point, one of these guys asked to see Jessie's cell phone. She handed it to him. He took out his cell phone and after fiddling with both phones, he gave Jessie's back.

He showed her his phone, and somehow, he transferred all of her information onto his phone.

Can that be done?

Regardless, I'm sure Jessie worried about that. As a result, she finally called her mom and me to see if we were okay. This bothered her so much that she threw her phone away. A blue light told her to do that, and it also told her to get on a bus to Denver.

We arrived in Seattle at about three-thirty in the morning. The ferries hadn't started their routes yet. We were going to have a two-hour wait, so I pulled up to a ticket booth and reclined my seat. Jessie tried to sleep, and I tried to sleep, too. Forget it. We were both too wired.

I decided to drive around Puget Sound to Poulsbo. Backing out of the ticket area, we drove south, across the Narrows Bridge, and arrived at home just before five o'clock. We both retired to our rooms, but we still couldn't sleep. When the sun rose, we decided to go out for breakfast.

"Dad, I want to go back to my apartment," Jessie said. "I'm afraid I might run into those guys, but I think I need to go home."

"Why don't you stay with me one more night? I just updated my service and have a new phone. You can have my old one. We can go to the AT&T store and have them erase my info."

"I really want to go to my apartment, Dad."

After breakfast, we went home for a while. Jessie put my old cell in her backpack, and I drove her to the Bainbridge ferry. She said she would go to an AT&T store and see if she could change it over to her account.

We arrived just as the ferry was ready to leave. Jessie jumped out and ran to the ferry. She made it just in time, but she forgot her backpack with the cell and her ID still inside.

Jessie called me from Seattle. She had borrowed someone's phone.

"I left my backpack, Dad."

"I know, hon. I'll take the ferry over and meet you at the depot."

"No, that's okay. I'll call Mom."

Jessie seemed to disappear after that call. I called her mom, and she drove to the apartment. Jessie wasn't there.

So, more freaking out and worrying. The key to her apartment was in the backpack as well.

I finally received a call from Jessie late that afternoon.

"Dad, I'm at the Poulsbo bus stop. Will you come pick me up?"

Early that evening—a January evening that at that time of day is already dark—I entered Jessie's room and immediately cleaned Panda's cage and emptied her litter box. I then walked over to her bag of food to feed her. Panda—as usual—ran to my feet and began doing figure eights around my ankles.

This time, she stopped abruptly and faced Jessie. Panda just stood there. I knew exactly what they were both thinking. For days, I had inundated Jessie with tales of my time with Panda. I thought she would be interested. Jessie had been silent.

I realized how foolish I was for doing that. Jessie was beginning to resent Panda. Panda picked up on the danger. They stared at each other. I placed the food bowl in front of Panda. She began eating.

"Hey, Jessie. I think I should put Panda in her cage and lock it for the night."

"OK," Jessie responded.

Panda had other ideas. Normally, Panda would play the "catch me" game. If she saw that she was winning, she would hop up to me and let me pick her up. Not this time. Panda was determined that she would not be caught.

My plans were not just to lock her in her cage; I was planning to take the cage and her to my room.

At first, I thought that having a pet at this point could be healing and comforting for Jessie. Something told me that wasn't the case.

Panda had not been locked in her cage for a long time. It didn't really matter. Panda planned to stay free.

I looked at Jessie and asked if it was okay to just leave Panda alone and let her run around. She said that would be fine.

Earlier that afternoon, Jessie and I had talked about our plans for the next day. Kukiko needed to pick up her sewing machine from a repair shop in Renton (just south of downtown Seattle). I told her I would take her.

Jessie could ride in with us, and after picking up Kukiko's machine, we could activate her phone and drop her off at her studio apartment.

When I first received Jessie's call for help, I was building stretcher bars for my paintings. The stretchers were already made; I just needed to rasp the inside edge so it wouldn't make a line on the painting.

I returned to rasping the stretchers. I actually enjoy making good stretcher bars. They need to be perfectly square and strong—well braced. It's like meditating.

As I was finishing my work, I heard a loud thump from Jessie's room. My first thought was to poke my head in her door, but I just had to finish this last side of the stretcher bars.

A few minutes later, I heard another loud thump. When I was finished, Jessie slowly walked into my room. Her forearms were pressed together in front of her, and her fists were clenched as if she were cold. Her fists were pressed against her mouth.

She pulled her fists away from her mouth and quietly said, "Dad, Panda died."

I just stood there stunned. I couldn't believe what I just heard.

"What?" I said.

"Panda died. I accidentally stepped on her."

"Where is she?"

"She's in my room."

I walked into Jessie's room but didn't see Panda.

"Where is she?" I repeated.

Jessie's fists were still pressed to her mouth.

"She's there. I put her in the backpack."

In the middle of the room was a small pink backpack that Jessie had used in kindergarten. It had a picture of a panda bear on it with the word "Panda" written above it.

I knelt down in front of it and unzipped the zipper. I reached in and pulled Panda out. She was heavy and warm. I had to reach under her with my other hand to lift her.

"After I stepped on her, she was still alive," Jessie said. "I stepped on her again—harder. I didn't want to see her suffer."

"Dad," she said, "I saw her spirit leave her body."

Panda was so beautiful! She was lifeless like a stuffed animal. I had to touch an eye. She didn't really look dead, but she was.

I placed her back in the backpack, walked out, and found a plastic bag. I put the backpack in the bag and tied it. I went outside and put her in the trash.

That might sound cruel, but I just needed to put her out of sight so I would never see her again. I couldn't cry. I was stunned to silence.

That little life was gone. The body meant nothing without Panda in it. I actually wished that if I died, someone would put me in a plastic bag and drop me in the trash. The body is just a remnant of what it once was.

I walked back into the house where Jessie was still standing, not knowing what to do.

"We need to clear everything out that belongs to Panda—the cage, her food, straw, everything. We need to do it now. I don't want to be reminded of her."

I wanted to erase the presence she once had in our home. I began carrying things to the trash or to the rafters inside the garage, pushed back so I couldn't see it. Jessie refused to help.

"Dad, I'm afraid you might hit me."

"Jessie, I won't hit you. I have never hit you, and I never will."

It was an odd night. It was surreal.

I went into my room and collapsed on my chair. Jessie followed me. She climbed up on my worktable and sat cross-legged. We talked late into the night. She told me more detail about the guys she met on the street—the guys who offered her alcohol and pot.

She talked about the strange blue light that was telling her what to do.

"Dad, before I called you, when I got off the bus in Kennewick, I was frightened. I didn't know what to do. A nice lady helped me find a hotel room. When she left, I was even more scared. I didn't like the room. It was dark and depressing."

Jessie said she went back outside and got back on a bus that she thought was going to Seattle. The bus just returned to the same spot. It just went around in a circle connecting the Tri-Cities of Kennewick, Pasco, and Richland.

"I tried a second bus. It did the same thing. This time, I noticed a Red Lion hotel. When I stepped off the bus, I walked to the Red Lion and checked into a really nice room. I thought, 'Now, this is the kind of room my dad would stay in.'

"I walked into the bathroom, filled the tub with hot water, and climbed in. I was going to kill myself. The blue light told me to kill myself.

"Then a thought entered my mind. I could kill myself, or I could call my dad.

"I decided to call my dad."

CHAPTER TWENTY

The morning after Panda died, Jessie and I climbed in my Dodge Ram and drove to Kukiko's house. I had promised to take Kukiko to Seattle to pick up a sewing machine she was having repaired.

It dawned on me that neither Jessie nor I had slept for three days. I still couldn't sleep. I was wide awake.

We picked up Kukiko and drove to the Bainbridge ferry.

There are a few options when you take a ferry to Seattle. For walk-ons and car passengers, it is free. Traveling from Seattle to any other destination costs money.

If your destination is downtown Seattle, it is better to walk onto the ferry. Seattle is relatively small in area compared to other cities. From the ferry, you can walk almost anywhere. If it is a little farther from the downtown area, there is always mass transit.

If you drive onto the ferry, they charge for the vehicle. From that point, you can leave your car and walk up to the main floor of the ferry where there is an abundance of seating. A food vendor provides snacks, meals, and coffee, as well as Northwest ales and wine.

You can go on the top deck where you can feel the wind on your face and look at the awesome scenery of Puget Sound—the city skyline, the mountains, and the many ships that use this scenic waterway and port.

If you have made many trips, you might just want to recline in your car seat and relax for the thirty-five minutes it takes from Bainbridge to dock in Seattle.

This particular day was one on which I was just happy to recline in my seat and try to relax. That was fine with Kukiko. Jessie was fine with it until we were halfway across the sound.

"Dad, I think I'll go upstairs and walk around. Is that okay?"

"Sure, it is."

Kukiko and I did our usual small talk. I hadn't told her about the things that had transpired in the last couple of days.

Then there was the announcement for drivers to return to their vehicles. The ferry was preparing to dock.

As it neared the dock, I suddenly became concerned about Jessie. She should have been back by now. Maybe she had decided to leave. Her apartment was only a fifteen-minute walk away yet Her backpack was still here.

Suddenly, the ferry's alarm went off, and people were moving to the railing on the port side to see what was happening. I knew immediately that it was Jessie. I hopped out of the truck and ran to the railing. Sure enough—Jessie had jumped off the ferry.

It is typical protocol that, when an incident like this occurs, the ferry completely shuts down—not to just rescue the jumper but to prevent the propellers from doing worse damage.

By the time I reached the railing, they had already pulled Jessie out of the water and a motorized raft sped up to the side of the ferry.

I was standing there when she was brought on deck, wet and shivering. We made eye contact, and she immediately mouthed the words "I'm sorry."

I tried to walk to her, but I was stopped by a crewmember. I explained that she was my daughter.

The ferry proceeded to dock, and an emergency crew quickly boarded. When they realized that she was with me, they asked if I had a vehicle onboard. I said yes; they looked surprised.

I was amazed at how quickly they had responded. A woman EMT approached me and asked if she could take my jacket to cover Jessie. I took it off and handed it to her. She then asked if I wanted her to ride in the back of the ambulance with Jessie. They had to remove her wet clothing as quickly as possible. I said, "Yes, of course."

An officer told me that there would be two police cars waiting for me when I drove off the ferry. I was to follow one. Another would be right behind me. They would escort me to the hospital.

I climbed back into my truck. An officer with a clipboard approached me.

"Has she done this before? Has anything else occurred recently?"

I told them about her trip to Kennewick and the incident with Panda. As I started to explain, I broke down crying.

"Maybe Jessie can finally get help."

THE VISION

When we arrived at emergency, Jessie was tied down to a gurney. I kissed her on the cheek and told her I loved her. I was relieved to see she was alright. Martha arrived forty-five minutes later.

Jessie would be under observation for a while. She was eventually moved to a room in the same area pending her assignment to a unit for treatment. There was a waiting area for family while the doctors and nurses tended to Jessie.

I had told Kukiko that we wouldn't be able to pick up her sewing machine today. She understood and went back to the ferry. Her son was waiting for her at the other end.

After six weeks, Jessie had the option of which parent she preferred to live with while she continued her outpatient treatment. She decided to stay with me. Jessie began regular therapy sessions with a social worker and an occasional meeting with her doctor to assess her progress. These sessions were at Kitsap Mental Health Services in East Bremerton.

There were three things that Jessie wanted to do when she was finally released from the hospital: to get her GED Certificate, take voice lessons, and get a membership at a local gym.

Very good choices, I thought. She was also cleared to drive, so I let her use the car to help her with these goals. She also needed to find a job.

Many people have told me that daughters are hard to bring up. Boys are easy. That was certainly true to my experience. The daughter part anyway.

Of course, I had missed being with Kevin as he grew up, but the first chance he had, he came out to Seattle to see me. He wanted to develop a relationship, and he did. During the twenty-six years that I have known him as an adult, he has developed into a man of courtesy, hard work, and love. I have always been able to communicate with him, and he has always called me "Dad." Kevin and his wife Annie, whom he met here in the Northwest, have four amazing sons. He was determined that his sons and I have a close relationship—a real grandfather and grandson relationship. I wanted that, too.

Kevin started work as a structural engineer in Seattle. When his boys were old enough to be involved in outside activities, he landed a job at Naval Submarine Base Bangor. The base was a short drive from his home, especially compared to his hour-and-a-half commute from his house in East Bremerton to Seattle. He wanted to spend more time with his family.

After a couple of years, the Navy sent Kevin and his whole family to Naples, Italy. He was gone for five years. He was a civilian contractor—a structural engineer who traveled to jobs in Europe, North Africa, and the Middle East.

It wasn't that easy for me to stay in contact with him. Kevin and Annie did get on Facebook, and that closed the gap. They had an open invitation for Jessie and me to visit them. As time flew by, I realized that Kevin's final year had almost ended. The time was quickly approaching for them to pack up and move back to the States.

Having retired from my business at the age of sixty-five, I had the time to take the trip to Italy.

The timing was perfect for Jessie as well. She had been released as an outpatient, but she was still struggling to find her way. I knew that this trip would be an experience she would never forget.

In the year following her psychotic break, Jessie found a job at Desert Sun, a tanning business. After two weeks, she lost the job because of a minor disagreement with a fellow employee. That's what I heard from Jess. It turned out that the business had a very high turnover rate, and Jessie was one of the many victims.

Jessie also had yet to realize the responsibilities and benefits of keeping a job. I wondered if her employer had actually sat her down and discussed things that needed to be improved on? Had Jessie been given a chance? Job-hunting was becoming a depressing ordeal for her.

So, the trip to Europe came at an opportune time. Jessie and I decided that our first stop would be Paris, France. Actually, the timing of our arrival was not the best. It was the same week as the terrorist attacks in Paris—Friday the thirteenth, November 2015.

However, the event didn't deter us from our trip. We found a quaint little hotel room across the river from the Louvre and two blocks from the Musée d'Orsay. Because we had the opportunity to take this trip, I wanted to spend time at these fabulous museums and wanted Jessie to experience them as well.

We found a fantastic restaurant a block from the hotel. Jessie's favorite food was on the menu: clams and oysters. It also had my favorites: escargot and French onion soup. The rest of the entrées and appetizers were also delicious.

When I traveled through Europe in 1988, there were two places I had missed that I wanted to visit. One was the Naples area, and the other was Venice. I had repeatedly tried to go to Venice, but railway strikes prevented it. There were other ways to get there, but I had a Eurail pass—already paid for. Taking another route was not in my budget.

Jessie and I spent four nights in Paris and caught the train to Rome early on our last morning.

The first leg of the journey took us to Milan. We had a two-hour layover and caught the next train to Rome after the sun had set. Jessie seemed to be disturbed and began crying. She seemed really uncomfortable. It concerned me. It might be a relapse. We couldn't connect to Wi-Fi on the train, but another passenger helped her connect. That helped.

When we arrived in Rome, we were both exhausted. Originally, we had plans to spend a day or two there to see the Colosseum and a few other major sights.

We decided to nix that. We found a hotel across the street from the station and headed to Naples early the next morning.

Actually, Naples wasn't our destination; it was a small town on the outskirts called Castel Volturno. Kevin and Annie were waiting for us.

We couldn't ask for better tour guides.

Close to ending their five-year stint in Italy, Kevin and Annie had plenty of time to explore the local sights, as well as visit many parts of Europe, including Venice.

The first order of business was to visit their favorite pizza restaurant. They described it as real Italian pizza, and it was awesome.

They decided not to take us to the ancient city of Pompeii. It was huge and tiring. Most of this city had been dug up well before modern-day preservation techniques. Our tour guides took us to Herculaneum instead. Only small portions of this city had been excavated, and the techniques were more preservation-oriented. I could only imagine what life had been like during that time.

Annie was a great guide. She was a walking history book.

Kevin took us on a day trip to the Amalfi Coast. That drive came highly recommended. He had been there enough times to have a favorite restaurant with his favorite dish—pasta with clams.

The next must-see sight was the Naples National Archaeological Museum. Annie insisted that we see this, even though it was late evening and we were pretty tired. It was in the heart of Naples—a cramped madhouse full of people and bumper-to-bumper traffic.

The art and artifacts from Pompeii and Herculaneum soon overcame our tiredness. This museum had the best quality Greek and Roman sculptures I had ever seen.

I was so proud of Jessie. She made sure I wasn't left behind as I hovered around the awesome sculptures. She continually came back to find me and make sure I was okay.

Other than these must-see sights in the Naples area, we just relaxed and enjoyed the small town of Castel Volturno. Jessie and I strolled through the streets to our favorite coffee shop in the mornings and enjoyed the hospitality of the owner. One day, there was a street market that had everything from clothes to knick-knacks to seafood and vegetables.

Kevin and Annie's four boys also added to the atmosphere. They were well behaved, animated, and provided light-hearted entertainment. I had brought them all Seattle Seahawk jerseys.

Then there was Thanksgiving. Kevin and Annie invited their friends to this yearly celebration. It was a wonderful day, and we met many nice people.

Annie also acted as our travel agent. Forget the train. We could take a short flight to Venice for forty-five dollars.

I gave her my credit card, and she booked a trip to Venice for Kevin, Jessie, and me. I relished being with my son and my daughter— in Venice no less. Kevin had been there a couple of times before, and he took over the tour. We ended up with an unbelievable room. It had a balcony hanging over a canal; the ceiling must have been fourteen feet high. A beautiful colored glass chandelier hung from this ceiling.

We meandered around the narrow streets, ate in fabulous restaurants, and enjoyed the art.

Besides the ancient Italian art, Peggy Guggenheim had a wonderful museum of modern art in Venice. I heard it was once her residence.

The highlight was spending half a day in the Doge's Palace. It was an amazing history lesson. I recommend you take the tour.

Venice was everything I had expected and more.

Jessie and I parted with Kevin after three days in that beautiful city. Kevin accompanied us to our gate at the Venice airport to connect with our return flight to the States from Paris. Kevin flew back to Naples.

We stayed in Paris for two more nights and chose the same hotel as before—with the Seine and the Louvre right outside our window. We hung out at our favorite restaurant. This was the relaxing time we needed before the long flight back to Seattle.

Jessie and I made an attempt to go to the top of the Eiffel Tower, but as we stood in line, Jessie felt sick. We caught a cab back to our familiar digs. One more visit to the Musée d'Orsay, and we packed for our flight the next morning.

There had been two bonding moments between Jessie and me in the last year. One was going through her ordeal with her so-called "psychotic break," and the other was our trip to Europe.

Our relationship definitely improved. I felt like we had our father-daughter relationship back—the relationship we had lost when Jessie turned thirteen.

We actually had conversations. Jessie eventually began helping around the house. We cooked meals together and discussed things. I could even relax and allow my humor to surface. My humor used to irritate her.

Claire and I—on the other hand—had a close relationship throughout her school years and well into college.

Claire and Jessie were both headstrong and stubborn to a fault. These were strong traits in their mother. I believe that these were not necessarily defects but traits that could be used as strengths if used properly. However, they were too easily used as self-destructive traits.

The thing I learned about Claire and Jessie was that they had both loved their dad as they grew up. I had delighted in being with them and sharing their experiences.

In their early years, I was as close as a father could get. I still remain close to them and am always there for them, but they have developed a fierce independence. They need to find their own lives.

Kim's story is a whole other ordeal. Along with Kevin, Kim finally had the opportunity to meet her biological father after eighteen years. They were both delighted to be with me, and I was delighted to finally be with them.

I realized that something was wrong in the early years of the new millennium. Up until then, Kim and I seemed to have a good relationship. This changed when her mother came down with breast cancer.

I had to hand it to Kim; she stood by her mother through her battle with cancer for fourteen years. Barbara fought hard, too. At one point, she kicked the disease only to have it reappear as bone cancer in her hip.

Barbara passed away in 2014. What a horrible road to follow—years of declining health facing the thought of death for over a decade and finally succumbing to it.

I wish that I had been given the opportunity to raise Kevin and Kim. I tried to have a close relationship with them. Barbara stifled each attempt or made it as difficult as she could—like the time when I traveled 1,200 miles to see them and was only allowed to be with them for twenty minutes while she stood in the same room with her arms folded, glaring at me.

If I could see my children as much as I wanted or even contact them by telephone, it would not fit with Barbara's story of labeling me as a deserter.

With Barbara living in Elk Mountain, Wyoming and my living on the west coast, it didn't give me much of a chance to defend myself. Barbara's family, acquaintances, and friends only heard one side of the story.

My daughter Claire began her freshman year at The University of Wyoming and majored in musical theater.

I expected her to attend a school in the state of Washington but Claire had other ideas. Because I was born in Laramie and had family there, the girls and I visited on several occasions. Claire fell in love with the campus.

When I realized that she was determined to attend school in this godforsaken place, I gave her my full support. One selling point was that I was a graduate of UW and she got a huge break on her tuition.

That first year, it was a requirement that she lives in the dorms. The following year, she wanted to live off-campus.

Kim had a son from a previous marriage. His name was Blaise. Claire and Blaise got along great on previous visits. Claire was therefore his aunt, and of course, he was Claire's nephew. They were the same age, so they decided they would be cousins.

There were several options for off-campus housing—the best being my brother Don's. He was part owner of an apartment complex and had some housing units around town.

When you send a daughter off to college, it is a great advantage to have family in the area. If it came right down to it, Claire could stay at her Uncle Don's house.

She really didn't want to impose on him, and she found out that Kim and Dave also had a couple of rentals. What Claire really wanted to do was get a place with Blaise. There was no break on the rent, and Kim and Dave's rental was a little more expensive than other options, but Claire really liked the idea of getting closer to her cousin. She also told me that she really wanted to get to know her half-sister, Kim.

If Claire was determined to get to know her sister, the only thing that could stop that would be if Kim had no interest in getting to know Claire.

Claire and Blaise rented a house together. It was Claire's sophomore year, and her high school sweetheart decided that he wanted to attend school in Laramie as well. Jason was a year behind Claire so he was required to live in the dorms. The following year, the Shannons decided to move Claire and Blaise to another rental. Jason would join them.

Blaise was in a heavy metal band, and he was an intense drummer. On one of my visits to the Shannon residence, Blaise was excited to show me his drums. To get more bass action, he had a double peddle and played with a double bass.

My opinion of Blaise was that he was a talented, polite, and intelligent person. It was always an honor to talk to him. I also liked the fact that he pursued his passion.

Even though Claire was getting financial assistance to go to school, I paid Claire's first-year rent for her Shannon rental. That meant dealing with Kim. I looked forward to having more contact with her; at least we would be communicating. This turned out to be deeply depressing. We talked over the phone on occasion. Unfortunately, our talks were extremely impersonal. I was merely a rent payer for Claire; it was strictly business. There was never a time when she asked how I was doing. I would often inquire about her well-being. I hadn't heard the word "Dad" since her first proud moment when she introduced me to her co-workers in the early nineties.

I finally told Kim and Claire that I wasn't going to continue to pay Claire's rent. Claire needed to do that with her financial aid. She was also working on a regular basis at a bagel bakery.

At the same time, I encouraged Claire to rent from my brother Don or find another rental to save money. Claire insisted on staying.

A year later, Claire and Jason did find a less expensive place and moved in. Neither Claire nor Jason had a vehicle. They carried most of their belongings to their new rental.

Their bed and some other items were a little too difficult to move by hand so they went to the Shannon family to see if they could get help.

They said "no" and slammed the door in Claire's face.

Later, Jason talked to me and said, "Wow, you really have a messed-up family!"

I said that they were no indication of what my family was really like.

When Claire and Jason called me and told me the story, I said to call Don.

Don made sure they got their items moved. That was family.

I have always been an advocate of counseling. I believe that talking to a professional therapist doesn't mean you have mental problems. It gives you insight about yourself from an objective person who is trained to help you confront your strengths and weaknesses. It helps you see things you may have been blind to.

While living in Evanston, Wyoming, I was sure that Barbara was convinced that I was having a relationship with Judy—the registered occupational therapist I worked under at the Wyoming State Hospital.

She was right in one respect. This was not sexually motivated but it was a relationship that evolved from honesty, caring, and communication. Those were the very things that Barbara and I lacked in our marriage.

Seeing a counselor cleared a lot of things up. I could stand back and realize what was happening.

Even now, as I approach old age, I have found occasion to seek counseling. I want to understand my role as a father, and I wonder why I haven't been able to maintain a permanent relationship with a partner in marriage. After all, I come from a family that stuck together through good and bad times. My brother and sister had this ability, and they—to this day—enjoy the comfort and stability of a good marriage.

I posed the question to the counselor I am seeing now:

"Why haven't I been able to make a marriage work after two tries? So, what is it about these two women I married and me? What's wrong with me? I have always wanted a partner, so we could share our lives together and support each other through life's ups and downs."

My counselor looked at me and asked, "So what do you think is similar about the two women you married?"

"Well," I said, "I think that they both lacked the energy or confidence to follow their dreams or interests. Neither had goals, and they were both threatened by the hard work and focus I put toward my art. Instead of supporting me, they tried to destroy my ambition. I think they both were very talented, and I tried to support that."

"The thing that stands out for me," said the counselor, "is that they both used your children as weapons."

Judy was the epitome of what I was like. She wanted to be a cowgirl. She moved to Wyoming, bought a horse, and was barrel racing in a rodeo within a year.

She wanted to move to Nashville and play music. She not only accomplished that but she also wrote songs and cut two records. She wrote a book about a tragic marriage and toured the nation giving talks and promoting her story. It wasn't just about herself. It was giving to others. It was giving to the world.

While we were working together, Judy would confront me on my bigoted and sexist behavior that I had no idea I was spewing. I grew up not knowing any better. She spoke to me in a way that showed that she cared for me. I didn't take offence to her remarks. It opened my eyes to this dark side of a naïve upbringing. I owe a lot to Judy.

So, that kind of woman is out there. I felt like the two women I married deceived me. At first, I believed that they had a passion to become someone who gives to the world, not just taking to satisfy their own greed and need to control others. After we were married, their true selves emerged.

Since the time I made the trip to Wyoming in the mid-seventies to see my children, I saw Barbara once.

In April 2004, Kevin and Annie had twin boys: Samuel and Steven. Barbara and her husband Steve drove out to Seattle from Wyoming to see the newborns. Barbara was told that I would be there with my daughters Claire and Jessie.

I drove up to the front door of the hospital and dropped my daughters off. They went inside while I parked the truck.

Barbara knew that I would be showing up soon, so she went out in the hall and hid. I walked down the seemingly empty hall toward Annie's room. When I began opening the door, Barbara came out from her hidden alcove and shouldered me as hard as she could against the sidewall from behind. Then she pulled the door open and walked in the room. She then stopped after entering and looked back as I walked in.

"Oh, my gosh, I didn't see you there."

Barbara had to lash out in some way.

CHAPTER TWENTY-ONE

I have always wanted to write my memoirs. There are probably a lot of people who want to do that but never get around to it.

That would be me, except that I realized I had a story to tell. At my age, I believe that writing my memoirs is a noble act, leaving a gift that any child should be proud to have—the story of the life of a parent or grandparent. I wish my father had done that.

Choosing a direction in art as my life goal was only possible because of my determination and passion. I had to believe in myself.

This has been a grand adventure. Life is a roller-coaster ride full of ups and downs, full of thrills and remorse. That is what life is supposed to be about. That is what shapes your spirit as you prepare to move on to whatever is next.

Having been born and raised in Wyoming and having chosen an art career are odd just by themselves. My period of time travel through this life included growing up in a sparse and isolated landscape of our nation. I experienced the magic and music of the sixties as a teenager, along with the effects and lessons of the Vietnam War.

My generation also lived in an environment of political turmoil and fear caused by the Cold War.

I had the experience of being in rock bands and I traveled extensively through North America and Europe discovering this thing called "Art."

Most important—to me—was the work I was able to do with the talents I was given. I did not waste them. Living and working in my studios were priceless experiences.

I had jumped out of the fishbowl called Wyoming and dove into the ocean. As a result, I not only learned a lot, I am still learning. A whole new world was open to me.

I painted like a mad animal and shared it with the world through galleries and any establishment that was willing to give me a one-man show. People who knew me only had to walk into my studio to see the passion I had.

So, here I am—retired and back to painting. My gift and my work will evolve from the experiences I was so honored to have—whether good or bad. They shaped who I am today. My paintings will reflect that history because I paint from my heart.

My work has been accepted in galleries, and my works—including small works and sketches—number in the thousands. The opportunities are there; I just need to take advantage of them.

I have jokingly said that my goal in life is to inundate my heirs with so many works of art that they won't know what to do with it all, especially if they are all quality pieces.

After all, my focus is on the experience and the process of making art. The end result is incidental.

THE VISION

I often look back at my two marriages. As I ponder these relationships, even though they were similar in many ways, the dynamics and outcomes were strikingly different.

Because of Wyoming law and because I crossed the border, I lost my right to have a relationship with my children from my first marriage. To go back and fight for the right to see them would have consumed time and vast quantities of money. My children would have needed to deal with the continual anger and resentment. My drive to pursue a career in art would have been seriously curtailed.

I will admit that Barbara and Steve did a great job raising our children, from what I hear. Kevin and Kim have turned into responsible adults.

My selfless act of allowing them the ability to grow up in a tight family without interference from me, greatly contributed to Barbara and Steve's ability to raise them the way they did.

Having me in the picture shouldn't have caused any adverse effects, but Barbara's intent to keep me from my children and punish me added an element that subsequently resulted in a negative situation.

My second marriage—twenty years after my divorce from Barbara—was just the opposite.

My rights were not taken away from me, and I was given the opportunity to fight tooth and nail to raise our two daughters.

This resulted in my costs exceeding $100,000 and throwing my daughters in the middle of an angry fight for custody. They could not be spared from this. They became victims of this anger. As in my first marriage, their mom used them as weapons.

Even after the divorce, they were not spared. I gave to them and supported them as much as I was able. The positive side was the countless memories and experiences I was able to share with them. My girls had the chance to know their father and their mother.

All of my children are now adults, well into their own lives and directions. They have chosen their paths and have a whole world yet to experience. I just need to back off and let them be who they want to be. They are old enough to make their own decisions.

I hope in the end that they will respect the choices I have made and understand that I will always love them.

My art speaks for itself. I don't need to describe it. Even though my philosophy is to continue looking ahead, my past artworks are as much my children as my son and three daughters are. My paintings and drawings have their own lives. These thousands of pieces could live many lifetimes beyond that of my descendants. I have no idea how many paintings I've sold or given away as gifts; there are many.

Once I visited a family in San Diego whom I hadn't seen in years. I was immediately drawn to the art on their walls. I walked up to a painting that caught my eye and said, "Wow, this is an interesting piece. Where did you get it?"

I looked at the signature. "Oh, yeah. I did that."

It's a strange thing to see a painting that you can't remember doing over thirty years ago.

The work I have done has been acknowledged in different ways. Four years in a row, I have been asked to give lectures at the University of Washington on the use of algebra and geometry in the fabrication of inflatable sculptures. These included a separate panel discussion with other professionals comparing our direction and accomplishments.

The Northwest College of Art and Design invited me to speak on art and careers. The Northwind Arts Center in Port Townsend asked me to give a three-hour lecture and demo of my painting process.

West Sound Academy gave me a one-man show that required giving the student body a lecture on my painting process and my life experiences as an artist.

I look at other artists' work and feel unique in this crowd. I paint from my mind, but my ability to do that is strengthened by continual studies of the landscape and the figure. Too many artists paint from photographs. They are wonderful paintings but show little of what is inside them.

I have realized that painting is a form of meditation. What feels like a few minutes during the painting process turns out to be hours that leave me with more energy than I started with.

I sit on my deck with a glass of red wine, looking out at the beauty of the Olympic Mountains, and contemplate the meaning of life. I seek only good thoughts. I have lived through a wondrous adventure.

I have learned so very much. Through the ups and downs, I have no regrets; those experiences were meant for my growth. I can move on to what awaits me with a clear conscience. Hopefully, I have learned my lessons.

There were many levels of enlightenment I experienced through painting, meditation, and reading Carl Jung.

I have also learned a lot from the acquaintances and close friends I have encountered through my life experience.

And let's not forget what the world, in general, teaches us. To understand it is to survive. We live on a huge sphere that enfolds us in a life-giving and sustaining envelope. It has its own laws and lessons. There are ferocious winds and extreme temperatures. Ocean waves can strike out in mountainous turmoil and sink the sturdiest ocean vessel.

It can also envelop us in an eerie calm with the warm rays of the sun coddling us to a point of forgetting how angry our planet could get.

What happened to my lifetime partner? Jung talks a lot about the anima—the female inside the male.

I believe I have become one with my female side. I feel like a complete person without having to put that load on a female companion and expect her to be the substitute for my weakness.

I stayed single for twenty years between my two marriages. During that time, I realized the calmness and confidence I felt by being alone with myself. I didn't need a woman to make up for the missing parts of my personality. I found her inside myself.

My decision to marry Martha after twenty years was definitely not because I felt I needed her. She became a friend and a comrade. We had great conversations and supported each other.

I also was excited about having children with her. I would love to raise my children. That opportunity was stolen from me in my first marriage.

Unfortunately, things changed for the worse with Martha. At least this time, I could fight for my kids and not have them taken from me.

THE VISION

Time continues to go faster the older I get. My son, a very wise man, said, "Life is like a roll of toilet paper. The nearer it gets to the end, the faster it goes."

Because I'm not on my deathbed yet, I immediately visited the lumber company and bought enough one-inch-by-two-inch pine to build ten more stretcher bars. I had enough linen to stretch over them. I launched into my next journey—into my imagination and the laboratory inside myself. We will see what comes out of it.

The first canvas I prepared was medium to large in size—53" X 55".

A week earlier, I coated the stretched canvas with rabbit skin glue—an old proven method I learned from the old masters.

The Titanium White primer was thicker than I thought. I thinned it down with turpentine as per the instructions on the container. It still seemed pretty thick. That's okay though—my criss-cross brush stroke created a texture that was appealing to me. It took a week to dry. The second coat was the same and it crossed the dried brushstrokes of my previous texture, giving the surface of the canvas movement even though it was solid white.

I laid the stretched canvas on the floor and began brushing earth colors in random areas—mostly yellow ochre and raw umber—using a lot of turpentine. I did the same with cerulean blue and alizarin crimson. They all mixed together where they met each other, creating different tones and shades.

After the pigment was applied, I wadded up an old tee shirt and dabbed the surface of the canvas. This absorbed some of the turpentine and left more textured shapes. The finishing touch was to sprinkle and splash more turpentine on the surface. It was then left to dry.

It was late evening and I wanted to do this initial step before I went to bed. The oil washes would be dry enough to begin the actual painting in the morning.

After turning out the studio lights, I strolled the fifty yards uphill to the house. Joey, my eleven-year-old vizsla, was waiting with unrestrained excitement as I walked in the door. Usually, she accompanies me to the studio but the fumes are a bit strong during this initial process.

I was excited to start a new painting but I was also tired. It wasn't like the old days when I was younger and stayed up all night and the following day, lost in the painting process. The life that each stroke of color I added to the canvas kept feeding my energy. It kept me in a constant state of "What comes next?"

I prepared myself for bed and crawled under the covers. Now that I am older, going to bed at night is one of my favorite activities—or non-activities. It depends on how you look at it. I can let go of my day and relax my mind and body. I would read, do a crossword, or inundate myself with the vast quantities of data from my cell phone. This activity doesn't last long. Within fifteen minutes, I am fast asleep.

My eyes popped open at 1:00 AM. This is normal for me. Every morning at around one, not only am I awake but I also can't go back to sleep. I can read a book for two hours, write, or watch a full movie. Sometimes, I stay up until the morning light appears and the birds sing their wake-up songs.

This morning was no exception. This time though, I could not get my mind off of the canvas I had prepared. The turpentine I used for the base colors would be dry enough so that I could hang it on my painting wall and see what images emerged. I already knew the basic direction I wanted to go, but I always look at the accidental shapes to see what the painting wants to say.

This nurtures the unconscious mind and releases the energy to create. It's like a relationship with a person. To control the whole thing will kill it.

The walk to the studio was dark and foggy. When Joey saw me put my hat on, she knew where I was going. She happily pranced around and took a twenty-foot lead—as some hunting dogs do. As we neared the studio, Joey's movement tripped the night-light so the entrance was well lit.

When I entered the room, the chill was overwhelming. In fact, it was downright cold. I placed some kindling in the wood stove and topped that off with larger pieces of wood. It lit easily and I left the door open until the fire could sustain itself.

The smell of the turpentine was still strong but the canvas was dry enough to hang on my painting wall.

I sat in my wicker chair to view the base painting.

Images danced across the surface. There were organic shapes that seemed to be filled with life. I wanted to keep those. I saw faces and animals—there were rocks, ravines, and mountains. All of these images were shaped better and were more alive than I could ever consciously paint.

My vision was to paint a Northwest landscape. My palette was already loaded with my chosen pigments. I painted the foreground trees in dark colors. The tops disappeared above the edge of the canvas with the detail of the roots and foliage dancing in detail below. The trees in the background were lighter in value and I painted them with light bluish grays to emphasize the depth.

There was an area at the bottom that leaned toward red and had clusters of circles caused by turpentine splatters. I emphasized them so that they looked like a nest of eggs and then painted red ants crawling along the surface.

The bottom was surrealistic, and this evolved into an impressionistic mountain landscape at the top. I fractured the reality of the two areas with a black space that I planned to cover with stars and galaxies.

My brush moved quickly from my palette to the canvas surface as I defined images and added color.

When I painted the black void, I added cobalt blue and a tad of warmth with burnt umber to the black pigment. That created a richer black.

As I painted this black area, I felt a strange dizziness. I have been around turpentine for forty years. I love that smell. Maybe it was finally getting to me. The funny thing was that my light-headedness seemed to dissipate when I moved to the more colorful areas of the painting.

When again I moved back to the black void, the world around me grew dark and I felt like I was losing consciousness. There was a strong sensation of no right side up or upside down.

Did I pass out? I felt wide-awake but there was no sense of reality that I could hold on to.

Huge dark spheres closed in on me and I felt a sudden fear. These spheres seemed to have no size. It was as if I had shrunk to the level of a microscopic particle that at the same time seemed so large that it encompassed the universe. I could also roll these dark particles between my thumb and forefinger. Size did not exist.

The feeling of falling overwhelmed me, but it was not a downward fall. It was an inward fall. My descent took me to a place that was smaller than an atom and continued to plunge even deeper.

New universes revealed themselves as small dots of light became galaxies. These galaxies became solar systems with planets and moons. Life forms and civilized societies emerged as did their fears, their loves, and ambitions. Their children had more children as did their children. Wars and natural catastrophes blew their world apart, then ended with a deeper awareness and evolution.

The universe became smaller yet as I continued to a microcosm of the wee universe I just experienced.

The darkness quickly evolved into a magnificent light. The world around me was lit to a brilliance that no darkness could penetrate. More spheres emerged from the light and human forms began to materialize inside each one. Each human was a universe unto itself.

A shocking revelation overcame me. I realized what life was about. The truth of our existence lay bare before my eyes and it was magnificent in its simplicity.

I know the meaning of our existence.

I felt a wetness on my face. I opened my eyes to Joey licking me. A faint morning light illuminated my room as I realized I was snuggled under my covers in my bed. How did I get here? I don't remember returning to the house and preparing for bed. Was I drinking? Did the fumes overwhelm me to the point of me becoming unconscious of my actions?

I crawled out of bed and slowly dressed as I searched my mind for any clue that would explain why I was here.

I put on my hat. That was the clue that told Joey where I was going. She danced around in uncontrollable excitement. I slid the side door open and began my walk to the studio. Joey took her usual lead to blaze the trail before us. The fog had not yet lifted and the air was chilly and moist.

I opened the door to my studio and it was even colder inside, holding in the air from the night before.

After turning on the light, I opened the small door to the woodstove to clean the ashes and reload it with kindling and logs.

That was unnecessary since I had already prepared the stove for a fire. All I had to do was light it.

In the center of the room was the canvas that I prepared the night before—lying on the floor with my initial color washes. The turpentine had evaporated so I picked the canvas up by the edges and hung it on my painting wall.

I sat in my wicker chair and gazed at my base painting. Images danced across the surface. There were organic shapes that seemed to be filled with life. I wanted to keep those. I saw faces and animals—there were rocks, ravines, and mountains. All of these images were more alive than I could ever possibly paint myself.

While I cannot remember or find the words to describe my vision of what life is all about, maybe hints will emerge from my paintings.

www.ingramcontent.com/pod-product-compliance
Lightning Source LLC
Chambersburg PA
CBHW050740080526
44579CB00017B/71